The Films of
Joel and Ethan Coen

The Films of
Joel and Ethan Coen

CAROLYN R. RUSSELL

McFarland & Company, Inc., Publishers
Jefferson, North Carolina, and London

Library of Congress Cataloguing-in-Publication Data

Russell, Carolyn R., 1958–
    The films of Joel and Ethan Coen / Carolyn R. Russell.
       p.   cm.
    Includes bibliographical references and index.
    ISBN 0-7864-0973-8 (softcover : 50# alkaline paper) ∞
    1. Coen, Joel. 2. Coen, Ethan. I. Title.
PN1998.3.C6635 R87   2001
791.43'0233'092273—dc21   2001030378
                                                   CIP

British Library cataloguing data are available

Manufactured in the United States of America

*McFarland & Company, Inc., Publishers
  Box 611, Jefferson, North Carolina 28640
   www.mcfarlandpub.com*

For Charlie

Contents

Introduction

If "knowingness is the soul of wit" in a contemporary culture steeped in irony,[1] Joel and Ethan Coen, whose work routinely traffics in meta-irony, are among those artists who best capture this zeitgeist. Bursting upon the independent film scene in 1984 with their stylishly inventive debut feature, *Blood Simple*, the fraternal team has since unleashed a small cascade of films which, as a body, reflect nothing quite so much as their desire to amuse each other. If the iconoclastic wittiness of their scripts and the sumptuousness of their distinctive visual style entertain audiences en route, the Coens are well pleased. They also seem to respect our ability to draw upon and extrapolate from the well of film historical and pop cultural sources required to decode the in-jokes at the heart of most compelling Coen moments. We remain, however, jostled backseat passengers on the Coens' cinematic joyride. Their mode of filmmaking may be compared to that of more mainstream Hollywood productions, which safety-belt the viewer in behind the wheel.

Joel and Ethan Coen are renowned for their like-mindedness, rendering their quest to amuse each other virtually indistinguishable from each pursuing his own idiosyncratic aesthetic compulsions. Vladimir Nabokov writes elegantly of the notion of the "ideal reader," an abstraction to whom the artist subconsciously directs her efforts—her own self. In the case of the Coens, this ideal audience for their work is made corporeal, each providing the other with a flesh-and-blood proxy for this theoretical entity.

Unsurprisingly then, those who collaborate with the Coens often note the extent to which they speak with a single creative voice; director Barry Sonnenfeld describes this synchronicity as "a two-man ecosystem."[2]

Though Joel is nominal director and Ethan producer, the two function interchangeably on the set and work together throughout every step of the filmmaking process. They finish each other's sentences, laugh soundlessly at each other's deadpan humor, and reportedly communicate regularly on a near-telepathic basis.

The Coens prefer to work with artists with whom they can enjoy similarly wordless but meaningful communion. Discussing the collaboration process, Ethan Coen says that "a lot is unspoken." Members of his and Joel's creative team "read the script and they get it, so a lot of the basic conceptual stuff is never discussed, because it doesn't have to be." Ethan elaborates further: "Some people, however much you talk, you sort of can't get it across. Or on a personal level you can't connect. So it's like a taste thing: you gravitate toward people who have similar styles and tastes. ... what's important is they get it ... they can feel their way through it, kind of like we can."[3]

The cabal that the Coens have assembled through the years, a brilliantly talented collective of people who "get it," makes an integral contribution to the process by which the Coen vision is realized onscreen. J. Todd Anderson, who has worked with the Coens since *Raising Arizona*, is responsible for storyboarding their films. (Storyboards are the panel sketches that depict a film's proposed series of shots.) The Coens' fanatical devotion to this practice is legendary. They storyboard extensively; relatively little camera coverage or dialogue is improvised on their sets.

The Coens prefer this procedure for several reasons. The first is economy. Low-budget filmmakers at heart, storyboarding is one way of maximizing the conservation of time and money. Joel explains:

> The only way to make a decent movie for no money is to be very, very prepared, and to be able to answer very specific questions about what you need to see and what you don't need to see—and therefore, what you need to spend money on and what you don't need to spend money on.[4]

The Coens are temperamentally predisposed toward this methodology as well. Says Joel: "We're not necessarily good extemporizers and we particularly prefer not to extemporize camera coverage on the set on the day we're going to shoot. It's just not the way we like to do it."[5] Finally, the Coens find that storyboarding is an efficient way to communicate their ideas to the people with whom they collaborate, which in turn allows for greater preparedness on their parts.[6]

Not that the Coens' colleagues of choice are apt to show up for work unprepared. The select troupe is composed of artists as meticulous as the Coens themselves. Sonnenfeld, the Coens' cinematographer on *Blood Simple*, *Raising Arizona*, and *Miller's Crossing*, has since become a major director himself, piloting such films as *The Addams Family* (1991) and its sequel (1993), *Get Shorty* (1995), and *Men in Black* (1997). Roger Deakins has been their cinematographer of choice since *Barton Fink*. Sonnenfeld and Deakins both have been masterfully adept at crafting the Coens' signature visual style while adroitly creating a unique aesthetic for each of the Coens' vividly idiosyncratic dreamworlds. Toward this end they have been aided and abetted by more Coen regulars: production designers Jane Musky (*Blood Simple* and *Raising Arizona*), Dennis Gassner (*Miller's Crossing*, *Barton Fink*, and *The Hudsucker Proxy*), and Rick Heinrichs (*Fargo* and *The Big Lebowski*). "Roderick Jaynes" has edited most of the Coens' films; the name is a pseudonym for the Coens themselves. Richard Hornung, who designed costumes for *Raising Arizona*, *Miller's Crossing*, *Barton Fink*, and *The Hudsucker Proxy*, contributes powerfully to the Coens' exuberantly stylized universes, as does Mary Zophres, who took over for Hornung on *Fargo* when Hornung was forced by illness to back out of the project. She designed for *The Big Lebowski* as well. Carter Burwell rounds out the Coens' talented band of regulars. His music graces all of their films; one can scarcely imagine a Coen film without Burwell's astoundingly elastic sense of what sounds right.

Parallel to the Coens' band of preferred crew members is the small crowd of performers who pop up in their films in parts both great and small. John Turturro, Frances McDormand (who is married to Joel Coen), John Goodman, Steve Buscemi, and Jon Polito constitute the core of this group.

Interestingly, the Coens tend to have specific actors in mind when they write a script. *Blood Simple*, for example, was written with the idea that M. Emmet Walsh would play the ultra-sleazy detective.[7] Steve Buscemi had his *Fargo* role written for him,[8] while *The Big Lebowski* was written as a showcase for John Goodman.[9]

The Coens write their screenplays in a manner as unorthodox as the films that result from them. Working without an outline, they begin with a hazy idea of an event that they intend to use as a plot point. They then take turns at the computer, one typing and one pacing, and begin to write scenes in chronological order; eventually, the script begins to gel in a particular direction.[10] The bulk of the plot twists and turns develop as a result of the brothers' penchant for writing in a manner described by Joel as "wildy style."[11] The term comes from an old Hollywood legend of which Joel is fond. The silent film director Mack Sennett is said to have routinely hired free spirits he called "wildies" who would attend script meetings and scream out crazy plot ideas, ideas that often, as the story goes, found their way into Sennett's movies. Joel and Ethan use the phrase to describe their version of Sennett's process. They paint themselves into a corner, plot-wise, then perform whatever literary gymnastics are necessary in order to paint themselves out.[12] The finished script will detail far more than dialogue and story. Their screenplays are renowned for their attention to such production factors as set design, camera angles and movement, and framing. Replete with such visual information, their scripts manage to convey a vivid sense of the finished film.

What fuels this venture is a confluence of sensibility that evolved during the Coens' childhood and adolescence in what they affectionately call "the United States' equivalent of Siberia."[13] In an age when the boundaries between the public and the private seem all but completely eroded, the Coens are noteworthy for their reticence surrounding their personal lives, past and present. What limited details the Coens wish to share are by now well-documented and consistent from account to published account.

Joel Coen was born in 1955 and Ethan in 1958 in St. Louis Park, Minnesota, a suburb of Minneapolis. They have an older sister, Debbie, who is a doctor in Israel. Their parents, Edward and Rena, are both academics; Edward taught economics at the University of Minnesota before his retirement, and Rena teaches art history at St. Cloud State University.

The Coens' childhoods, by all accounts happy, are remarkable only for the amount of time devoted to the ingestion of books and movies. One local late-night television show in particular consumed a good deal of the brothers' attention, feeding them a steady diet of wildly variegated old movies. Joel remembers that the show might run a Fellini film one night and *Son of Hercules* the next.[14] This eclecticism was a defining feature of their early exposure to all media. They read James M. Cain and Aristotle and watched Doris Day comedies alongside art-house double features. It is easy to make a connection between their youthful indiscriminate consumption of disparate forms and the disjuncture that is a constituent stylistic component of their films.

Eventually the boys sought a more proactive role in their entertainments. Buying a Super 8 camera with money earned mowing neighborhood lawns, the brothers gathered a small group of friends and began to make movies themselves. They remade some of their favorites, and created such original classics as *Henry Kissinger: Man on the Go* and *The Banana Film*, considered by the few who have seen it to represent "the pinnacle of the Coens' Super 8 years."[15]

Joel graduated from high school in the mid-seventies and entered Simon's Rock College in Massachusetts before transferring to New York University's acclaimed film program. His thirty-minute thesis film, *Soundings*, anticipates the eccentricity that will mark his later work; in it, a woman makes love to her deaf boyfriend as she fantasizes aloud about another man.[16]

After graduation Joel attended the University of Texas at Austin for a brief period before abandoning its graduate film program for New York City. There he worked intermittently as a production assistant on various projects before landing a job as assistant editor for Sam Raimi. Together they worked on Raimi's *Fear No Evil* and *The Evil Dead*, low-budget horror films famous for their imaginatively kinetic camerawork. Raimi would become a good friend of the Coens, as well as a future collaborator.

Ethan also attended Simon's Rock College after high school, eventually transferring to Princeton University where he studied philosophy. Following graduation in 1980, Ethan joined his brother in New York City, where he embarked upon a series of temporary jobs. One of the longest of these was a position as a statistical typist at Macy's department store: "It was," says Ethan, "a long road that had no end."[17]

The Coens began to write together in their spare time and were eventually able to sell a script called *Suburbicon*.[18] By the time the Coens were ready to begin their first feature film together, a crucial transformation had taken place. Joel and Ethan Coen had become the Coen brothers, a double-brained, quadruple-handed creative entity that would pump new blood into the independent film scene and foreground the ascension of a new kind of post–studio age, film school–educated auteur.

Like many of their contemporaries, the Coens make films that are highly self-conscious of their relationship to preexisting film forms. Their movies rely upon a base of knowledge, cultural and film historical, that is presumed to be shared between themselves and their viewers. Though their films may be taken at face value, appreciating their playfulness depends upon this common frame of reference.

Just as their movies rest upon a shared production of meaning, filmmakers and viewers collaborating together by way of a common vocabulary grounded in the aesthetic past, so do they rest upon a shared notion of identity. Coen films are the products of artists acutely aware of their status as auteurs; their branding of their films with a strong authorial signature is a highly self-aware enterprise. Less self-conscious but no less significant an activity is the process by which viewers participate in constructing the Coen brand, anticipating the arrival of and responding to their films with a set of expectations based on the Coens' highly visible trademark style.

So consistent are the paradigms of the architecture that underpins the Coens' stylized dreamworlds (*Fargo* provides the exception that bold-faces the rule) that the duo may be said to have invented their own genre. The conventions of this exotic beast are detailed in the pages which follow, but may be summarized by Joel Coen himself: "You start with things that are incredibly recognizable in one form, and then you play with them."[19]

ONE

Blood Simple

Blood Simple, Joel and Ethan Coen's 1984 debut feature, heralded the arrival of a new kind of independent film, one which would unabashedly combine the strategies of the art-house cinema with those of popular entertainment cinema. The Coens earned the right to make their own rules as Joel explains:

> We did it entirely outside Hollywood. To take it a step further, we did it outside of any established movie company anywhere.... We wanted to make the movie, and the way we did it was the only way we could have done it. The main consideration from the start was that we wanted to be left alone, without anyone telling us what to do.[1]

Financing for the film came from 168 private investors; most of its $1.5 million budget came from their home state of Minnesota, with additional funding from New York, New Jersey, and Texas.

After the film's completion in 1983, the brothers attempted to secure distribution from several major studios. Because the film defied easy categorization, "too gory to be an art film, too arty to be an exploitation film, funny but not quite a comedy,"[2] Hollywood passed on the opportunity. Circle Releasing, a small firm considerably east of Hollywood, eventually bought distribution rights; the Washington, DC–based company backed a film that would eventually win a Grand Jury Prize at the United States Film Festival, as well as an Independent Spirit Award. Besides appearing on many top ten lists of 1985, *Blood Simple* was also honored by the National Board of Review as one of the year's best films. A critical hit, the film enjoyed modest commercial success, returning approximately $5 million.

The Coens cite the works of James M. Cain as the primary inspiration for the film's narrative; Raymond Chandler and Dashiell Hammett also occupy key positions in the Coens' pantheon of pulp fiction writers whose fervid tales of passion, blood, and guilt fueled their drive toward *Blood Simple*'s imaginative revisioning of the form. The film's title is, in fact, taken from Hammett's *Red Harvest*; the term refers to the state of mind-numbing confusion which follows an act of murder. Undoubtedly, however, the film is most beholden to the Coens' youthful fixation on the movies they watched incessantly, voraciously. Joel Coen relates, "*Blood Simple* utilizes movie conventions to tell the story. In that sense it's about other movies ... us[ing] the medium in a way that's aware that there's a history of movies behind it."[3] Each frame of *Blood Simple* is imbued with this awareness; it is responsible for a layer of uncommon aesthetic richness in a film defined by its multilayered approach to storytelling.

The deserted, faded scenes of rural Texas which open *Blood Simple* function as both establishing shots and the projected mindscape of the film's initial narrator, a private detective named Loren Visser (M. Emmet Walsh). Visser's mournfully stark and depopulated landscapes mirror his worldview, enunciated in the guttural slurred speech appropriate to a man who, throughout the film, cannot muster the enthusiasm to keep flies from landing on his head:

> The world is full of complainers. The fact is, nothin' comes with a guarantee ... something can all go wrong. Go ahead, complain, tell your problems, ask for help ... and watch 'em fly. In Russia they got it mapped out so that everyone pulls for everyone else. That's the theory anyway. What I know about is Texas, and down here, you're on your own.

Out of this perspective will flow the choices, interpretations, and actions of a man who, like the other characters in the film, will be unable to transcend his limited frame of reference; the consequence of this limitation will be that everything will, indeed, "all go wrong."

Blood Simple inaugurates the Coens' trademark use of highly stylized filmspace; the familiar closed universe of film noir is immediately recognizable as the visual context of Ray (John Getz) and Abby's (Frances McDormand) taut conversation. We are in the back seat of Ray's car, observing the pair as Ray drives Abby out of town. Their outlines are barely visible as layered shadows compete with the refracted gray light of the rain-spattered windshield. Passing cars generate additional fleeting illumination, filling the entire frame with hot white flashes that introduce the film's credits. The tightly framed scene anticipates the claustrophobia

Private detective Loren Visser (M. Emmet Walsh) ponders murder in *Blood Simple.*

which characterizes much of the film, while its low-key chiaroscuro light-ing forecasts the film's neo-noir visual style.

Abby tells Ray that her first anniversary gift from Marty (Dan Hedaya) was a small, pearl-handled .38; she says that she thought she had better leave before she used it on him. Confidences are exchanged; mutual attraction is discovered. We see Ray's face for the first time as he turns around to look at the Volkswagen that appears to be following them; Ray's squinting paranoia is a harbinger of things to come. Abby and Ray wonder what next to do. The camera cuts to their lovemaking at a nearby motel, commenting ironically on the inevitability of their decision. There has quickly been established a link between violence and eros, a quintes-sential noir coupling. The archetypal noir sexual triangle is also estab-lished; the volatile instability of this geometry is made clear when Ray takes an unsettling call from Marty in the motel room. Early on, the film makes clear its own imperatives, related but not necessarily beholden to generic paradigms: each act, each event, will result in a subsequent act or event that will propel the story forward in an almost surrealistically tight chain of cause and effect. Ray and Abby head back to town in order to pursue their romance, aware that Marty knows of their affair.

The source of Marty's information confronts his employer in the office of Marty's bar, the Neon Boot; the country love song playing on the bar's jukebox comments ironically on the scene which follows. The private detective fidgets in his chair as he faces Marty, who is initially found with his boots crossed atop his desk in an iconographic Western pose. Here is the first of what critic Roger Ebert describes as the Coens' favorite image: "crass, venal men behind desks."

Marty is surprised by the photographs Visser has taken, having only requested surveillance and a phone call. He is also discomfited by the detective's leering satisfaction with the seamier aspects of his job; Visser's account of the evening's activities is more information than Marty wants. Marty fingers the photographs in a manner both suggestive and somehow pathetic. Seeking to reinstate the balance of power in their relationship, Marty opines that "in Greece, they would cut off the head of the messenger that brought the bad news." (The Coens will iterate a minor obsession with heads and hats throughout their work.) If the repellent private investigator justifies his ruthless and bloody brand of capitalism by invoking a private dreamworld he calls Russia, Marty judges himself benevolent through comparison with the customs of a place he imagines to suit his purposes. The fantastic status of both geographies mirrors the similar status of the world in which they conduct their violent transactions; it is a Texan dreamworld, a minimalistic, ultrastylized, synthetic Texas-of-the-mind.

The racist detective tells Marty that "it ain't such bad news ... you thought he was colored. You're always assuming the worst." Marty dismisses the investigator. Visser scoops his silver Elks Man of the Year lighter off Marty's desk before leaving; it is an object upon which the camera has chosen to linger. Its glitter is prominent against the matte texture of the dark room. Many shots in this scene are lit solely by the neon lines of saturated color which emanate from various signs and from the room's jukebox; the resulting images are colorful without sacrificing their dark tonal quality.

Marty turns toward the two-way mirror which separates the office from the bar, and in one of the Coens' most playful transitions, the camera follows his gaze through the glass and into the room beyond. We meet Meurice (Samm-Art Williams), Ray's African-American co-bartender and presumably the target of Marty's suspicions. Meurice plays Neil Diamond's "I'm a Believer" on the jukebox, a favorite tune of his which will resonate powerfully when later its context is altered. Meurice chats with a new female acquaintance; the two collude together in order to repel Marty's crude advances toward the woman. Marty lies too, denying knowledge of Ray's whereabouts the night before; Meurice has had to cover for him behind the bar.

The next scene begins with a Kubrickesque tracking shot as the camera follows Marty's dog's progress through a narrow hallway. Interestingly, the perspective of the lens places the camera at the height of a person walking slightly behind the animal, personifying the Coens' authorial presence in the film. We are in Abby and Marty's house; Abby is preparing to leave her home and her marriage. Ray approaches the dog warily though the German Shepherd is friendly; it will be Ray's fate to consistently miscalculate potential sources of danger. Ray plays pool and examines family photos. His index finger traces the outline of Abby's picture, recalling Marty's earlier action and making clear the phallic connotations of the gesture. Abby locates the object of her search: her gun and her bullets. She is ready to leave the opulence of the house for a motel, but when Ray suggests she stay with him, she agrees.

Against Abby's advice Ray goes to the Neon Boot. A slow tracking shot moves forward along the length of the bar, rising to accommodate the drunk passed out on the bartop before lowering itself back into its tracking position along the surface of the serving area. The visual joke is characteristic of the film's black sense of humor; this kind of wry authorial commentary is responsible for many such darkly amusing turns.

Behind the back of his building, Marty broods and contemplates the disposal of various objects as they are hoisted into the large incinerator which backs up to his property. Its blazing roar mingles with the electrified crackle of a bug zapper; the sounds are exaggerated in order to convey Marty's internal state. Ray joins him, initiating a confrontation which will change both their lives.

Ray wants the money Marty owes him. Marty refuses, calling Abby "an expensive piece of ass." Marty offers Ray a "refund" if he will tell him who else Abby has been sleeping with. When Marty inadvertently triggers a smile from Ray by sarcastically referring to him as a marriage counselor, recalling an earlier conversation between Ray and Abby, Marty's low-voltage wrath intensifies. "What are you smiling at?" Marty snarls. He continues:

> I'm funny? Right? I'm an asshole? No, no, no, no, no, no, no. I'll tell you what's funny. What's funny is her. What's funny is that I had you two followed. Because if it's not you she's sleeping with, it's someone else. And what's really going to be funny is when she gives you that innocent look and says, "I don't know what you're talkin' about, Ray—I ain't done anything funny." But the funniest thing to me right now is that you think she came back here for you.

Marty warns Ray off the property, threatening to shoot him if he returns.

"Fair notice," Marty intones ominously, staring again at the incinerator as a body-sized rolled carpet is thrown into its flames.

Once more we observe Ray from the back seat of his car; he stares at his house, where Abby waits. That he has been influenced by Marty's warnings is made clear during his subsequent interaction with her. As he enters the house she is replacing the telephone receiver, having just answered a silent call from Marty.

> Ray: *Who was it?*
> Abby: *What?*
> Ray: *On the phone. Who was it? Was it for you?*
> Abby: *I don't know, he didn't say anything.*
> Ray: *How'd you know it was a he?*
> Abby: (after a pause) *You got a girl? Am I screwing something up by being here?*
> Ray: *No. Am I?*
> Abby: *I can find a place tomorrow and I'll be out of your hair.*
> Ray: *Well, if that's what you want to do then you ought to do it. You want the bed or the couch?*

Limited by frames of reference which mediate their respective readings of each other's words, Ray and Abby have no idea of the extent to which they lack proper context for the other's remarks and thus have misconstrued their meaning. Nearly all of their subsequent dialogue will be characterized by this kind of disconnection.

Marty stews in his office rather than returning home, remaining in an environment where he feels a measure of control rather than facing his empty house. Abby meanwhile lies awake on Ray's living room sofa. The shot of Abby is an arresting one. A predominant noir visual motif involves the mapping of the human face with stark contrasts of light and shadow, producing startling, sometimes grotesque patterns; the image of Abby's "masked" face is so highly emblematic of this technique that its iconography verges on parody.

Cross-cutting among Marty, Abby, and Ray reveals the restlessness of each. Abby rises and glides to the bedroom to join Ray; the image of her white-nightgowned form as she floats down the hallway is the first of many which will suggest the conventions of the horror film.

Ray draws Abby down to him. In a lyrical long take, they remain below the frame while the camera remains still, observing the street outside Ray's bedroom window. The light slowly changes; as morning arrives, Abby rises to resume her original position within the frame. Such formal exercises are plentiful throughout the film, focusing our attention on the

Coens' mode of storytelling, the dramatic purposes to which the medium of film may adroitly be put.

A slow tracking shot follows Abby into the living room where she notices Marty's dog; as she struggles to interpret the animal's presence, Marty attacks her from behind. The camera focuses on Abby's fallen compact, another glittery object thrown into high relief. Abby attempts to reach her gun, which has spilled out of her purse onto the floor. Marty drags her backward away from the weapon; he taunts her, making clear his intention to rape her. As Marty propels the struggling Abby out the door, the camera races diagonally across the front lawn to meet them. The short scene which follows is a blend of quick cuts and extreme hand-held close-ups; the staccato rhythm of these images heighten their impact. The sequence strongly recalls William Wyler's similar scene in his 1965 adaptation of John Fowles' novel *The Collector*. Abby is able to successfully defend herself, breaking Marty's index finger (an appendage noted in this film for its phallic symbolism) and kicking him in the groin. Marty doubles over in pain and vomits. Ray arrives, armed with Abby's gun. As Ray and Abby embrace, Marty speeds off in his car; his attempt at a vehicular grand gesture is thwarted, however, when he is forced to turn around and retrace his path—Ray's street culminates in a dead end.

Marty's splinted finger is the focal point of the film's next shot as Marty crosses a parking lot to meet Visser; the teenagers drinking there rib him about breaking his "pussy finger," driving home the visual metaphor somewhat heavy-handedly. Marty and Visser talk in the front seat of the detective's Volkswagen. Visser serves up some loathsome joking conversation calculated to provoke Marty's sore ego. Marty tells the detective that he has a job for him. "Well, if the pay is right and it's legal, I'll do it," Visser says. Marty tells him that the job is "not strictly legal." "Well," Visser says, "pay is right, I'll do it." Marty tells the detective that the job involves his wife and "that gentleman." "The more I think about it," he says softly, "the more irritated I get." Marty waits for Visser to voice aloud what he can only bring himself to imply; hearing the actual words, Marty looks ill. Visser calls Marty an idiot after he solicits double murder but is willing. The detective appears less concerned with the deed than with a worry that Marty will jeopardize them both by going "simple" on him. Marty asserts that the $10,000 he is willing to pay him will provide the basis for trust between them. Visser notes that "in Russia, they make only fifty cent' a day. " Marty looks puzzled by the bizarre non sequitur but listens closely to the detective's instructions regarding an alibi and covering a money trail to the murders. Before leaving, Marty tells Visser to make sure the bodies are not discovered; he suggests the incinerator behind his bar. "Sweet Jesus, you are disgusting," muses the detective. His contempt for Marty is not only ironic considering his own moral character but will, in retrospect, seem a clue to his private game plans.

Abby rents a loft. She goes to the bar to ask Meurice to "keep an eye on Marty and Ray, make sure nothing happens." Meurice asks Abby if it's ever occurred to her that he's "the wrong person" to ask; the remark renews a question concerning Abby and Meurice's history. Before Abby leaves, Meurice tells her that she need not worry for a while—Marty has gone to Corpus Christi for a few days.

That night Abby wakes up terrified—she thinks that Marty is inside Ray's house. Ray tells her not to worry: the house is locked. She lies back down while the camera lingers and rack focuses upon the view through the bedroom window, a convention of cinematic grammar which contradicts Ray's assurances. Ray and Abby discuss Marty's psychiatric peculiarities. Abby offers an interesting assessment of Marty's and Ray's differing patterns of communication. She says they both seldom speak, but that Marty's unspoken words are "usually nasty" while Ray's are "usually nice."

Her comment is evocative within its context, for *Blood Simple* is a film which will continually interrogate the nature of spoken language and the limitations of its capacity to convey human reality. Ray convinces Abby to suspend such speculation; in an echo of their earlier scene together Ray pulls her down to him. As Abby moves out of the frame, the detective's battered Volkswagen is seen through the bedroom window; our view of its menacing presence has been obscured by Abby's form.

Like so much of the Coens' mobile camerawork, the camera which glides through the house to the front door where Visser fumbles with the lock recalls the pointed subjectivity of Welles and Hitchcock. The detective quietly breaks in and takes Abby's gun from her purse, noting that its cylinder has three bullets in it. He creeps heavily through the house, moving in and out of shadow. Unexpectedly, he leaves. He walks around the house, finds the bedroom's window, and peers in at the sleeping couple. The frame fills with a flash of hot white light.

The detective calls Marty from a pay phone to tell him that the deed is done and that he is ready to collect the money Marty now owes him. They meet at the bar. Visser slaps his monogrammed lighter on Marty's desk; almost immediately Marty drops his recently caught fish on top of it. Visser gives Marty a photograph that shows Ray and Abby in bed together, posed as we have last seen them; they are bleeding from multiple gunshot wounds. "Dead?" Marty asks. "So it would seem," replies the detective. Revolted by the dead fish Marty has placed in front of him, Visser moves the two closest away from him, further obscuring his view of the lighter. Meanwhile, Marty is once again struggling not to be ill. Marty tells Visser that he is going to be sick and, still holding the photograph, goes to the restroom at the back of his office. Visser asks for his money and again questions Marty to make sure that he has kept quiet about their deal. The shot of Marty as he kneels before his safe blends archetypal images of the noir and horror genres. He looms above the camera, his face nearly filling the frame; garish lines of wavy color form a lurid backdrop for his head. As Marty removes money from the safe, he slides a piece of paper into its recesses. He reassures Visser that he need not worry about issues of security. Calling their relationship "an illicit romance," Marty extends the metaphor: "We have to learn to be discreet," he says, "trust each other … for richer or poorer." "Don't say that," says Visser. "Your marriages don't turn out so hot."

Their marriage of convenience will prove no exception. Marty tells him to count the money and go, extending the enveloped photograph and piles of cash across his desk with the heel of his boot. The detective declines to count the money. "I trust you," he says, before pulling out Abby's gun and shooting Marty, whose florid face registers stunned disbelief. The wound emits a slow trickle of blood; one leg loses its balance against the desk and crashes to the floor. The detective kicks Abby's gun across the room, its metal glinting evilly against the wood flooring. Twice the camera contrives to afford us a visual perspective denied Visser: we can see the glitter of his silver lighter beneath the aging fish on Marty's desk. The detective leaves, and the camera moves to record the scene he leaves behind; the overhead shot is punctuated by blackscreen swipes as the revolving ceiling fan interrupts the image.

The scene which follows is marked by a gothic sensibility. The first image is very stylized; the darkened bar is lit by neon color in a beautifully composed shot which focuses our attention on the smoked glass of the front-door window. In a grippingly effective use of a frame-within-a-frame design, this window becomes a miniature screen against which is projected a suspenseful shadow play. Mist obscures the outline of a car; its headlights magnify the silhouette of the figure which approaches the door. The door opens; it takes a moment for us to recognize the backlit form as Ray's, an image which forces a shocked reevaluation of our earlier perception of events. Here is the first of several bodies which will, in *Blood Simple*, rise from the dead.

Ray has returned to the bar for the money Marty owes him. Finding the cash register empty, his attention snags on the light seeping through the cracks of the closed office door. As he moves toward the light, the camera assumes an extremely low Wellesian perspective of Ray's boots as they disturb the carpet dust. The sound effect which pervades the film, that of the ceiling fan pulse/heartbeat, fuels the tension of the moment as Ray discovers Marty, who appears to be sitting in his chair, his back to the door.

Ray slowly walks toward Marty, who has not responded to his less-than-polite salutation. There is suddenly a burst of sound and color as Ray accidentally kicks Abby's gun across the room, discharging a bullet which lodges in a wooden post inches away from his leg. Two bullets from Abby's .38 are now accounted for. The camera pirouettes a close ninety degrees around Ray's stunned face as he takes in the fact that Marty has not reacted to the event. Ray turns on harsh fluorescent overhead lighting and absorbs the scene before him. He recovers the gun and recognizes it as Abby's. He places the gun heavily upon the table, near the concealed lighter; metal objects in the film—gun, lighter, compact—seem weighted by the testimony they bear, false and otherwise.

As Ray prepares to move Marty's dripping body, he hears Meurice come into the bar. Ray shuts the light and locks the door; his presence goes undetected by Meurice and his companion, who begin to enjoy themselves out front. Meurice's song, Diamond's "I'm a Believer," gets played on the jukebox, providing an ironic counterpoint to Ray's subsequent attempts to remove all traces of murder from the office.

It is a task to which Ray nearly proves himself inadequate. Using his nylon windbreaker to clean blood off the floor, Ray seems to actually increase its volume; his ineptitude at the gruesome job is bizarrely comic. The work goes slowly to the sounds of intermittent laughter from the bar. Finally finished, Ray places the gun in Marty's coat pocket and drags the body from the room. He incinerates the bloody cloths he has used and drives off with Marty in the back seat.

Ray drives through the night mist of a dark agrarian dreamscape. Listening to a radio evangelist, he is suddenly aware of other sounds—Marty is breathing heavily from the back seat. Ray skids to a stop, bolts from the car, and careens across the vertical lines of a plowed field. His disorientation is matched by the scene's aesthetic; Ray is isolated in a perspective drawing of hell. He returns to the car. The radio provides a mockingly jaunty tune as aural backdrop to Ray's next shock: the back seat of the car is now empty, though bloodstains attest to its most recent occupant. Ray finds Marty crawling down the road, away from the car. Unsure, Ray seems to ponder various scenarios before removing a shovel from the car. Before he can bring himself to strike Marty, Ray spots a truck on the horizon, heading straight for them. In a riveting sequence Ray hoists Marty out of the truck's path with only seconds to spare; Marty celebrates the moment by vomiting yet again. Ray shoves him back into the car.

A horizontal pan across a field's furrowed plow lines exudes an American gothic expressionism; we hear the sounds of a shovel hitting dirt. Ray drags Marty into the grave he has dug by the light of his car. Marty makes feeble motions as he lies in the trench. Unbelievably, he extracts Abby's gun from his coat pocket. Slowly, painfully, Marty pulls the trigger, but the chamber is empty. As Ray reaches for the gun, Marty fires again at point-blank range; once more, the chamber is empty. The six-chambered gun has been fired four times now, discharging two bullets; there remains, therefore, a final bullet in one of the gun's last two chambers. Ray pockets the gun. Though earlier his ambivalence toward his situation had been palpable, it appears to have been resolved by Marty's attempt at self-defense; Ray buries Marty with accelerating vigor. Marty's muffled screams are truly bloodcurdling as they compete with the soundtrack's eerie slasher-flick music and Ray's amplified gasps of exertion. The scene is pure horror; like much of *Blood Simple*, it recalls Joel Coen's earliest filmmaking experience in this genre.

Dawn finds Ray exhausted; the unspeakable intimacy with which he has "bedded" Marty finds expression in the image of him leaning against his car, smoking a cigarette. The camera then delivers one of the film's best visual ironies. An aerial shot of the scene registers curved tire tracks which traverse perfectly parallel lines of plowed field; they lead directly to the spot where Marty has been dispatched to an early grave. The dark humor of the scene is intensified when, in a nod to Hitchcock's car-in-the-lake *Psycho* sequence, Ray is unable to start his car's engine to make his escape. And, in the best Hitchcockian tradition, we are made complicit in Ray's crime, breathing a sigh of relief when the engine catches and Ray is able to flee.

Ray has just survived the most horrifying night of his life and committed a most heinous crime, all for love of Abby. Ray calls her, initiating a conversation hopelessly hindered by the fact that each is limited by restricted spheres of knowledge.

> Ray: *Abby? You all right?*
> Abby: *Ray? What time is it?*
> Ray: *I don't know. It's early. I love you.*
> Abby: *You all right?*
> Ray: *I don't know ... I better get off now ...*

Abby: *Well, I'll see ya. Thanks Ray.*
Ray: *Abby...*
(Abby hangs up.)

Abby perceives Ray's call as an oddly timed Valentine. Ray believes he has just committed a horrible murder in order to save Abby from the consequences of her botched attempt. For Abby, the most salient aspect of the conversation is "I love you." For Ray, Abby's "thanks" validates his reading of events.

Ray goes to Abby's loft. Meanwhile, Visser makes two crucial discoveries. Destroying the simulated murder photos, he realizes that Marty has held his back, has duplicitously retained the incriminating photo Visser showed him. He also for the first time misses his lighter. The detective breaks into Ray's house and goes through Abby's purse, clearly suspicious that Ray and Abby are somehow involved in the disappearance of two crucial pieces of evidence linking him to Marty's murder.

Back at Abby's loft, Ray has fallen asleep in a chair facing her bed; Abby awakens him accidentally. The verbal interaction which follows is pivotal. Just as the detective has been launched in a new direction through the mute testimony of absent objects, so will the lives of Abby and Ray be forever altered by their respective interpretations of the words which follow.

Abby: *Whyn't ya get into bed?*
Ray: *I didn't think I could sleep—I'm surprised you could.*
Abby: *You called me this morning.*
Ray: *Yeah. I just wanted to let you know everything's all right. I took care of everything. Now all we have to do is keep our heads.*
Abby: *What do you mean?*
Ray: *I know about it, Abby. I went to the bar last night.*
Abby: *What happened? Was Meurice there?*
Ray: *I cleaned it all up. But that ain't important. What's important is what we do now. I mean we can't go around half-cocked. What we need is time to think about this, figure it out. Anyway, we got some time now. We gotta be smart.*
Abby: *Ray—*
Ray: *Abby, never point a gun at someone unless you mean to shoot him. And if you shoot him, you better make sure he's dead 'cause if he ain't he's gonna get up and try to kill you. Only thing taught us in the service that was worth a g'dam. Where the hell's my windbreaker?*
Abby: *Ray, just tell me what happened.*
Ray: *That ain't important. What's important is that we did it, that's the only thing that matters. We both did it for each other. That's what's important.*

Abby: *I don't know what you're talkin' about—I mean, what are you*
      talkin' about? I haven't done anything funny ...
Ray: *What was that?!*

Ray freezes at Abby's last question, for Marty has warned him that
Abby will use just those words when she is confronted with evidence of
her sexual betrayal. Her question and his response are perfectly under-
standable given their respective subjective frames of reference.

Having no knowledge of what has transpired, Abby assumes Ray and
Marty have had a fight. At Ray's advice concerning murder she is horrified
and mystified—she believes that his speech regarding making sure a man
is dead is the ranting of a man thinking aloud, confessing a recently committed deed. Ray does not really pay much attention to the discrepancy
between what he believes she has done and her attitude toward it until
the end of their dialogue—and then he believes, without a doubt, that she
cannot be trusted.

The phone rings. The low cutting monotone with which Ray orders
Abby to answer it, as if she might try to avoid doing so, makes his mis-
trust of her clear. Abby answers; there is silence on the other end. When
Abby says, "It was him," Ray asks who. When Abby answers, "Marty,"
Ray's confusion is comical; a fragment of stupefied laughter escapes him
as he contemplates the incompatibility of her answer with his reality.
Having unintentionally raised Marty from the dead yet again, Abby asks,
"What's going on with you two?" The gulf between them is conveyed
visually as they face each other from opposite ends of the large room, the
space between them bisected by the vertical line of the loft's stovepipe.
Concluding that Abby's caller is a rival suitor, Ray tells Abby to call who-
ever it was back and leaves, after depositing Abby's gun on a table by the
door. Abby is, of course, stunned by Ray's behavior. A quick cut to the
detective as he hangs up the telephone identifies Abby's actual caller.

Meurice's index finger is centered in the frame as he activates his telephone message machine. Meurice listens to Marty's voice on tape; Marty
tells Meurice that he is back from his trip and that there is money missing from the bar. He tells Meurice that he suspects Ray; this call is obviously Marty's means of covering the funds he has paid Visser. The long
take concludes with Meurice's finger centered in the frame once more, turning off the machine; a match cut to Ray's index finger in the same position follows, as Ray probes an especially large bloodstain on the upholstery
of his car's back seat. When Meurice drives up, Ray hastens to cover the
seat with a towel. Meurice freezes Ray still with his question regarding whether or not Ray has been to the bar; when he realizes Meurice is

discussing theft, not murder, he relaxes enough to smile incongruously in the face of Meurice's accusations. Meurice berates Ray's "obviousness," saying that only Meurice, Ray, and Abby have keys to the safe. He also mentions that Abby has warned him about Ray. Having contributed greatly to Ray's growing confusion and paranoia, Meurice departs on a note of warning. The scene concludes with an aural callback joke: we hear the squeal of tires as Meurice discovers the street's dead end. As Ray moves out of the frame, the camera reveals bloodstains surging up through the thin cloth draped across his car seat.

The detective breaks into the bar and discovers that Marty's body is missing. Uttering a startled "Damn!" he attacks the safe in the office. The composition of the shot ironically foregrounds the location of his missing lighter; in the background Visser attempts to recover some of the evidence he now believes is being amassed in order to implicate him in Marty's murder.

Abby arrives at the bar, forcing the detective to abandon his indelicate operations on the safe. While the detective hides in the men's room, Abby surveys the recent damage perpetrated by the detective. It is obvious to her that someone has searched the office and tried to break open the safe after having forcibly entered Marty's inner sanctum. Seeing Marty's fish on the desk, she understands that Marty has at some point returned from his trip. Abby stands still, assembling the mosaic of clues the scene presents. The look in her eyes suggests her growing turmoil as she attempts to piece together a narrative capable of organizing her data. In a lyrical and disturbing shot, Abby's free-falling disorientation is made manifest onscreen. In a dizzying illusion, her head appears to float backward and down onto her pillow, simulating a fall from her standing position in the bar's office to lying prone on her bed in the loft. This lovely effect is followed by what proves to be a dream sequence. Marty is resurrected from the dead, once more, to warn Abby about Ray and to vomit copious amounts of blood onto the floor of Abby's new home. The sequence communicates her current point of view: Ray is somehow involved in the disappearance of her husband and may well represent a danger to herself. "You left your weapon behind," intones Marty, throwing her the silver compact last seen during his attempted rape; the linking of the compact with the line previously spoken by Ray symbolizes his threat. The dream sequence also drives home how prepared we have become for the unexpected to occur in this film; when we first see Marty, the idea that he may somehow have survived his ordeal, risen from the dead yet again, is not inconceivable.

Abby goes to Ray's house; she finds him in the process of moving out. He asks her to join him. She replies that she has to know what has happened first. As Ray puts the knife he's been using to cut packing string in his pocket, Abby delivers her hypothesis: Ray has broken into the bar to get his money, and he and Marty have had a fight. Ray looks vaguely ill at what he perceives is either her duplicity or her insanity. He tells her that he's been feeling sick—he can't sleep or eat. "When I try ... ," he falters. "Truth is, he was alive when I buried him," he tells Abby. As Ray and Abby face each other, a newspaper is thrown against the glass door just behind them; its surreal report is that of a gunshot as Abby's perspective shifts yet again. Fearful and confused, she hurriedly exits Ray's. As she leaves, she sees the bloodstains in the back seat of Ray's car.

Abby goes to Meurice's house. She tells him that something has happened between Marty and Ray. Meurice tells her that he believes Ray has stolen money from Marty. Meurice has put distance between himself and recent events by "retiring" from his job. When Abby expresses her fear that Ray may have killed Marty, Meurice assures her that Marty is alive; he offers Marty's phone call following the "robbery" as proof. He tells her to stay away from Ray—"the man's gone nuts"—and offers to search for Marty.

Ray goes to the bar. Noting the condition of the office, he opens the safe and finds the doctored "murder" photo Marty kept. The image of his face haloed by wavy horizontal lines as he makes his discoveries establishes a visual link between him and Marty by recalling the previous similar shot. He puts the photograph on Marty's desk, next to the fish which still cover Visser's lighter. The desktop is now littered with objects whose decontextualized presence or absence has deluded, deceived, and initiated fateful action. Ray leaves the bar. Getting into his car, he notes the decrepit Volkswagen parked behind him, half a block away.

Ray leans against the huge window in Abby's darkened loft; the shadowed image suggests a protesting figure imprisoned. Abby arrives home and turns on the loft's lights. Ray tells her sternly to turn the lights off. She does so, though she tentatively questions Ray's directive. The next shot observes a rifle trained on Ray from a building across the street; the gun is lowered when the loft goes dark. When Abby again asks why, Ray indicates that someone may be watching. Shakily, Abby manages to ask, "So, what'll they see?" She turns on the lights. "Just leave it off, you can see in!" Ray says, moving toward her. "If you do anything, the neighbors will hear!" Abby warns, in a near-whisper. Ray finally understands that Abby is afraid of him. Ray conveys his love to Abby seconds before a rifle blast shatters the window. Blood blossoms through the cloth of Ray's shirt where he has been mortally wounded.

Abby is dumbfounded as she stares at Ray's body on the floor. Her gaze shifts to the loft's broken window and then beyond, to the windows which face hers from across the street. She is terrified; her fear freezes her motionless. Our point of view is again from behind the rifle as its bearer reloads and trains its sights on Abby. Abby seems to hear the sound, leaping out of the line of fire just as the gun is refired.

Abby scrabbles across the loft's wooden floor. The sound of footsteps in the loft across the street alerts us to her impending peril—her assailant is coming after her. Abby darkens the loft once more by throwing her sandal at the light bulb on the ceiling; once she feels safer, she moves to Ray's still body. She hears glass breaking, then footsteps. We see her grab toward the body on the floor. Abby's fearful gaze is glued to the loft's front door; she hears someone approaching. She runs into the bathroom. Visser enters the loft. "You got some personal property of mine," he says, searching Ray's lifeless body. He finds nothing. "Now I don't know what the hell you two thought you were gonna pull off!" Visser snarls. He bashes Ray in the head, offscreen, in what seems to be an attempt to ensure that this particular corpse stays put.

Abby has been focusing on the bathroom's only exit, a window several stories off the ground. When Visser enters the bathroom, Abby is gone, the window open. Visser divines that Abby must have gone next door through the window. Leaning against the window frame in Abby's bathroom, he extends his gloved right hand through the window, feels along the brick exterior wall until he reaches the window next door, and begins to open it. In the apartment next door, Abby grabs the hand, flattening it against the sill. She slams the window frame down, clamping the hand in place. She then thrusts the knife she has removed from Ray's body into Visser's pinioned hand, skewering it to the sill. Visser screams and struggles.

From the loft's bathroom, Visser begins firing bullets through the wall which separates him and Abby (they are on opposite sides of this wall in adjacent apartments). Each bullet hole allows a beam of light into the room where Abby has sought refuge; the angled rays illuminate the impaled and bleeding hand. The detective begins to pound the wall he has weakened; meanwhile, Abby quietly returns to her own loft. Visser succeeds in punching through the wall and sets about removing the knife piercing his right hand with his left. In the film's most indelible image, the two disembodied hands conduct a macabre struggle; Visser is able to free himself with a stomach-turning wrench of the weapon.

Abby enters her loft. She picks up the gun Ray has earlier deposited on the small table near her door, and she moves into a steadied position on the floor, against a wall. Visser hears her from the bathroom, though he cannot see her—the bathroom door obscures each's view of the other. Pausing to put his hat on, Visser moves toward the door. Glancing at Ray's murdered body, Abby steels herself to fire. She shoots through the door, discharging the gun's third and last bullet, and says, "I'm not afraid of you, Marty!" An overhead shot shows the bloodied detective, lying face up on the floor with his head under the sink. Visser laughs maniacally as the irony of the situation begins to dawn. "Well, Ma'am," he retorts, "if I see him I'll sure give him the message!" We are afforded the detective's optical perspective in a final slow motion shot. As he lies dying, his entire universe has collapsed toward a single instant as he waits for a drop of condensed moisture to fall. The shot is an extension of his attention but rivets ours as well, forcing a recognition of our need for closure. The shot ends, however, before gravity prevails, frustrating our need and his.

It is significant that Abby's survival experience includes no moment of epiphany. Completely in the dark at the end of the film, she will never understand the true nature of the events which have transpired, for enlightenment is dependent upon the multiple perspectives of those already dead, who have themselves died in states of incomprehension or misapprehension. In *Blood Simple*, subjectivity is lethal baggage.

Blood Simple initiates what critic Peter Biskind has called the Coens' "pull-their-wings-off disdain" for their characters.[4] Relatedly, detractors note that the Coens tend to create characters which seem peculiarly bloodless. Both charges are true, and both are related to the distancing effects of the Coens' highly formal film style. *Blood Simple* is the first of many films which will be narrated by a flamboyantly expressive subjective camera, one which will "emphasize its own presence in the composition of every shot, and in the movement from one shot to the next."[5] This strategy heightens our awareness of the Coens' presence behind the lens and of the artistic vision which guides them.

The Coens' stylistic strategies so emphasize their authorship of the world before us that we are seldom, during the film, unaware of their roles as storytellers. The self-conscious flourishes of the camera intrude upon our ability to be drawn into the storyworld of the film and impede any impulse to develop emotional bonds with the film's characters. The more conscious we are of the storytellers' manipulations, the more the human figures in the film recede as objects of empathy and identification (or disgust and revulsion). They become purely aesthetic constructs, the Coens' wittily deployed chess pieces. Rather than responding with emotion to these characters, we begin to study them with the same ironic detachment with which they are observed by the camera. We bond instead with the agency responsible for the story*telling*. That is, we become emotionally and intellectually invested in the narrational process that delineates the fictional world presented to us, rather than being drawn into it ourselves.

The Coens will, after *Blood Simple*, continue to make films whose formalist techniques will forestall emotional involvement with their characters. The consequence of this strategy is that the true stars of *Blood Simple*, and of every Coen brothers film, are the Coens themselves. John Harkness writes that "the Coens' strengths lie in a stylization that reduces or even eliminates the human presence from the frame."[6] It is a testament to the Coens' idiosyncratic talent that their films often render this presence superfluous.

Blood Simple's composite identity has also aroused strong reaction. The film is strenuously allusionist, drawing heavily from the images and coded conventions of many genres. These generic vocabularies are plundered by the Coens with exquisite skill and an enthusiasm born of an unapologetic love of mass culture.

Film noir plays a large role in the Coens' theatre of generic convergence. Myriad are the references to noir genre conventions; the visual style of the film is possibly the most assertive of these references. Other quintessential noir elements are woven throughout the film: the great motivational triad of love, lust, and money; the voice-over prologue by a hard-boiled detective; the sexual triangle of husband, wife, and lover; the alluring female who inspires violence; the heady mixture of romance, paranoia, and jealousy; attention to cigarettes and their rituals of flame and fire; the declaration of love before death; the homoerotic subtext of certain verbal exchanges between Marty and the detective; and the aura of fatalism which permeates the text.

The other genres invoked and displaced in *Blood Simple* involve similarly widely understood cinematic signs and motifs. For example, our first glimpse of Marty is a parody of "town sheriff" iconography: the shot originates with the tip of his cowboy boots, which rest atop his desk. Conventions of the Western abound in the film. The loquaciously corrupt Texas outlaw, reconfigured here as the private detective, is a stereotypic Western figure. The wide-open landscapes of endless horizons which visually dominate his opening monologue are also familiar, as is the saloon where he and his employer conduct their repugnant negotiations.

Blood Simple has a dark comic edge; the timing of events and laughable/horrible miscommunications contribute toward a sensibility which at times feels almost screwball. Its mix of violence and comedy is, however, a purely postmodernist hybrid form, one that the Coens are especially adept at exploiting.

Much of *Blood Simple* is indebted to the horror genre, the form which launched Joel Coen's film career. The goriness of the film is quite spectacular. Blood drips from not-quite-dead bodies to collect in viscous pools and to seep up through cloth intended to cloak evidence; blood is wiped and smeared and vomited and spit. Vomit itself constitutes a virtual thematic motif of Marty's; when he is not throwing up, he is wiping his mouth, trying not to. A body is buried alive while screaming, having arisen from the dead in a most horrifying fashion; a woman cowers in fright, her back up against a wall, as she awaits the terror of the unknown. The skewered hand scene speaks for itself.

The Coens' exuberant mix of generic strategies executed with arthouse style has occasioned criticism in some quarters. Joel Coen's favorite bad review suggests that *Blood Simple* has "the heart of a Bloomingdale's window and the soul of a résumé."[7] In an interview with *Film Comment*'s Hal Hinson, Coen succinctly addresses this issue:

> If somebody goes out to make a movie that isn't designed primarily to entertain people, then I don't know what the fuck they're doing. I can't understand it. It doesn't make sense to me. What's the Raymond Chandler line? "All good art is entertainment and anyone who says differently is a stuffed shirt and juvenile at the art of living."[8]

Not only *Blood Simple*, but all of the Coens' subsequent work will make evident this philosophy.

Blood Simple is a highly original work; paradoxically, much of its invention flows from its unique appropriation of film historical source material, from specific allusionist images and camera moves to surgically altered bits of generic paradigms. Throughout the film the Coens gleefully underscore their attention to the codified devices and conventions of cinematic grammar. These strategies, alternately exploited and subverted in *Blood Simple*, presume upon a base of knowledge and experience that is shared between the filmmakers and their audiences; if the Coens are, to use one writer's phrase, "determinedly ironic about their own devices," they expect their viewers to be as well. Hinson summarizes this aspect of the film well. He writes:

> The filmmakers assume that the audience grew up on the same movies they did, and that we share their sophisticated awareness of conventional movie mechanics. But the Coens don't play their quotations straight; they use our shared knowledge of movie conventions for comedy. The movie has a wicked, satirical edge—there's a devilish audacity in the way these young filmmakers use their film smarts

to lure us into the movie's system of thinking, and then spring their trap, knocking us off-balance in a way that's both shocking and funny.[9]

With *Blood Simple* the Coens initiate the intersubjectivity which will mark all of their films: reciprocal recognition of film aesthetic history played as ironic in-joke. The Coens, however, never let their audiences forget their authorial power. As Hinson indicates, they are just as likely to use mutually held expectations of genre or film grammar to thwart and frustrate, shock and entertain-by-subversion as they are to reward this shared knowledge by adhering to conventional deployment. Their dream-worlds may be familiar, but they are never predictable.

CHAPTER 2

Raising Arizona

In 1985 Joel and Ethan Coen began writing the second of the four films they owed Ben Barenholtz at Circle Releasing Company, the independent production company which allowed the brothers to pursue their work unfettered by bureaucratic interference (an unlikely scenario had they signed with a studio). The finished script produced a flurry of corporate activity as the previously dismissive studios vied with each other for distribution rights. Twentieth Century–Fox edged out the competition, securing the rights to what would become one of the Coens' most crowd-pleasing and financially successful movies. Produced for under $6 million, *Raising Arizona* would generate more than $22 million in ticket sales.

Returning at higher salaries were several friends whose careers had been boosted by their collaboration with the Coens on *Blood Simple*. Co-producer Mark Silverman, production designer Jane Musky, associate producer and assistant director Deborah Reinisch, and cinematographer Barry Sonnenfeld all signed on for the Coens' second feature, as did musician Carter Burwell, whose bluegrass score is central to the artfully controlled chaos of *Raising Arizona*.

The Coens wanted their second film to be a striking departure from their first. Concerned that they might be pigeonholed as film noir specialists, they aimed for something as removed from *Blood Simple* as possible. They wanted, says Ethan, to make a film that was "*sui generis.*"[1]

Fueled by an utterly postmodern comic sensibility, *Raising Arizona* succeeds dramatically in demonstrating their versatility. Achieving, in Ethan's words, "fast-paced and funny, versus slow and punishing,"[2] the film nevertheless represents an audacious deepening of the aesthetic evident in *Blood Simple*. Sonnenfeld has noted that "topics are incredibly unimportant to them—it's structure and style and words."[3] Their idiosyncratic attention to those priorities lends their work a distinctive continuity, a persistence of vision that bridges the pulp fiction–inspired *Blood Simple* and the sweet screwball looniness of *Raising Arizona*.

As in *Blood Simple*, *Raising Arizona* opens with a voice-over narration. In the Coens' first film, the role of the detective as narrating agent is limited to this initial speech in what is both a nod to the conventions of film noir and a structure joke, since this voice-over is not coherent in terms of the film's narration. (The short voice-over prelude usually indicates that the rest of the film "serves as sort of a linguistic event, as the narrator's speech even when there is none."[4] In *Blood Simple*, the Coens subvert this device.) *Raising Arizona*'s narrator recounts story action throughout the film. The Coens embrace this conventional strategy and its subversive possibilities; not since Terrence Malick's masterpieces *Badlands* (1974) and *Days of Heaven* (1978) has a storyworld narrator's mediation been so ironically at odds with storyworld circumstance. The juxtapositioning of this character's subjective perceptions with the images generated by an equally subjective camera provides the film with many of its most madly comic moments.

We hear *Raising Arizona*'s narrator and protagonist before we see him, a fitting introduction to a character who seems to exist most fully in the language he uses to describe his world. H.I. McDunnough (Nicolas Cage) introduces himself ("call me Hi") a second or two before we see him photographed and booked into the county jail in Tempe, Arizona. He describes it as a day he'll never forget, for there he meets Ed ("short for Edwina," she barks in marine-like fashion), the woman of his dreams (Holly Hunter). The sequence which follows is marked by the characteristic dissonance between H.I.'s take on the realities of his cartoon universe and the events he purports to describe. On the way to his prison cell he analyzes his situation. "Now prison life is very structured, more 'n most people care for. But there's a spirit of camaraderie that exists between the men like you find only in combat maybe, or a pro ball club in the heat of the pennant drive." He says this as he is escorted down a dank corridor—passing one of his fellow convicts, a 450-pound man with a mop and pail, H.I. glances at him. The convict hisses back.

Quick scenes follow H.I. as he attends a prison group therapy session and a meeting of his parole board. Freed from prison on the board's recommendation, H.I. is next shown in the parking lot of a convenience store, which he prepares to rob. He blames the impulse on President Reagan, whose misguided economic policies H.I. charitably attributes to his advisors.

Back at the police station again, H.I. is photographed by a weeping Ed, whose fiancé has left her for "a student cosmetologist who knew how to ply her feminine wiles." Before he is escorted back to a prison cell, H.I. engages Ed's rapt attention with an indirect declaration of love.

Raising Arizona's characters are tragicomically transparent in their relationships to the cultural representations that dominate their lives. Their self-identities originate in the stereotypes, images, and phrases they have appropriated from various mass cultural sources. The clichés, bromides, and homilies that comprise much of the film's rhythmic dialogue take on a mad intensity when the Coens orchestrate their utterance in disjunctive contexts. The scene which follows H.I.'s return to "life inside" exemplifies this motif. During a prison therapy session, the psychologist notes that most men H.I.'s age are getting married and raising families; they would be unwilling to accept prison as a substitute. "Well," opines one of the convicts (John Goodman), "sometimes your career has got to come before family." This same fellow will later explain his prison break by asserting that "the institution no longer had anything to offer us."

In a very funny scene, the Coens lampoon the legendary food fantasies to which convicts are said to be prone. H.I. attempts to benefit from his therapy sessions through contemplation of the therapist's remarks, but, he laments, "prison ain't the easiest place to think." As H.I.'s voice-over ends, his cellmate's droning reminiscence becomes audible. "And when there was no meat," he intones, "we ate fowl. And when there was no fowl we ate crawdaddy. And when there was no crawdaddy to be found, we ate sand." "You ate what?" asks H.I. "We ate sand." "You ate *sand?*" H.I. repeats incredulously. "That's right," his cellmate tells him.

Paroled yet again by a board which implores him to stop hurting himself with his "rambunctious behavior," H.I. is drawn inexorably back into his old line of work. As we see him fleeing across a convenience store parking lot, police sirens blaring in the background, H.I. waxes philosophic on the ideological arguments which orbit "the incarceration question."

As the narrating H.I. ponders this issue, we watch him try frantically to access his getaway vehicle; he has locked himself out. He gives up and runs off into the night.

The next shot finds H.I. back in the hands of the law. The camera lingers on his newly acquired Woody Woodpecker tattoo, an image which single-handedly references the film's aesthetic paradigm. Reunited with Ed once more, H.I. puts a ring on her finger following a flirtation comprised of mutual appreciation of prison humor and hand-to-hand contact as H.I. is fingerprinted. Ensconced once again in familiar surroundings, H.I. tunes out his cellmate's reveries of the glories of meals past in order to consider his life. He thinks of Ed and of a brighter future which, he says, is only eight to fourteen months away.

Chastised by his parole board for his recidivism, then released, H.I. makes his way to where Ed is processing incoming arrestees. "I'm walking in here on my knees, Ed, a free man proposin'," he declares before greeting an acquaintance being photographed in handcuffs. Ed and H.I. are married.

Some quick shots of the wedding (criminals on the groom's side of the room and police on the bride's side) mark the film's transition to H.I. and Ed's married life.

"Ed's dad staked us to a starter home in Tempe," H.I. informs us over a long shot of a trailer surrounded by dusty desert. H.I. gets a job at a factory where he drills holes in sheet metal and listens to the reminiscences of his coworker (M. Emmett Walsh, in a fine comic cameo). Noting the similarity between prison life and his current routine, H.I. nonetheless delights in his home life with Ed. "These were the happy days, the salad days as they say, and Ed felt that having a critter was the next logical step," H.I. relates as he attends to the desert plants in front of their trailer, attired in Bermuda shorts and a fishing hat. Ed knits for the baby to come. H.I. expresses Ed's feeling on the subject: "Her point was that there was too much love and beauty for just the two of us, and every day we kept a child out of the world was a day he might regret later having missed."

Alas, H.I. and Ed wait in vain for offspring. In one of the film's most memorable sequences H.I., whose speech patterns are as stylized as the visual images they accompany, describes his and Ed's ordeal. He speaks in a sweetly droning, pseudo-biblical, quasi-mournful ecstasy of verbiage; Howard Cosell meets Billy Graham. The film brings the desperate poetry of his words and the events they purport to narrate into a vertiginous proximity which incites high humor.

The scene begins with Ed driving up to the trailer with the siren of her police cruiser screaming. She is crying hysterically. "I'm barren," she sobs. H.I.'s reaction shot is a memorable one. The camera lurches from overhead, swooping downward to rest at H.I.'s face level, a kinetic reference to sinking hearts and felled hopes. His voice-over begins at the end of this shot and continues through the next. H.I. and Ed sit in front of a doctor's desk, which is covered with paraphernalia. Pills of every color and size, surgical scissors, plastic models, baby bottles, tiny plastic containers of medicinal drops, birth control devices, and a child's plastic stethoscope are featured items. The doctor, who looks much like George Burns in a white coat, gesticulates ineffectually with his cigar toward an illustration of the female reproductive system. During his explanation, Ed continues to sob uncontrollably; no sound is heard, however, except for H.I.'s voice, and the sinister whispering of the wind (a wickedly funny touch). H.I. relates: "At first I didn't believe it, that this woman, who looked as fertile as the Tennessee Valley, could not bear children. But the doctor explained that her insides were a rocky place where my seed could find no purchase. Ed was inconsolable." H.I.'s fervently nonscientific explanation of their ill luck is endearingly entertaining within its context.

H.I. and Ed are unable to adopt because of H.I.'s criminal past; H.I. laments that "biology and the prejudices of others conspired to keep us childless." Ed and H.I. fall into a depressed state. Ed takes to her bed, while H.I. morosely notes that even his job "seems as hot and bitter as a dry prairie wind" despite the lurid tales delivered by his shiftless coworker. (A story concerning a man who somehow ends up with a sandwich in one hand and a severed head in the other is evidence of the Coens' fascination with the topic. In *Blood Simple*, this same actor plays a detective who suggests that if his head were cut off he'd simply crawl around without it.) H.I. assesses the depth of his despair. "I even caught myself driving by convenience stores," he says, and pauses. "That weren't on the way home."

H.I. and Ed's hopes for a family are revived when they learn of the Arizona quintuplets, babies born to Nathan and Florence Arizona, an unpainted-furniture mogul and his wife. H.I. declares:

> Now y'all without sin can cast the first stone. But we thought it was unfair that some should have so many while others should have so few. With the benefit of hindsight, maybe it wasn't such a hot idea. But at the time, Ed's little plan seemed like the solution to all our problems, and the answer to all our prayers.

H.I.'s voice-over is accompanied by the McDunnoughs' careful preparations for the course of action Ed has prescribed. As they drive off into a surreal southwestern sunset, aluminum ladder secured firmly to the roof of the car, the film's credits appear onscreen as Carter Burwell's banjo and vocal hillbilly music swells.

The Coens use their eleven and a half minutes of pre-credit backstory to establish a staggeringly rich sense of stylized story environment, as well as to deliver a vast amount of story and character information. The staccato onslaught of short scenes works to imbue the film with a breathless sense of propulsion. Following the credits, the film's style changes. The quick shuffle of scenes shot by a fairly static camera gives way to longer scenes and sequences dominated by a flamboyantly mobile camera. This highly subjective mobile camera will investigate highly subjective filmspace. The Coens and their cohorts have fashioned a minimalistic, ultrastylized, closed universe wherein the earthy tones of the Southwest merge with the cotton candy hues of the fairground. While the film nominally situates itself in Tempe, Arizona, its filmspace delineates an imaginary geography which combines the architectural style of a theme park with the contours of a Warner Brothers cartoon. It is pure synthetic postmodern fabulism, a projected world where each image is metaphoric and highly allusive.

The crime docudrama is spoofed during a short sequence immediately following the film's delayed credits. The Arizonas are pictured in their aggressively symmetrical living room. A title informs us that we are privy to "The Arizona Household." "Wednesday, April 12" appears next, followed by an interesting and humorous metalepsis (Gerard Genette's term for the breaching of narrative levels). Nathan Arizona, Sr., is yelling at an employee via telephone. After what is obviously a query from the other end of the line, Nathan Sr. ostentatiously raises his wrist to look at his watch. He says, "It is now precisely," he pauses, during which time a title appears on the screen: "8:45 p.m." "Eight-forty-five in the p.m.," Nathan Sr. says.

During Arizona's phone call, the couple have noted but not heeded some strange thumps from above; a cut to the nursery reveals the source of the disturbance. H.I. is trying frantically to keep the children from crying. Toward this end he holds each baby in turn while performing a shuffling dance, hoping this dipping and bobbing will help. Baby-cam shots pepper the sequence which follows (cinematographer Sonnenfeld filmed while being dragged on a blanket across the floor), a surreally choreographed attempt by H.I. to restore the hiding, crawling, and jumping babies to their cribs. Mrs. Arizona interrupts her reading of Dr. Spock's baby care book to check on the children. She is puzzled to find all five boys sitting up, in perfect alignment.

Ed cries out in disappointment when she sees H.I. approach the car empty-handed. She is highly unsympathetic to his pleading explanations. She rolls up the car windows, locks the doors, and orders him to return to the Arizonas'. "Don't you come back here without a baby!" she barks like a drill sergeant. "They got more 'n they can handle," she says, repeating the headline of the local paper's coverage of the story, apparently choosing to take it at face value.

H.I. does indeed return for a baby, climbing up his ladder to the nursery window, where he is gurgled at by one of the babies who gazes at him over his mother's shoulder. Once again, bouncing baby point-of-view shots are humorously effective.

Ed is overjoyed when H.I. returns triumphant. "Here's the instructions," H.I. says, throwing the Dr. Spock volume in the car after carefully handing the child over to Ed. "He's beautiful," Ed near-cries. "Yea," says H.I., "He's awful damn good. I think I got the best one." Ed has an attack of conscience which she overcomes with H.I.'s help.

Like the other characters in *Raising Arizona*, Ed has created herself out of the cultural representations which saturate her world. In her military-like response to the challenges of working within a predominantly male culture, in her heightened reaction to the news that she is infertile, and in her fervent, felonious drive toward motherhood is evinced a subjectivity which bears the genetic imprint of daytime talk shows devoted to the exploitation of sensationalized "women's issues." Nowhere in the film is this idea more pointedly demonstrated than in the moments following the kidnapping. "I love him *so* much," Ed sobs twice mere seconds after beholding the purloined toddler. "I know you do," empathizes H.I., respectful of and transfixed by the enormity of her parental feeling.

H.I. readies their home for little Nathan Arizona, Jr.'s arrival. After rearranging crib items, stashing what might be dirty laundry under bed pillows, hiding his *Playboy* magazine under the mattress, and playing "Home on the Range" on their record player, they welcome the appropriated child to his new home.

The new parents exult in their changed status. Ed vows that they will provide their child with a life that will be "decent and normal from here on out," and H.I. leaps to "preserve the moment" in a family photograph. The resulting photo suggests that H.I. will need to make some adjustment to his new role; he looks like a man recently electrocuted in the bosom of what he refers to as "the family unit."

In a bizarrely comical spoof of the birth process, H.I.'s therapy session convict buddies break out of prison. The larger of the two erupts from the muddy earth, struggling with great effort to rise from the depths below. He screams in the rain as he emerges, then screams again as he stands erect in the driving rain and lightning, filthy but victorious. With a flamboyant gesture, he reaches back down into the mud and pulls the other out, feet first. They howl in the murk before retiring to a gas station bathroom to pomade their hair. Satisfied with the effects of their primping, they steal a car.

Back at the McDunnough residence, Nathan Jr. is peacefully asleep along with H.I. and Ed, who have fallen asleep while sitting up and gazing at the infant. A knock at their door startles them awake; a voice tells

Ed (Holly Hunter) and H.I. (Nicolas Cage) celebrate an extralegal home-coming in *Raising Arizona*.

them to admit the police into their home. H.I. grabs his gun in response, while an alarmed Ed solemnly warns that "they ain't gonna split up the family." The rapidity with which she is able to switch her self-identity (from drill sergeant to victim of infertility to kidnapper bent on balancing the scales of "justice" to mother defending the sanctity of her family) is rivaled only by the sincerity with which she assumes each role. The result is vastly entertaining.

The night visitors prove to be H.I.'s convict friends Gale (John Goodman) and Evelle Snopes (William Forsythe); they conduct a raucous reunion while Ed looks on disapprovingly. Gale and Evelle are curious about Nathan Jr. The lack of consensus between H.I. and Ed concerning the child's recent history draws suspicion from the two criminals. H.I. deflects their attention from his family by inviting them to sit down, an invitation which they accept with alacrity. Ed, however, is upset both at the odor the men have brought with them, having hit the main sewer line as they tunneled out of prison to freedom, and with the fact that they are fugitives. She refuses to allow them to stay. Gale wonders aloud who wears the pants in the family (clearly, in the case of his own partnership with Evelle, he does), eliciting an alarmed reaction from H.I. Thunder outside the trailer underscores his panic at being caught between two worlds. Talk of H.I.'s "short leash" propels H.I. into a discussion with Ed on the merits of human charity. Ed relents, allowing the convicts to stay a short while.

That night H.I. has a dream. He drifts off thinking about "happiness, birth, and new life" but once asleep is haunted by what H.I. describes as "a lone Biker of the Apocalypse, a man with all the powers of hell at his command." As H.I. describes this apparition of evil destruction, images of his dream fill the screen. The sequence which follows showcases some of the Coens' most audacious camerawork. Its style is strongly reminiscent of that of their friend and former mentor Sam Raimi.

Leonard Small, the Biker-Thing-from-Hell (Randall "Tex" Cobb), is a cross between the *Mad Max* trilogy's (1979–1985) Road Warrior and *Taxi Driver*'s (1976) Travis Bickle, with a little *Carrie* (1976) thrown in for good measure. He emerges from roaring flames clad in metal, leather, and— unspeakably vile—seemingly newly skinned fur. He leaves a blaze of fire in his wake as he roars down the highway, blowing up bunnies with hand grenades and shooting sunning lizards off rocks. Flowers spontaneously incinerate as he flies by on his motorcycle. Nowhere is the comic-book aesthetic which defines the film more evident than in this sequence. Small sports a tattoo which reads "Mama didn't love me"; his tiny bronzed baby shoes jingle at his side near his ammunition belt. The tattoo links H.I. with our protagonist; the demonic Small is H.I.'s doppelgänger, let loose upon the world as a consequence of H.I.'s guilty imagination. H.I. explains,

> He could turn the day into night and lay to waste everything in his path. He was especially hard on the little things, the helpless and the gentle creatures. He left a scorched earth in his path, befouling even the sweet desert breeze that swept across his brow. ... I don't know if he was dream or vision, but feared that I myself had unleashed him, for he was the fury that would be, as soon as Florence Arizona found her little Nathan gone.

The camera records Small as he careens Evel Knievel–style out of the desert toward town but does not follow. In response to H.I.'s tremulously voiced anticipation of Florence Arizona's reaction to her son's abduction, the camera races up the Arizonas' driveway, tracking up and over tricycle, parked car, and ornamental fountain. The Arizona family manse is a cross between the Flintstones' house and Camelot; plastic-looking palm trees leading to the front door finish its surreal opulence. The camera shoots up the abandoned ladder to the nursery and flies through the window straight toward the tonsils of Florence Arizona, whose mouth is open wide in preparation to scream her grief and terror at finding Nathan Jr. gone.

H.I. wakes from his dream to find Ed consoling the baby, who she says has had a nightmare. "Somehow it's a hard world for the little things," H.I. mumbles as he watches the sun rise.

The next scene finds Nathan Arizona, Sr., promoting his unpainted furniture business during the press conference devoted to his son's kidnapping. The reporters' feeding frenzy includes such queries as whether or not the grieving parent would care to comment on the rumor that his son has been abducted by UFOs. "Don't print that, son," Nathan Sr. pleads. "His mama reads that, she's just gonna lose all hope."

The second of the Coens' "crass, venal men behind desks" has an uproarious exchange with the law enforcement officers assigned to his son's kidnapping; the local police and the FBI compete with each other over issues of jurisdiction while Nathan Sr. maligns the competence of both. The scene concludes with the frustrated father succumbing to a temper tantrum any toddler would be proud of; he screams and throws things and questions whether or not law enforcement can distinguish "between a lead and a hole in the ground."

Cut to a hole in the ground: Gale and Evelle's point of egress. A throng of police mill around the site while German Shepherds investigate. They are joined by the Apocalyptic Biker, who spares the life of a rabbit in deference to his company. He moves on to the gas station restroom recently vacated by Gale and Evelle. The camera swoops between their abandoned pomade and Small's twitching nostrils to convey the biker's bestial powers of smell.

Back at the McDunnoughs', H.I. is caught between Gale and Ed's growing antagonism. Ed requests that the convicts make themselves scarce while they entertain their "decent friends." H.I. contemplates leaving with the convicts; a look from his wife occasions a change of heart.

H.I. and Ed prepare themselves for their guests. A floor-level shot of H.I.'s feet as they are shoehorned into white top-stitched loafers below lemon casual trousers gently lampoons southwestern leisure attire.

We are introduced to Glen (Sam McMurray) and Dot (Frances McDormand), who have come to visit with their children. Glen and Dot pause at the front door to exclaim over the McDunnoughs' blessed event; behind them, their offspring vigorously attack H.I.'s car. Once inside, Dot waxes poetic over little Nathan Jr. She suggests they name the child Jason. "I just love biblical names," she gushes. H.I. and Glen talk out in the kitchen. While Glen mangles ethnic-slur jokes, H.I. monitors the activities of Glen's kids. Words cannot do justice to the nihilistic comedy of this scene as these children spin off into a frenzy of lunatic destruction.

Oblivious to the needs of her many children, who respond to parental neglect by perpetrating acts which range from the grossly unhygienic to the near-homicidal, Dot terrifies the McDunnoughs with her command of soundbite medical lingo. Especially humorous are her dire prognostications regarding childhood vaccinations and her warnings concerning the baby's educational and financial future.

By the time H.I. and Glen take a stroll through a desert which looks as though it came packaged with a Barbie doll, H.I. is nearly undone by the enormity of his fatherly responsibilities. H.I.'s quick transformation from beaming family man to beast of burden crushed by the cares of fatherhood is wonderfully executed by Cage, whose hangdog features are able to register an astounding variety of shades of torment.

Cage's physical inertia plays perfectly in *Raising Arizona*; its stasis provides great textural contrast to the baroque liveliness of his characteristic mode of storytelling and the frenetic pace of the film itself.

H.I. confides to Glen that he feels suffocated. Glen empathizes before suggesting his and Dot's solution to the pressures of family life: wife swapping, or "swinging" as Glen puts it. H.I. responds by punching Glen to the ground while growling his vehement rejection of the idea. The scene ends as Glen, fleeing H.I.'s wrath, runs face first into a cactus. This stunt is accompanied by an especially rich squashing noise; like all of *Raising Arizona*'s sound effects, it might have been patched in from a Road Runner cartoon.

Out for a ride that evening Ed despairs that H.I. has ruined their friendship with Glen and Dot, "decent folk" in her opinion. Glen is also H.I.'s foreman at work—she guesses he will now fire H.I. and where, she asks, does that leave their "entire family unit?"

H.I.'s demeanor changes as they drive by his favorite convenience store. He notes that the baby needs diapers. "I'll be out directly," he says with suspicious light-heartedness. "Mind you stay strapped in," he says ominously before entering the store.

H.I. has snapped and embraces a familiar palliative to medicate his mounting anxiety. Armed and stocking-masked, he tells the teenager behind the register that he'll "be taking these Huggies and whatever cash you've got." The youth alerts the police by pressing a panic button below the counter, initiating an alarm which compels Ed to take note of H.I.'s activities in the store. H.I. orders the teenager to hurry after Ed screams at him through the window; he confides that he seems to be "in Dutch with the wife." Ed drives off, leaving H.I. to fend for himself. To make matters worse, the young store clerk begins to fire a gun at H.I., as do the arriving police. (H.I. never loads his gun with bullets for, as he has explained to his parole board, he doesn't want to hurt anybody.)

There follows a surreally funny chase scene through the streets and backyards of a dreamlike suburban obstacle course. A camera races across the ground to simulate a charging Doberman's point of view; H.I. survives by virtue of having frozen in place a half inch out of the chained animal's reach. H.I. keeps running, the store clerk and police cruiser in hot pursuit. The Doberman joins the chase, having pulled his chain stake out of the ground. Ed, upon hearing gunshots, relents and tells Nathan Jr. that they are going to pick up daddy. H.I. hijacks a man in a truck. "Son," the man says upon making H.I.'s acquaintance, "you got a panty on your head." In a hilarious shot, the truck driver screams as he spots the gun-crazy teenage clerk blocking their path. The teenager shoots out the windshield of the truck, but before he can fire again he is toppled by the Doberman, who by now has acquired a posse of canines. Swerving to miss the youth, H.I. and the truck driver nearly hit the police car, which has never ceased firing at them. As the truck comes to a halt, H.I. is thrown through the glassless windshield onto the front lawn of a house. The police cruiser pulls up, and the officers open fire. H.I. takes off through the house, a police officer in pursuit; a shaky mobile camera follows the chase.

As little Nathan Jr. cutely cowers in the back seat, Ed maneuvers the car toward H.I., who is pursued by a shooting policeman through a supermarket. H.I. is trying to replace the Huggies he has dropped at some point during his getaway. Not only must H.I. evade this dedicated policeman, he must also avoid the dog pack racing through the aisles. A rifle-toting grocer gleefully joins the hunt; the injured look on H.I.'s face as he measures this latest threat is priceless. H.I. makes it out of the store and is rescued by Ed, who delivers a right to H.I.'s jaw as soon as he is seated in the vehicle. They argue over the quality of their family life, which Ed thinks is poor. H.I. tells her to accept him as he is and as Nathan Jr. does; he urges her to adopt an "I'm O.K., you're O.K." philosophy. On their way home they pick up the package of Huggies dropped in the heat of the chase.

When they get home Ed delivers an ultimatum to Gale and Evelle who, she believes, exert a "bad influence" to which H.I. is increasingly prone. Once Ed and the baby retire to the bedroom, Gale and Evelle try to recruit H.I. into their plan for a bank heist. "You're young and you've got your health," observes Evelle. "What would you want with a job?" They say they know he is partial to convenience stores but urge him to follow the prison therapist's advice regarding ambition. They intend the bank robbery to be the starting point of a crime spree "to cover the entire Southwest proper. And we keep going until we can retire. Or we get caught. Either way, we're fixed for life." Gale tells H.I. that he must perpetrate crime in order to be true to his own nature. The camera closes in on H.I.'s face before the image dissolves into that of the Demon Biker; again, the conventions of film grammar suggest this fellow to be H.I.'s darker impulses made corporeal.

H.I. leaves Ed a poetic note explaining his decision to return to the life of an outlaw; his words are accompanied by a montage of images which observe the simultaneous activities of various characters. H.I. writes that "he cannot tarry"; he feels the forces of "bad trouble" gathering about him, trouble which he hopes to spare Ed and Nathan Jr. by leaving.

Meanwhile, Small has tracked the baby to the McDunnoughs'. He goes to Nathan Sr.'s office where he makes an appropriately satanic entrance. He identifies himself as a bounty hunter with the instincts of a bloodhound. Small wants more than the $25,000 reward Arizona has posted; denied this money, he threatens to find the child and sell him to the highest bidder. Small reaches out and catches a fly by the leg midflight, a feat which establishes his blood-sucking monster pedigree. Recognizing Evil when he sees it, Arizona refuses Small's extortionate offer. Before he can phone the police, Small is gone.

Glen visits H.I. and demands Nathan Jr.; he and Dot have discovered the child's identity but would rather raise the child themselves than force the McDunnoughs to give him back. Unfortunately, Gale and Evelle overhear Glen's bellowing. They grab Nathan Jr., saying that it is "just business"—they intend to return him for the reward. There ensues a bizarrely comical fight between Gale and H.I. So imaginatively filmed is this sequence that the altercation seems animated rather than choreographed. The fight thoroughly destroys the trailer, which like the other sets in *Raising Arizona* functions tropologically. It is designed to reflect the McDunnoughs' outsider status; the flimsiness of the trailer's interior walls is emblematic of how tenuous is their hold on the "normal" life of "the family unit" in Reagan's America. The fugitives leave H.I. bound to a chair and abscond with little Nathan Jr. They return briefly to grab Dr. Spock's baby care book. H.I. screams his anguish, a sound which penetrates the far corners of their desert neighborhood.

Ed returns home and frees H.I., who repudiates his past and vows to devote himself to his family. He sets out to find Nathan Jr.

Gale and Evelle, meanwhile, are much taken with their new charge. Evelle robs a convenience store on their way to their bank job, obtaining diapering instructions from the clerk before pulling his gun. In their haste to flee the scene of their latest crime, they drive off with an infant-seated Nathan Jr. poised on the roof of their car. When they discover their deed they scream in tandem with misery. They rescue a miraculously unharmed Nathan Jr. from the road's double center lines and vow to never leave him again. No longer willing to trade the child for the reward money, they rename him Gale Jr. and welcome him to their family.

H.I. and Ed have an emotional scene as they look for the missing boy. Ed cares for nothing save the safe return of the baby to his parents; she and H.I., she says, are finished. They have been living, she says, "in a fool's paradise."

The apocalyptic bounty hunter finds a discarded picture of the bank Gale and Evelle plan to rob. A match cut to the bank itself follows. Gale and Evelle decide that taking the baby with them as they rob the bank is more prudent than leaving him behind. Their heist is plagued with verbal mishaps, but they leave triumphant, unaware that their sack of money contains an activated pressurized canister of dye marker. Seconds before it explodes in their car, they discover that they have once again left Nathan Jr. behind. They nearly collide with the McDunnoughs, who question the two convicts and snatch the Spock book out of the dye-drenched car. H.I. and Ed drive off, ignoring the pleas of Gale and Evelle, who wish to join their search. "It's our baby, too!" they shriek pitifully.

The next shot reveals the infant-seated Nathan Jr., serene as he observes the world from his place on the twin yellow lines of the roadway. A fireball in the background of the image announces the arrival of "bad trouble." Small rides out of the flames toward the child as H.I. and Ed approach from the opposite direction in their car. "What is he?" breathes Ed. "Do you see him too?" whispers H.I. Small scoops the car seat up from the pavement and secures it to the front of his bike; he then delivers a rifle blast to the windshield of H.I. and Ed's car. The sound effects which accompany Small's maneuvers are heightened in the extreme; each click and clank resonates malevolently.

The showdown between Small and H.I. (a conflict between H.I.'s outlaw impulses and his nobler, more civilized, domesticated self) is a showcase of cartoon punishment; improbable angles and wildly mobile camerawork capture this epic struggle. One of the sequence's best gags includes a race through the bank, where customers and employees are still face down on the floor as per Gale and Evelle's instructions. During the melee H.I. discovers, hidden from view by Small's weapon-laden vest, a Woody Woodpecker tattoo over Small's heart; the connection between the two combatants is made even more explicit.

In a spectacularly destructive explosion, Small is vanquished by H.I., who apologizes to the biker seconds before bits of the creature are scattered all over the road. A close-up of Small's bronzed baby shoes is accompanied by the echo of an infant's cry. This testament to the importance of parental love rings poignant, even amidst *Raising Arizona*'s cartoon nuttiness.

H.I. and Ed replace Nathan Jr. in his crib, having entered the Arizonas' nursery by ladder once more. Only the bedraggled and charred book of baby care they place beside the happy child suggests his adventures during his sojourn with the McDunnoughs. Nathan Arizona, Sr., enters the room and is overjoyed to see his son. Despite his heightened emotional state, Arizona cannot help but remain true to his nature. He tries to substitute unpainted furniture for the reward money he thinks H.I. and Ed deserve. The McDunnoughs refuse the reward and confess their true roles in his son's disappearance. Arizona is sympathetic to their troubles and not only declines to press charges but offers the stricken couple some sweetly sound marital advice. His declaration of love for his own wife is as surprising as it is touching.

That night H.I. has a dream, a montage of visions of the future which include Gale and Evelle's return to the secure womb of prison life, Glen's continuing absence of any clue, and the happy youth of Nathan Jr. Even further into the future H.I.'s dreams take him, to a cozy home where H.I. and Ed are surrounded by children and grandchildren; lovingly they embrace as they gaze upon the joyful family created by their union. This gathering occurs, in a place "if not Arizona, then a land not too far away, where all parents are strong, and wise, and capable, and all children are happy and beloved. I don't know," H.I. muses, "maybe it was Utah." The sweetness of the moment dissolves into acerbic wit, and the final credits roll.

Like *Blood Simple*, *Raising Arizona* reflects the Coens' signature disinterest in writing multidimensional characters with whom viewers can connect emotionally. The film's characters are incarnated abstractions deployed as special effects in a film where each element, including each actor, exists to serve style. Though they may fail to elicit sympathy or trigger emotional involvement, they are hypnotic creations whose stylized linguistic adventures contribute mightily toward mapping the film's exotic cinematic terrain.

Raising Arizona continues *Blood Simple*'s preoccupation with the spoken word. The film is redolent with characters who appear to have composed themselves from language appropriated from various sources. Their clichéd speech reveals the pop cultural foundations of their existence, the extent to which the culture offers prefabricated identities easily accessible through its predigested images and ready-made phrases. The Coens gleefully offer up their verbal commonplaces within contexts that alter their significance in ways that inspire typical Coenesque lunacy laced with irony. Inadvertently, perhaps, the Coens illustrate an interesting idea: the postmodern conception of identity, wherein self is not "a pre-given entity or essence, but ... [is] produced in the signs, narratives, fictions and fantasies that make up the social world,"[5] is eloquently articulated in the hyperstylized cartoon world of *Raising Arizona*.

If with *Raising Arizona* the Coens lampoon a culture wherein subjectivity originates in the popular clichés of fast-food commercials and talk-show confessions, its portrait is not without affection; their unique take on the pressures of work and family is an absurdist vision that is somehow ultimately sustaining.

Like *Blood Simple*, *Raising Arizona* maintains an exquisite balance between its key forms of address, authorial and generic. That is, the authorial subjectivity of the camera is once again emphasized as the agency which interprets the flow of the film's stylized generic worlds. The surplus meaning generated by this signature Coen strategy produces content at least as important as the literal meaning of the film's audiovisual images.

Raising Arizona represents to a greater degree than *Blood Simple* the postmodern incoherent text, what Robert Venturi calls "the difficult whole. ... various parts, styles, or sub-systems are used to create a new synthesis."[6] This new synthesis, composed of elements freed from their original narrative sources, produce what is called a "decentered" text. Guiliana Bruno suggests this idea in her definition of pastiche: "an aesthetic of quotations pushed to the limit ... an effacement of key boundaries and separations, a process of erosion of distinctions."[7] *Raising Arizona* represents one of American cinema's most vivid examples of this aesthetic strategy. The film utilizes a mesmerizing amalgamation of generic paradigms to deliver its breathless ballad of love, loss, and redemption. As always, the Coens presume upon a base of shared knowledge of the generic worlds they revisit and revamp.

The prison movie genre is prominently referenced in *Raising Arizona*. Archetypal images displaced in the Coens' quasi-animated universe include those of the booking and fingerprinting process and of prisoners lying in their bunk beds while shadows pattern their tormented faces. The confrontation with parole board members is, in *Raising Arizona*, a wacky tribute to a story element of the genre rarely given screen time; garnering comic honors as well is the Coens' rendition of a relatively new convention, the prison group therapy session. Finally, every great prison film deserves a boffo prison breakout scene. The Coens' version of this staple component is extremely funny, as is its reversal in H.I.'s last dream sequence.

The crime docudrama enjoys a brief life in the film, as do the conventions of the male buddy film, realized in the relationship between the felonious Snopes brothers. The Western genre is lightly touched upon as well. Carter Burwell's twangy score links the film to this tradition, as does H.I.'s central conflict: the clash between the savage and the civilized is an archetypal Western generic theme.

Apocalyptic science fiction/horror is given a high profile in the film. The *Mad Max* trilogy is an especially strong intertext, courtesy of Leonard Small. Conventions of the biker movie grace these sections as well.

The slapstick/screwball, comedy of manners, and romantic comedy are forms giddily subsumed by *Raising Arizona*. Of these genres, the screwball comedy enjoys the greatest amount of attention to its generic paradigms. The Coens' second film revisions quite a few of them. Its hyperkinesia and chaotic narrative structure are constituent elements of the form, as is its collection of (beyond) eccentric characters. Screwball comedies are known for their Depression-denying sensibility. Interestingly, H.I. invokes the Reaganomics of the eighties as his personal nemesis. Other screwball conventions skewed in the film include the physical nature of its visual jokes, the domestic conflict at the heart of the film, and its attention to issues of class as rendered in the differences between the Arizona and McDunnough households.

The criminal-couple subgenre is also given a comical turn. Ed's hilarious admonishments concerning H.I.'s initial failure to secure an infant renders her a surreal Bonnie to H.I.'s dementedly philosophical Clyde.

Finally, the film may be seen to address the aims of social satire; *Raising Arizona* delivers scathingly amusing commentary on a variety of topics. Arizona's disinclination to ignore the advertising potential of the press conference devoted to his son's kidnapping speaks volumes about a certain brand of American capitalism. What passes for traditional middle-class values and how often shallow are the hallmarks of such are lampooned well. Glen and Dot, who Ed describes as the kind of "decent people" with whom they ought to socialize, emerge in the film as sexually deviant, parentally dysfunctional, would-be blackmailing criminals. They are, however, among the few characters in the film who at no time brandish a gun. In *Raising Arizona* both likely and highly unlikely types are able to produce lethal weapons at a moment's notice as the brothers Coen take a swipe at America's cultural romance with gun violence.

Raising Arizona is a highly entertaining example of postmodern bricolage; its fervid absurdisms incorporate and transcend the conventions of many disparate film forms. The wonder of this film is that its highly formal edifices do not preclude its loopy warmth; *Raising Arizona* is as close to a Valentine to their audiences as the Coens are likely to ever send.

Critical reaction to the film was largely positive. David Denby of *New York* had been one of *Blood Simple*'s greatest admirers; his review of *Raising Arizona* rings not only with high praise but with the satisfaction of having been proved right in his previous assessment of the Coens' talent. Their second feature, he writes, makes clear that "the Coens are the real thing"; their "deranged fable of the New West" turns "sarcasm into a rude yet affectionate mode of comedy."[8] Richard Corliss of *Time* calls the film "exuberantly original,"[9] while David Ansen of *Newsweek* calls *Raising Arizona* a "wild-card comedy [that] knows where it's headed every inch of the way. It's a hoot and a half."[10] Other reviewers, such as David Edelstein, noted the warmth and integrity with which the Coens soften the edges of their satire.

A minority of critics disliked the film for what they perceived as its mean-spirited disparagement of the film's characters. Sheila Benson, one of the most influential of these critics, complained of its cold detachment, a criticism which had dogged *Blood Simple*. She writes that while "*Raising Arizona* is miraculously adept technically ... it remains so cool at its center. There is always the sense of the filmmakers' superior distance from these maddened hayseeds." Ultimately, Benson wrote, the wizardry of the film "is in the service of a really cretinous humor and a deeply condescending viewpoint."[11] The Coens refute this charge of condescension. Regarding their take on the film's portrayal of life in Tempe, Ethan responds: "Of course its not accurate. It's not supposed to be. It's all made up. It's an Arizona of the mind."[12]

Raising Arizona pleased most critics and audiences and was highly profitable to boot; it is the only one of the Coens' first five films to do better in the United States than in Europe. The film represents a critical step in the filmmaking career of the two brothers, allowing them, as one writer put it, "to sneak into the cinematic mainstream."[13] Ethan offers a typically deadpan explanation of the leap from *Blood Simple* to *Raising Arizona*. "It's like a real cheap and shameless bid at making a commercial movie. We decided to sell out and that was the first decision."[14] The second might have been not to sacrifice their formal brilliance to this goal. The result is an inspired marriage of comedy both high and low.

CHAPTER 3

Miller's Crossing

The complexity of the Coens' third feature reflects a healthy respect for their viewers. *Miller's Crossing* (1990) is an extremely verbal film; the spectator's appreciation of the storyworld action (both implicit and explicit) turns upon an ability to follow rather complicated linguistic events.

Loosely based upon Dashiell Hammett's *The Glass Key* and its screen adaptations of 1935 and 1942, *Miller's Crossing* is a stylized revisioning of the thirties gangster film. As such, it pulses to the beat of its generic antecedents: cause and effect, transgression and retaliation, crime and punishment. Set in an anonymous northeastern city during Prohibition, the film pays ironic tribute to the "dirty town" premise of Hammett's *Red Harvest*, and to "a celluloid place called Gangland ... populated by mobsters and molls, tommy guns and T-men ... bootleggers and bootlickers ... cutthroats and crooked politicians."[1]

Beautifully photographed by Barry Sonnenfeld, the film resonates with visual references to films from *Little Caesar* (1930) and *The Public Enemy* (1931) to *The Godfather* parts 1 and 2 (1972 and 1974); Sonnenfeld's thickly textured amber images especially recall cinematographer Gordon Willis' work on *The Godfather* films. These generic allusions are integrated within the hermetically sealed, meticulously stylized universe that Coen characters typically call home. In his landmark essay on "The Gangster as Tragic Hero," Robert Warshow describes the milieu of the movie gangster as "that dangerous and sad city of the imagination." The Coens exploit the fact that the thirties gangster film was always played out in such a world, classical-era location shooting being a phenomenon associated with wartime technology. They go further, though, not only foregrounding the artificiality of *Miller's Crossing*'s eastern city but suggesting the stylized minimalism of a Warner Brothers studio lot. They present essences on the screen, a sort of visual synecdoche wherein a charmed glimpse represents the mythical whole.

According to the Coens, *Miller's Crossing* originated with two key images. The first was a dreamed vision of a black hat touching down in a forest clearing, then rising with the wind to soar upward toward the trees beyond. (When the film's star, Gabriel Byrne, queried Joel Coen about the symbolic significance of the hat in *Miller's Crossing*, Joel helpfully replied, "The hat is very significant."[2]) The second image depicted overcoated urban gangsters conducting a malign transaction in a wood. The incongruity at the heart of both images is consistent with the film's central tension; as always, the Coens strike an audaciously idiosyncratic bargain between the subjective dreamworld that distinguishes their vision and the film historical dreamworld upon which they draw for inspiration and mischief.

The film opens with an aural image: ice is dropped into a glass. The film's initial visual image follows, that of the glass being filled with the illegal liquor that constitutes the bedrock business of the city's head crime boss, Leo (Albert Finney). The first scene of the film involves other business, however. In a nod to the opening of Francis Ford Coppola's *The Godfather* (1972), Johnny Caspar (Jon Polito) has sought an audience with Leo. He is seeking permission to kill a man who has double-crossed him. A man lingers behind Caspar, having built a drink in the dark recesses of the amber- and leather-toned room; upon hearing the name of Caspar's intended victim, the man moves forward, crossing the length of the room to stand behind Leo. As Caspar makes his fevered argument the camera slowly pushes in toward his floridly animated face; its shining intensity is a marked contrast to the lush gold and brown textures of the room's stylized, aggressively masculine thirties interior. As Caspar's plea draws to a close, the camera reveals for the first time the faces of the other men in the room. Leo's face registers a stolid intractability. Backing Leo is his right-hand man and the brains behind Leo's gangland throne, Tom Reagan (Gabriel Byrne); his pale face reflects a brooding attention to the discussion at hand. Eddie "The Dane" Dane (J. E. Freeman), Caspar's second-in-command, radiates menace as he glowers from beneath the brim of his fedora.

The hilariously over-the-top comic monologue that Caspar delivers is effectively at odds with the somber elegance of Barry Sonnenfeld's lush photography. The scene is also noteworthy for its double helping of the type of crass, venal man who Roger Ebert notes the Coens love to place behind desks. Caspar orates:

Joel and Ethan Coen.

I'm talkin' about friendship, I'm talkin' about character, I'm talkin' about—hell Leo, I ain't embarrassed to use the word—I'm talkin' about ethics. You know I'm a sporting man. I like to lay an occasional bet. But I ain't that sporting. When I fix a fight ... I figure I got the right to expect that fight to go off. ... But every time I lay a bet with that son of a bitch Bernie Birnbaum, ... he's selling the information I fixed the fight ... Bernie ain't satisfied with the honest dollar he can make off the fix. ... So, back we go to these questions—friendship, character, ethics. ... It's getting so a businessman can't expect no return from a fixed fight. Now if you can't trust a fix, what can you trust? For a good return you go bettin's on chance, an' then, you're back with anarchy, right back in the jungle. That's why ethics is important, what separates us from the animals—beasts of burden, beasts of prey ... ethics. Whereas Bernie Birnbaum is a horse of a different color, ethics-wise, as in he ain't got any.

When asked if it might be someone else selling him out, Caspar assures Leo that no one else is involved "who ain't got ethics." To whom does he refer? The fighters paid "to tank out," other bookies, other mobsters. Caspar says it's a matter of "character." He says he knows it's Bernie selling him out, "'cos ethically, he's kind of shaky."

The conversation of which the above is part is conducted by story-world participants with no sense of irony because those concerned accept Caspar's terms. Friendship, character, ethics, trust, anarchy—these are concepts which are not stable in and of themselves but depend for their meaning upon the consensus of their "user" community. As in *Blood Simple* and *Raising Arizona*, the Coens gleefully exploit the comic territory which gaps between familiar phrases and contexts that utterly undermine their ability to express the ideas and values with which they are normally associated.

Caspar negotiates in his plea an interesting construct concerning notions of order versus chaos. When gangsters break gangster rules, they risk "anarchy," an orderlessness that puts them "right back in the jungle." He says it is this sense of "ethics" that "separates us from the animals." However, in the next part of his speech, his language conveys what he really means by anarchy. Among the denizens of the underworld, clear agreements and covenants must govern the rules of its world, otherwise, there is no distinction between "beasts of burden" and "beasts of prey." In other words, gangland "ethics" allow and perpetuate a system whereby the gangsters are allowed to be beasts of prey, while average law-abiding citizens are the lower-echelon, too-stupid-to-know-it beasts of burden, suckers. (Nonofficial gangsters, or possibly "official" gangsters, such as policemen and politicians, form an interesting community sandwiched between mobsters and average folks. They are corrupt, like the mobsters, and like them, understand and adhere to the rules of the underworld, yet, like average folks, they have no power to set agenda, or initiate action.) Anarchy is, according to this conception, a state wherein mobsters retain no special status. Likewise, in the gangsters' lexicon, the word "character" refers to predictability within a given situation, while a man may be said to be "of principle" if he insists on paying his own gambling debts. "Friends" are strategic allies, a flexible status subject to political changes of fortune.

Leo suggests that a man called Mink may be responsible for Caspar's problem. The Dane immediately and vehemently denies the possibility. Caspar concurs, noting that Mink is Eddie Dane's "boy." The significance of this description is soon made clear—the Coens will transform the homoerotic subtext and ambiguous sexual triangulations of *The Glass Key* into explicit, plot-motivating relationships in *Miller's Crossing*.

Recapping the basic thrust of Caspar's speech, Leo grunts, "So you want to kill him." "For starters," deadpans the nightmarish Eddie Dane. Leo nevertheless denies Caspar and Dane his blessing. Tom looks languorously startled by Leo's response. Caspar tells Leo that he's telling him of his plans "as a courtesy" rather than asking permission. He intends, he says, to pursue Bernie's murder despite Leo's wishes to the contrary. Leo threatens Caspar after detailing the extent to which his corrupt grip on the city allows Caspar's businesses to operate in peace. Caspar is nearly apoplectic at Leo's dismissive contempt. The multiethnicity of Leo's organization (a contrast to what one writer has called "the blood-mysticism of Coppola's Sicilians"[3]) is emphasized in Caspar's retaliatory rant. Caspar is not one to neglect the opportunity to characterize his colleagues by ethnic slur, nor does he avoid referring to himself in this fashion. Caspar and The Dane leave Leo's office on none-too-friendly terms.

"Bad play, Leo," Tom advises. Leo attributes Tom's opinion to jitters over a gambling debt he owes a thug named Lazarre and offers to pay the debt for him. "Call me a big-hearted slob," he says, reaching for the phone. Tom declines Leo's help. He says he'll square himself with Lazarre. "That's why God invented cards," he notes. Tom grabs his hat and coat and leaves but not before making a final appeal to Leo. "Think," he says, "about what protecting Bernie gets us. Think about what offending Caspar loses us." "Oh come on, Tommy, you know I don't like to think," Leo says. "Well think about whether you should start," says Tom. Quickly there has been established what will be a structuring thematic pattern in *Miller's Crossing*: the binary opposition of heart and head, of feeling versus thinking.

The credits arrive accompanied by a lyrical realization of the Coens' seminal windswept hat image; the imagery of this scene will resurface later in the film as the content of an enigmatic dream of Tom's. The camera faces skyward as it slowly tracks beneath the stark limbs and leaves of motionless trees against a blanched sky. These images are replaced by a black hat, which fills the frame as it falls gently to the ground. The title credit appears over this image as Carter Burwell's lilting Celtic melody turns dark. The sound of the wind becomes prominent as the hat sails off.

Tom is awakened the next morning by a friend. He learns that he has been unlucky in his attempt to win the money he owes. When he is told that he has lost his hat to Verna and Mink in a bet he lurches offscreen to be violently ill. Though his friend cautions him against it, he places a new bet with Lazarre on a horse race.

The next scene finds Tom at Verna's (Marcia Gay Hardin) door. She refuses to give him his hat, which she says she has won fairly. She slams the door in Tom's face after inquiring if the retrieval of his hat is the sole purpose of his visit. She relents when Tom asks for a drink. The next shot centers on Tom's hat. Light plays over its surface as the camera pulls back to reveal the mirror behind, which reflects the image of Tom as he lies smoking in his bed.

A knock at his door rouses Tom. He carefully closes his bedroom door and moves through the early morning moonlight to greet Leo. "What's the rumpus?" he asks his boss, the first of many times this question will be uttered (one of the bits of jazzy slang in the film that originates with the Coens). Leo apologizes for the lateness of the hour and asks to come in, a man clearly with much on his mind.

Over drinks they talk, facing each other in sturdy armchairs at one end of Tom's spartan, precisely ordered living room. According to production designer Dennis Gassner, Tom's apartment was designed to mirror the inside of Tom's head.[4] Tom asks if Leo has reconsidered "cutting Bernie loose." Leo says that he can't and moves on to his uppermost concern. Verna, he says, is missing. Leo says that because of the current situation, he is worried. "Verna can take care of herself," says Tom, "maybe better than you can." "What does that mean?" asks Leo, discomfited. Tom, too, is uneasy; he avoids the question by attending to their drinks. Leo will not let it pass and repeats the question. Tom unflinchingly gives Leo his considered opinion. "It's a grift," he tells him. Verna is with Leo in order to save her brother Bernie from harm; Leo is the "angle" she is playing to this end. Leo thinks Tom judges Verna too harshly. In any case, he says, he doesn't like to hear his friends run down, even, he says, by other friends. "Friendship's got nothing to do with it," snaps Tom. "Well, see you'd do anything to help your friends like you'd do anything to kick your enemies," explains Leo, the man ruled by his heart. "Wrong, Leo," says Tom, the man ruled by his head. "You do things for a reason," he argues, though he will soon violate this code of his and, in the process, prove his own point.

Leo says that Tom doesn't understand what is in Verna's heart. In *Miller's Crossing*, "heart" is the antonym of "head," which is nearly synonymous with "hat." These words recur in the film's dialogue with a rhythmic intensity that stops just short of drawing conscious attention to its dialectic between intellect and emotion. "If she's such an angel, why are you looking for her at four o'clock in the morning?" asks Tom. Leo tells him that he has hired a detective named Rug Daniels to follow Verna around and "keep her out of trouble." A quick cut to Tom's face reveals some emotion working below its surface. Leo tells Tom that he has lost contact with both the detective and Verna and asks for his help in locating his errant girlfriend. He is especially worried, he repeats, because of the situation with Caspar. Tom delivers a final warning concerning both Caspar and Verna, and Leo leaves, traversing what seems an endless expanse of open interior space to reach Tom's door.

Tom broods for a moment before heading back to his bedroom. He

Bernie (John Turturro) makes himself at home in *Miller's Crossing.*

sits on the edge of his bed; behind him Verna wakes. Her presence reveals the source of Tom's certainty that Verna is no good for Leo, as well as his repressed alarm at learning of Leo's surveillance.

Verna is relieved to learn that Tom has said nothing of their affair to Leo. She asks if Tom has put in a good word for her brother. Tom says that he didn't. "You said you would," says Verna. "I said," says Tom, "I'd think about it." Tom asks her if she noticed Rug Daniels the evening before; Verna says no. When Verna asks Tom what he and Leo discussed, Tom replies, "I told him you were a tramp and that he should leave you." Verna calls Tom a son of a bitch and hurls a shoe at him. Her effort concludes this scene of cozy domesticity.

A wordless, macabre comic sequence follows. A shaggy dog, head cocked quizzically, stares at something offscreen; a cut to a young boy occupied similarly is next. The object of their attention is then revealed: a staring corpse is slumped against an alley's brick wall, gray toupee askew. The boy appears fascinated by this clump of artificial hair. He snatches it off the dead man's head, and he and the dog run out of the alley. In the background the soundtrack's incongruous cheerful whistling blends with the peal of church bells, augmenting the scene's strange humor.

The screen goes dark as the church bells fade into a raucous conversation conducted in a foreign tongue; the next scene fades into this aural backdrop. Such sound bridges are plentiful throughout the film. Tom is reading a newspaper at a busy lunch counter. The paper imparts two important pieces of information. It identifies the alley's toupeeless corpse, who we can safely surmise must be Rug Daniels, as a "policeman's aide" killed in a gangland slaying. Tom, however, seems more interested in a story concerning the sad fate of the horse he has bet on.

Tom goes to the Shenandoah Club, owned and operated by Leo's organization. Just inside its doors he is greeted ("What's the rumpus?") by Mink (Steve Buscemi), who conducts a rapid-fire beseechment delivered as a single long sentence. He is conveying a message for Bernie, who wishes to speak with Tom but is understandably squeamish about appearing in public. Tom notes that Mink's relationship with Bernie would be a source of distress to Eddie Dane. Mink is bug-eyed with panic at the thought that The Dane might learn that Mink and Bernie are "amigos," it being unlikely, as Tom points out, that The Dane is an "understanding type."

Tom enters Leo's office to find his boss in conversation with the mayor and the chief of police; the two elected officials amuse themselves by waxing jocular on the subject of the corrupt regime from which they derive their power. Leo tells Tom that Verna has shown up and is downstairs in the club. "Ya hear about Rug?" he asks. "They took his hair—Jesus, that's strange," he muses. Leo believes that Caspar is responsible for Rug's odd demise. His meeting with the two city officials is, in fact, a strategy session dedicated to dealing with Caspar. Leo wants to shut down Caspar's businesses, which are as illegal as his own, though such action would inevitably lead to an all-out war between Leo and Caspar. Tom is adamantly opposed to this course of action and insists that "giving up Bernie Birnbaum is a pretty small price to pay for peace. Business is business," he says. Leo and Tom argue about how to best deal with Caspar, while the mayor and his chief of police shift uncomfortably in their seats. Rising, the mayor timidly tells Leo, "We can *dangle*, Leo, if you prefer." The self-conscious precision with which he appropriates the gangland idiom makes for a great moment. After Leo screams at him to remain in the room, he and Tom continue their discussion. Leo is still pushing for a war; Tom reminds him that Caspar has played by the rules, whereas Bernie has broken them. Not only that, says Tom, but they have more to lose in a war than Caspar does. "The two of us have faced worse odds," asserts Leo. "Never without reason," says Tom. "It helps to have one." Tom leaves disgruntled. Leo swears and pounds his fist in frustration.

Recovering, he tells his minions that "the goddamn kid's just like a twist." The line is one of many that suggests the complex emotional undercurrents which bind Tom, Leo, and Verna.

"Get me a stiff one," Tom says, striding purposefully through the crowd at the Shenandoah; a swish pan culminates in a shot of the bartender to whom his request is directed. The bartender is the same individual who has previously roused Tom from his drunken stupor and who has placed bets for Tom; his French accent contributes further to the multinational dimensions of the film's key figures. The man counsels Tom to get the money he owes Lazarre and, when asked, informs Tom of Verna's whereabouts.

Tom storms the ladies' powder room. A fluid tracking shot monitors a surprised group of gowned women as they flee the room. Verna sits at a vanity, working at her makeup. She listens to Tom's description of Leo's misguided, in his opinion, affection for her. Verna responds by saying that she likes Leo. "He's honest, and he's got a heart." Tom argues that Leo is committing a huge tactical error due to Verna's intervention on Bernie's behalf. He asks Verna to "quit spinning Leo in circles and point him where to go." He says that if Leo knew of their relationship, she'd lose her influence; Verna counters by asserting that the impact of this information would cut both ways. Verna acknowledges that her romance with Leo originates in her desire to save her brother. She defends Bernie's character and allows that there is little she wouldn't do to help him. Tom suggests that the previous evening's amorous activities were part of this campaign and insultingly insinuates that Verna would never shirk the opportunity to play a viable angle, no matter how low. Verna calls Tom a "disgusting scum-head," which inspires an ambiguously motivated kiss before she delivers a strong right to Tom's jaw. The scene concludes with a slow tracking shot of Verna's undulating form as she heads toward the door.

As Tom enters his apartment, the telephone is ringing. He wearily deposits himself in a chair opposite another. Before picking up the telephone he tosses his hat onto the tip of one of his crossed shoes. We hear a distant voice mumble something about money through the receiver; Tom asks for more time. The camera has been slowly moving forward toward Tom's seated figure. A close-up of his face coincides with his offer to Lazarre who, he says, can send his minions over to break his legs. "I won't squawk," he says, sharpening his focus on something before him. "Hello Bernie," he says, indicating the audience to whom his pointed lesson in consequences has been directed. Bernie (John Turturro) sits opposite him, his presence having been earlier obscured by the chair's height and the camera's willfulness. "What's the rumpus?" asks Bernie. "Come on in, make yourself at home," answers Tom dryly.

Bernie is there to plead his case, which rests on the notion of friend-ship. He says that since he and Tom are both in trouble, it is an especially difficult time to be abandoning crucial friendships. Tom refers to Leo's involvement with Verna as Leo's payoff for continued loyalty to Bernie and asks what's in it for himself. Bernie displays an unusual sense of the allegiance he says he prizes so highly in a darkly amusing exchange. Tell-ing a revolting story about Verna, he refers to her as "a sick twist." Tom informs Bernie that she speaks highly of him. Bernie replies, "Yeah, well, you stick by your family." Bernie is willing to help Tom with his debts if Tom will stop causing trouble for him with Leo. He repeatedly notes that "a guy can't have too many friends." Tom wonders how Bernie can be making money despite being cut off by Caspar. Mink, it emerges, is responsible for the continued flow of information regarding the crooked bets that end up profiting Bernie rather than Caspar. Bernie asks if they have a deal. Tom says he'll think about it. Bernie disappears after osten-tatiously checking the corridor in both directions.

Tom places yet another bet despite the fact that even the bookie jokes about his losing streak. Two gangsters, emissaries of Caspar's, materialize in order to escort Tom to see their boss. Arriving at Caspar's warehouse office with the two thugs, Tom is treated to a slice of Caspar's domestic life; the sequence is a comical send-up of the classical gangster's devotion to family. Caspar gets down to business after their departure. Like Leo and Bernie before him, he cites the value of friendship and offers to pay Tom's gambling debts if Tom will give him Bernie Birnbaum. He appeals not only to friendship but to Tom's sense of justice; Tom knows, says Cas-par, that "it's the right thing to do." If Tom will do this, says Caspar, they can all be friends again, a condition which he describes as "a mental state." Tom says that he'll think about it. Caspar allows that it is fine to think about it but tells Tom that unless he agrees, he won't be in any shape to leave the building. "Would that be," asks Tom, "physically, or just a men-tal state?" Stung, Caspar and his associates leave the warehouse, except for the larger of the two thugs. This actor, Mike Starr, bears an uncom-mon resemblance to William Bendix, his counterpart in *The Glass Key* (1942).

Tom watches as the man prepares for his work by fastidiously remov-ing hat, coat, and suit jacket; he further readies himself for action by rum-pling his hair, a gesture which seems to involve more rite than expedience. As the huge man moves toward Tom, Tom indicates that he too needs a few moments to prepare for his ordeal. The man effects a gesture which conveys his understanding and respect for Tom's request. He stands flat-footed, facing Tom, arms down at his side, and waits. Tom begins to remove his coat, then grabs his chair and heaves it off the floor to bash it against the man's head. He does not, however, continue his assault; rather, he stops still and waits to see what will next happen. His action is not a ruse to gain leverage in their battle but a social experiment; he is curious as to what will be the results of his transgression. The man looks absolutely stunned at Tom's betrayal. He wipes blood from his face and stares at it, unbelievingly. "Jesus, Tom," he says, and he sounds both hurt and perplexed, as a child might be at some unprovoked insult. The childlike aspect of this response is reflected also in his exit; stalking toward the door to get reinforcements he resembles nothing so much as a huge child withdrawing from a playground, feelings hurt. The potency of this scene relies upon ironic incongruity. It is, therefore, truly fitting when it turns out that he has gone to fetch his much smaller colleague for help. The two deliver a terrible beating to Tom, the worst of the blows landing seconds before invading policemen reach them. The screen blacks out, as does Tom.

He is revived by the police, who are in the process of "interrogating" Caspar's thugs, a bloody process. Out front, in Caspar's club, police are destroying everything in sight—Leo's retaliation against Caspar. Tom leaves the building to join the chief of police, who is monitoring the mayhem. In a comic exchange, the chief humbly conveys his opinion that Leo's stubbornness on the issue of Bernie Birnbaum is bad for everyone concerned. Tom is quick to remind him of his place, which is firmly under Leo's thumb. The policeman backpedals furiously in the face of Tom's anger. Meanwhile, the chaos of the bust escalates as machine-gun fire is exchanged.

Tom muscles his way into Verna's apartment; a single minor facial blemish gives surreally slight testament to the physical abuse he has recently suffered. Verna calls the police, ostensibly to dislodge Tom; he avails himself of her phone call to order extra protection that night for Leo. Tom tells Verna about Rug Daniels. Verna is less than moved by the news. Tom and Verna's witty, noiresque banter is at its best in this scene. Tom describes Rug as "not a bad guy if looks, brains, and personality don't count." "You better hope they don't," retorts Verna. Tom relates his theory of recent events. He reasons that since Caspar has so recently tried to purchase Tom's help in smoothing things over with Leo, Caspar has not yet begun to wage war. It is, therefore, unlikely that Caspar killed Rug. Tom tells Verna he thinks that either she or her brother, "Saint Bernard," killed Rug, who was in a position to tell Leo about their affair, news which might cause Leo to undergo a change of heart regarding his support of Bernie. When Verna protests that Tom "knows her a little" and wonders how he can believe her a murderess, Tom replies that "nobody knows anybody, not that well." Tom says he came to Verna in order to hear her justification of the murder. Verna says Tom is there "for the oldest reason there is" and urges him to admit that he is jealous of her relationship with Leo. Tom does his best to dispel this belief. Verna then notes that she's never met anyone else "who made being a son of a bitch such a point of pride." She tells him that some day he'll pay a price for it. The scene ends with their rough embrace; Verna throws his hat to a chair, where the camera lingers.

A match cut from Verna's billowing curtains to the billowing drapes of a richly appointed room begins the film's most notorious passage. The mellow sentimental strains of "Danny Boy" compete with the sounds of an offscreen beating, while the camera slowly pans away from the window, past objects which give mute testimony. Gun, lighter, pack of cigarettes, and cup of coffee sit on a table, providing an explanation for the image upon which the camera finally rests. The man who has been caught off-guard during a break lies prone next to his overturned chair. A small lake of blood pools beneath the man's body. His cigarette ignites the newspaper he had been reading. His killer moves on, unaware of the incipient blaze he has left behind. He opens the front door of the house to admit a compatriot with machine guns.

A cut to a phonograph playing the "Danny Boy" recording is followed by a shot of Leo as he lies in bed on his back, hands behind his head, listening. Leo smokes a cigar, eyes closed with the pleasure of the music; meanwhile his assassins mount the stairs. Leo pauses in his reverie. He smells smoke and finds its tendrils rising from beneath his bedroom floorboards. Puzzled, he pauses for an interminable moment while the gunmen below draw closer to his chamber. Leo looks at his gun on the night table, then at the door. His enemies have ascended the stairs and are now in the hallway outside his room. Without hurry he slippers his feet and stubs out his cigar. The tension built by the sequence's cross-cutting is then broken by a cathartic eruption of action. The two killers break into the bedroom, machine guns blazing; simultaneously Leo grabs his gun and rolls underneath the bed. He shoots one of the men in the leg and delivers a bullet to his brain when the man falls. Taking the dead man's machine gun, Leo races out of the room. Avoiding gunfire, Leo throws his machine gun out an open window and follows; the weapon clatters along the slanted roof before falling to the ground with near-balletic grace. He grabs the gun and stands at the ready in front of his burning house, waiting for the assailant still inside to show himself. As the gunman's silhouette appears in the window, Leo opens fire. In a bizarrely attenuated marionette-like dance, Leo's would-be assassin seems to dangle midair;

caught between the force of a lengthy stream of bullets from Leo's machine gun and the kickback generated by the involuntary firing of his own machine gun, the corpse is grotesquely animated by a series of macabre contortions. It is the film's visual equivalent of *Blood Simple*'s skewered hand sequence. Leo remains cool; he returns fire at a moving car full of gunmen as "Danny Boy" reaches an emotional crescendo. He calmly pursues the car with machine-gun fire until the vehicle explodes. As the record comes to its melancholy finish, Leo surveys his vanquished enemies. He pulls out his half-finished cigar from the pocket of his dressing gown and puts it in his mouth with satisfaction.

Leo and Caspar officially at war, Tom assesses the previous night's damage before conferencing with Leo, who is struggling to understand the sudden unavailability of his elected sycophants. Tom tells him that the mayor and the chief of police are running scared. Tom reminds Leo that he counseled him against hitting Caspar's place and displays characteristic insight. "Last night made you look vulnerable," he argues. "You don't hold elected office in this town. You run it because people think you run it. Once they stop thinking it, you stop running it." Leo jokes in the face of this warning. Tom urges Leo to take Caspar seriously and to avoid going "toe to toe with that psychopath." Tom attempts to overcome Leo's unwillingness to confront his shrinking power base. He reminds Leo that no police intervened at his house the night before, though he ordered them there. He counsels Leo to give up Bernie, placate Caspar, and wait for Caspar to show a weakness they can exploit. Leo tells Tom that he plans to propose to Verna, which precludes the possibility of giving up Bernie. Tom's face registers only the slightest of reactions to this news; his gaze shifts momentarily, his eyes haunted. Leo is reconciled to Tom's disapproval of his relationship with Verna; consequently he is at first dismissive when Tom discloses his hypothesis concerning Rug's murder. Tom asks Leo to trust him. Leo is still hesitant. Tom bolsters his argument by telling Leo of Verna's motivation for the killing—he confesses their affair, which Rug was in a position to expose. Leo looks stunned, then utters a single heartbroken syllable before turning his back on Tom. Moments pass before Tom rises and goes to the door, pausing to look back at Leo. The expanse of floor between them emphasizes the gulf that now separates them. Tom leaves. A tracking shot precedes Tom down the gangster-lined corridor; behind him, Leo emerges, removing his coat. Leo proceeds to beat an unprotesting Tom down the corridor, down a vast flight of stairs, and into the main ballroom of Leo's club. Throughout the one-sided fight, Tom keeps careful track of his hat, several times retrieving it and maintaining a hold on it against all odds. The violence ends when Tom accidentally executes a comic grapple with a woman of operatic proportions; in the wake of her scream Tom's bartender friend intervenes, and Leo is content to have Tom thrown out after a formal public "kiss off."

Back at his apartment Tom makes a phone call to Caspar's camp, requesting a meeting. Verna arrives and announces that she and Leo are through. She denies involvement in Rug's death again and wonders why Tom must "always take the long way around" to get what he wants: she suggests that Tom both implicated her in Rug's murder and confessed their affair to Leo in order to be with her.

Tom and Verna are in bed. Tom tells her of a dream he had once. He is walking in the woods when a gust of wind blows off his hat. Verna interrupts with her guess at the dream's conclusion—Tom runs after the hat which changes into something else, "something wonderful." "Nah, it stayed a hat," says Tom. "And no, I didn't chase it. Nothing more foolish than a man chasing his hat," Tom tells her, oblivious to the irony of his comment. Much of his time has recently been devoted to just this activity, as though keeping his hat means keeping his head, both literally and figuratively.

As Tom gets ready to go out, Verna suggests that Tom and Leo might still have a future together. Leo, she says, has a big heart. Tom refutes this possibility. Verna then suggests that she, Tom, and Bernie leave town together, a scenario Tom finds equally unpalatable. Tom tells Verna that he should find Bernie to warn him that his situation is increasingly more dangerous, and Verna tells Tom where Bernie is hiding. She then expounds upon their betrayal of Leo; she and Tom are, she says, "about bad enough to deserve each other." Tom remains cryptically detached during Verna's rueful character analysis.

In a visual redux of the earlier scene with Leo, Caspar is playing host to the mayor and the chief of police as Tom arrives at Caspar's new office. As usual, Eddie Dane lurks malevolently in the background. Tom presents himself to Caspar for work. As proof that he has switched sides, Tom offers up Bernie's whereabouts, adding that they might also find Mink there, since Bernie and Mink are, says Tom, "cozy as lice." Eddie Dane is not at all pleased to hear that he has been two-timed and defends Mink's honor. Caspar tells Eddie to find Mink and tells Tom to find Bernie. When they do, he says, his men will "take care" of Bernie.

Tom is at the wheel as Caspar's men force a crying and pleading Bernie into the car. They drive out to woods known as Miller's Crossing, where Tom learns that it is to be his test of loyalty to kill Bernie himself. Realizing that Tom has never killed a man, the gangster delivering Caspar's orders raises his eyes in exasperation before tutoring Tom in the art of gangland murder. "Your first shot puts him down," the man says. "Then you put one in his brain. Then he's dead. Then we go home." Tom grasps the gun as if it were a scorpion.

Tom walks Bernie into the woods while Bernie maintains a steady hysterical pleading for his life. The scene is a tour-de-force for actor John Turturro, whose character delivers a shockingly effective monologue filled with the abject terror of the condemned. He begs for his life with naked fear; his pleas are completely devoid of any semblance of dignity or pride. "Look into your heart," he cries. "I'm praying to you." This wailing litany is repeated again and again.

Tom spares Bernie's life, whose face registers a near-crazed ecstasy at this reprieve. Tom orders Bernie to disappear forever in payment for his mercy, a promise Bernie affirms before he flees through the woods. A long shot of Tom as he stands for a moment in the clearing has the smudged graininess of a faded oil painting; the desolate place where Tom finds himself alone mirrors the inner landscape of a man who has broken faith with a code that has heretofore governed his existence.

An ultrastylized long shot of a city street finds Tom in a phone booth. He calls Mink and tells him about Bernie's death. He adds that Eddie Dane is looking for him and that Caspar knows that Mink conspired with Bernie to hijack his "honest fix." Tom tells him to lay low until Caspar calms down and then to implicate Eddie Dane in the gambling scheme. Tom assures Mink that if he follows his instructions he'll convince Caspar to go easy on him. Tom turns from the telephone into the fist of one of Leo's men. The man politely hands Tom the hat he has knocked from his head and delivers Leo's message: Tom is to steer clear of the brewing conflict or receive no special consideration. Tom's irreverent response elicits another blow to his head. As in other such scenes, the violence leaves Tom's face virtually unmarked.

Caspar and Tom meet again. Caspar tells Tom that he thinks Tom was right; Mink's low profile has convinced him that Mink conspired with Bernie to rob him, though Eddie Dane continues to reject this idea. Tom tells Caspar that before he died Bernie told him that Eddie Dane and Mink set him up to take the fall for their double-cross. He wonders aloud to Caspar whether The Dane is really having difficulty locating Mink. After a short speech to review the values he holds dear, Caspar lets it be known that though The Dane bears murderous intent toward Tom, he believes that The Dane would never cross him—they share a history. Tom suggests that such history might fade beside the eternal "wild card": love. Caspar says he understands about the Dane and Mink but refuses to entertain the possibility that The Dane is crossing him.

Caspar and Tom's meeting is interrupted by the excited entrance of Caspar's young son. Displeased by his son's lack of self-control, Caspar backhands the child viciously across the face. The father then comforts the child, adopting a bizarrely dissociated stance. "Whatsa matta, somebody hit you? Kids," opines Caspar, "you gotta be firm." The sequence is, like so much of the Coens' humor, funny/horrible. Tom is asked to locate Mink so that Caspar may interrogate him.

The wail of Caspar's son is an appropriate sound bridge to the next scene, which opens with a glove smashed into the face of a boxer. Tom reads the paper in a gym; over his shoulder we read headlines which indicate that Leo's power and influence are ebbing. Verna arrives to meet Tom. Tom tells her to leave town for a few days in order to avoid the approaching mayhem. He tells her he will join her later. Verna is worried—she can't find Bernie and asks if Tom was able to locate and warn him. Tom says that he warned him and that Bernie has left for parts unknown. Verna thanks Tom with a smile and a kiss. Tom watches her leave with a mixture of his characteristic cerebral mournfulness and regret.

Eddie Dane sees Verna leave Tom's company and follows her home. He breaks into her apartment and questions her about Tom's activities. He also asks her why she is carrying on with the man responsible for her brother's death, information which Verna seems to immediately accept. Two of Leo's men rush the apartment; The Dane uses Verna as a shield as he shoots both men. The scene is played for comedy even as it illuminates the dark corners of the psychopathology that passes for personality in The Dane. Verna escapes. "I'll track down all you whores," mutters The Dane in an unambiguous show of his personal sexual politics.

A match cut once more from Verna's fluttering curtains to those in Tom's bedroom finds him ruminating and smoking. When he hears someone enter his apartment, he responds with studied nonchalance, slowly moving toward his living room, then sagging against a door as he takes in the scene. A man sits in the dark. "Hello, Bernie," says Tom. "Come on in, make yourself at home." Bernie's greeting perfectly completes the reenactment of their earlier meeting when Bernie was, as now, an uninvited and unwelcome guest.

Bernie acknowledges how awkward his reappearance must be for Tom. He says that he was going to keep his end of their bargain, but his recognition of the "play" Tom had inadvertently handed him compelled him to reevaluate his position. If he leaves, he says, he has nothing. If he stays, he says, he's got Tom, who has everything to lose if Bernie appears publicly. Noting that Tom is not, for once, cracking wise, Bernie moves on to express the grudge he bears Tom. He has a "painful memory" of himself at Miller's Crossing, prostrate and humiliatingly weak. He also resents the fact that Tom fingered him in the first place and brought him to Miller's Crossing to be killed. "You didn't, I know," Bernie half giggles, "you didn't shoot me." "But what have I done for you lately?" cracks Tom. Bernie says he wants to see Tom sweat a little. "When you smart me," he tells Tom, "it ruins it." Bernie takes his gun and prepares to leave, but not before he orders Tom to kill Caspar in return for Bernie's continuing silence concerning his stay of execution.

The door has barely closed behind Bernie before Tom grabs his hat and his gun and, barefoot, leaps out his bedroom window in order to reenter his building. He races down a corridor, gun extended; his progress is abruptly halted by Bernie's outstretched foot. Tripped, Tom takes a header while his gun goes flying. Kicking him in the head, Bernie taunts Tom. "What were you gonna do if you caught me? I'd just squirt a few and then you'd let me go again."

At the Shenandoah Club Tom speaks to his bartender friend, asking him if any bets have been placed on any long shots. Seconds after he receives the bartender's information, the club is raided by the police. As a new member of Caspar's team, Tom is allowed to leave the club without incident.

Outside the club, Tom and the chief of police commiserate over the disruption of the status quo, which had been so profitable for all. Tom asks the chief about a boxer named Drop Johnson, who the bartender says has placed a heavy bet on an unlikely contender. The policeman tells him where to find this man before he confides to Tom that he believes Caspar to be as crazy as Leo. Gunshots break out in the club behind them.

Tom is muscled off the street and into a car where Eddie Dane waits. Eddie tells Tom that he thinks he's "as straight as a corkscrew," a spy in the enemy camp. The Dane delivers a growling speech filled with the venom of his hatred for Tom, who looks slightly more pale than usual when he hears that they are bound for Miller's Crossing in order to verify the death of Bernie Birnbaum.

Once again the camera trolls through the muted woods of Miller's Crossing. The Dane and Tom walk behind Caspar's men, one of whom provides an operatic accompaniment to the proceedings. The Dane makes it clear that if Bernie's body is missing, Tom is a dead man. Tom moves forward through the woods with an unsteady gait. His terror overpowers him, and he vomits against a tree, convincing Eddie that his suspicions are true. The Dane begins to vent his antipathy toward Tom in physical blows, a sadistic prelude to the execution he is now sure will follow. He draws his gun and aims it; a second later one of Caspar's men indicates that they have found a body. The face of the body has been obliterated, the result, the gangsters assume, of Tom's incompetence in such matters.

Tom tracks down Drop Johnson and questions him about the fight. Tom supposes that Johnson is working with Bernie, a theory bolstered by the hat Bernie has left behind at Johnson's. Tom tells Johnson to tell Bernie to get in touch with him.

The Sons of Erin social club is bombed by a group of thugs and police; a charred body sails from the club into the street in a stylized arc of choreographed horror. A man emerges from the ruins of the club waving a white handkerchief; he is promptly gunned down by a gangster, whose colleagues, thugs and police alike, laugh at the victim's death throes. A gun battle ensues, a nightmare version of a Keystone Kops episode.

Tom visits the mayor, who has his hands full attempting to placate Caspar, who is there to secure jobs for some relatives. In a hilarious exchange, the mayor tries to explain the unfeasibility of Caspar's plan. Placing people "on the pad," the mayor argues with painstaking patience, involves attending to certain matters of form. "There's a way we do things," he insists, "hallowed by usage and consecrated by time." Caspar cares not a whit for the protocols which lubricate the gears of corrupt city politics. He accuses the mayor of disloyalty, a charge Tom appears to support. Caspar ejects the mayor from his own office and takes his place behind the mayor's desk to mull over recent events with Tom.

Tom intensifies his campaign to convince Caspar that Eddie represents a threat. Tom mentions the upcoming fixed fight and suggests that The Dane is perpetuating the myth that Bernie is alive not only in order to rid himself of Tom, but so that he might have a patsy to take the fall for his own grift. "Nobody knows anybody, not that well," Tom tells a skeptical Caspar. Caspar is in an agony of philosophical despair over the ethical questions posed by his need to choose between Tom and The Dane; both recommend double-crossing the other. Tom provokes a rage in Caspar which he is able to defuse with a few well-chosen words. Caspar blames his volatility on the stress of his new leadership role.

Tom gets a call from Bernie; he learns that it was Mink who shot Rug Daniels, and it is Mink lying dead in Miller's Crossing. Tom tells Bernie that their deal is over. He says he's leaving town and orders him to meet him at his apartment with a payment of $2,000 to ensure he doesn't tell Caspar he's still breathing.

Tom receives a terrible beating just outside his door from Lazarre's men—payback for unpaid debts. Relations between all involved are amiable, however; it is understood that the gangland code which prescribes their behavior has nothing to do with personal feelings. In fact, says one of the men, Lazarre likes Tom and has told them they need break none of his bones. Tom sends his best regards back to Lazarre.

"What's the rumpus?" asks Caspar, greeting him at the door of his kitschily opulent home. Tom tells Caspar he has spoken with Mink and that Mink will be at his apartment later, citing the appointment he has arranged with Bernie. Tom says that Mink has confirmed The Dane's treachery and has told him that The Dane will be gunning for Caspar that night. Tom suggests a preemptive strike against The Dane. Caspar's elaborate facial contortions reflect his extreme confusion. Caspar tells Tom that they have located Leo. Suddenly, shockingly, they are interrupted by the distinct vocal stylings of The Dane; he has, it appears, been in the room during the entire interview. The scene which follows owes more to the horror genre than the gangster saga.

The Dane has been tracing Tom's movements about town; in the course of this activity he has learned much. He has, in fact, brought a thoroughly beaten and interrogated Drop Johnson to see Caspar. The camera zooms toward the faces of Johnson and Tom as mutual recognition of their peril registers. The Dane says that it is Mink's body out in the woods and accuses Tom of his murder. Quick cuts to high angle shots of Caspar during The Dane's furious summation accentuate Caspar's agony of uncertainty. The Dane begins to choke the life out of Tom, a procedure he performs with great relish; he is, however, interrupted by Caspar's intervention with a fireplace iron. Caspar has finally made a choice between his two seconds. Screaming a catalogue of The Dane's sins, Caspar pulverizes The Dane's head with an iron shovel. The exaggerated cartoon sound effects which accompany this attack find a visual match in the drippy goriness of the scene. The camera zooms in on Tom's face to record his shocked response before returning to Caspar's crazed visage. Caspar is distracted by the sound of Drop Johnson's steady screaming, a sound effect which could have been grafted from *Raising Arizona*. Completely over the edge, Caspar advances toward the hysterical boxer, intending to "give the man something to holler about." The camera zooms back from a close-up of Johnson as Tom manages to quiet him. Comically, the flow of noise is stemmed as if by an electronic switch. Persuaded to spare Johnson, Caspar sets his sights on Mink. Tom convinces Caspar to honor the agreement he has made with Mink, using Caspar's finely honed sense of ethics to craft his argument. Johnson begins screaming again, alerting Caspar and Tom to Eddie Dane's bloody attempt to rise from the floor. The screaming continues as a zooming camera records Caspar's response, a bullet to the brain.

Tom grabs his hat and leaves his place at a coffee shop at three-thirty in the morning, a half hour before the rendezvous at his apartment. He is waylaid outside by Verna. Soaking from the rain and distraught, she accuses Tom of using her to set up Bernie's death. In a heartbreakingly bereft voice, Verna laments that "Bernie's friends didn't really like him." Her comment betrays a vulnerability rooted in an existence that predates her current role as gangland moll; she uses the word "friend" as a civilian might. Tom surprises her by explaining that giving up Bernie was the only solution he could think of to save Leo; though they are "through," he tells her, he still cares about Leo. Tom tells Verna, truthfully, that Bernie isn't dead. Verna responds by telling him that he is "a lie, and no heart," an ironic evaluation under the circumstances. Though Verna threatens Tom with a gun, she cannot bring herself to kill him. The camera lingers on her retreating back as she walks off into the rain, disconsolate. Like Tom, her hard-edged veneer conceals the soul of a disillusioned romantic.

Tom arrives home seconds after Caspar enters his building (called the Barton Arms, in honor of the title and protagonist of the Coens' next filmscript, already completed) and dismisses Caspar's driver. Two shots are fired as Tom advances toward the front door; once inside Tom notes first the hat marooned in the middle of the hall staircase, then the body crushing the second-floor banister. Mounting the stairs Tom identifies the body—it is Caspar. Bernie is heard giggling on the second floor. When Tom arrives Bernie notes that Tom has set him up to be killed by Caspar "to avoid a little dirty work" himself. When Bernie asks if Tom had cared who killed whom, Tom professes to have assumed Bernie would come out the winner since he came prepared for blood—Tom's, that is. Asked why he thinks he's not still Bernie's target, Tom replies that with Caspar gone, there is no longer any problem between him and Bernie. He asks for Bernie's gun. He says he needs it to frame The Dane for Caspar's death; it is also the gun responsible for two other murders. Bernie confides that Rug's murder was "a mix-up" and hands the gun over to Tom. Tom finds cash and a gun on Caspar; Bernie chatters in response to Tom's efforts to clear up minor details of certain events which continue to puzzle him. As in *Blood Simple*, however, none of the film's storyworld characters ever know everything, a privilege reserved for the viewer.

Tom leans against the wall; the low angle shot is notable for its iconographic purity. Tom explains to Bernie that framing Eddie Dane won't work because The Dane is dead. Bernie must, therefore, take responsibility for the killing. When Bernie protests that it will be his word against Tom's, Tom chillingly replies, "Not necessarily."

Bernie wonders why Tom means to kill him—there is, he notes, no angle in it for him any longer. He begins a reprise of his performance in Miller's Crossing. "Look in your heart," he cries. "What heart?" asks Tom and shoots him point-blank in the brain. The cerebral strategist has turned killer. The shot reverberates with a surreally prolonged echo—longer than the duration of time it takes for a man to lose his soul. Tom arranges the scene to reflect a scenario which describes Bernie and Caspar killing each other. The scene concludes with Tom phoning Lazarre's organization. He tells them he has the money he owes and that he wants to place a new bet.

Tom attempts to visit Leo but finds him occupied with the mayor and the chief of police—the status quo has been restored. Tom stops by Bernie's funeral, attended by Leo, Verna, and a rabbi. Verna tells Tom to drop dead; Leo tells Tom that she is under a lot of strain. Verna drives off, leaving Leo and Tom to walk and talk. Leo announces his and Verna's engagement, and Tom congratulates him. Leo says that he wishes he had understood earlier that Tom's betrayal was a ruse; he expresses his gratitude. Leo proposes that Tom purposefully orchestrated the argument that precipitated their estrangement. Tom is noncommittal, admitting that he doesn't always understand what motivates his behavior. The remark is a testimony to a profound inner sea change. Nobody knows anybody, Tom seems to be saying, not even himself.

Leo delivers a heartfelt entreaty for Tom to return to his old role in his organization; he tells Tom that he forgives him for his dalliance with Verna and wishes for things to return as they were before. Tom rejects Leo's apology as unasked for and unwanted. He tells Leo goodbye, and the men stare at each other for a long, ambiguous moment. Leo leaves, his back retreating toward an avenue of trees. Tom watches him go. The camera considers Tom as he adjusts his hat on his head. His eyes are haunted. Tom is, at the end of the film, completely untethered, distanced from the entanglements of romance, finance, business, and friendship. Most significantly, he is removed from himself. The final shot of the film delicately delineates Tom's alienation. It is a stark portrait of a man self-exiled not only beyond the borders of his world but beyond self-knowledge. Accordingly, the film's denouement evokes no sense of closure but generates instead a tension born of that rarest of Coenesque devices, identification.

Miller's Crossing represents, for Joel and Ethan Coen, a rather restrained, lyrical deliberation. Its pacing is, more often than not, elegiac; long takes inform its static compositions with a cerebral mournfulness that mirrors its protagonist's chronic state of mind. As if to compensate for the film's neoclassically composed images and meditative rhythms, the

Coens underpin *Miller's Crossing* with an elaborately conceived narrative structure. Intricate patterns of repetition characterize this structure. Doubled events, thematic dichotomies, parallel relationships, and reiterated snippets of dialogue afford the film a substantive weight despite its essential irreverent ebullience. It is as though the Coens' characteristic onscreen energy has been displaced and consolidated beneath *Miller's Crossing*'s lacquered surfaces. The film is, of course, sporadically punctuated by the kind of self-reflexive formal devices most associated with the Coens. Black-screen transitions, cartoony swish pans, obtrusive tracking shots, highly mobile camera movement, and self-conscious match cuts are used judiciously throughout the film to highlight certain narrative events.

Sound bridges pepper the aural text, as do ironically commentating sound effects. The most prominent aural effects in the film, however, are surreal and are emphasized as the purely subjective sound images of the filmmakers. The sound of roaring wind often accompanies close, interior compositions; moments of tension are highlighted by synthetic, self-consciously hi-tech, "otherworldly" sound effects. Often the soundtrack is characterized by a cartoonlike exaggeration of effect: the sound of frying flesh after a bullet pierces a body, the digitized, mechanical scream of a witness to a brutal murder. The climactic violent confrontation among Caspar, The Dane, and Tom combines all the formal devices which periodically rupture the surface calm of *Miller's Crossing*.

These formal techniques are deployed with a certain amount of irony in the service of a larger ironic stance toward the film's source material—what John G. Cawelti, writing of generic transformation, has called a "puzzling combination of humorous burlesque and high seriousness."[5]

In *Miller's Crossing* Gabriel Byrne as Tom Reagan provides the "high seriousness"; just about every other element of the film is humorous burlesque. Tom is displaced from what should be his storyworld reality: a true "nostalgic reincarnation of an earlier genre" which "set[s] its highly traditional generic content in a slightly different context, thereby giving us both a sense of contemporaneity and of pastness."[6] Instead, Tom is a dislocated, dissonant figure whose existential angst seems to originate within the film's storyworld but which resonates beyond; his earnest tragic hero is trapped in a Ren and Stimpy cartoon.

Miller's Crossing relies, as do all Coen films, upon a shared frame of reference between filmmakers and audience; this intersubjectivity allows for a complex and witty deployment of generic conventions. There is a sharp sense of ironic glee in the Coens' strategic manipulations, which work well because they are rooted in clear affection for and appreciation of the classic modality. Caspar's unceasing agony of philosophical self-scrutiny is, for example, a wickedly funny reinvention of prototypical gangsters famous for their incapacity for self-reflection.

Equally transgressive humor informs the death-by-tommy-gun of Leo's would-be assassin. The scene not only burlesques countless moments of Production Code–inhibited classic gangster films but also mocks the hyperreal graphic violence which so pervades the modern gangster epic. The gangster's traditional devotion to family is lampooned by the Coens in Caspar's schizophrenic attention to his unfortunate son. Similarly, generic themes and motifs that are traditionally subtextual are in *Miller's Crossing* the targets of overt comedy: capitalism, the myth of the ruggedly individual self-made man, and corruption on both sides of and including the thin blue line. Confused sexuality is often an undercurrent in gangster dramas; in *The Glass Key* (1942) and Howard Hawks' *Scarface* (1932) this theme is especially pronounced. *Miller's Crossing* uses its tortured sexual geometries overtly to propel its narrative.

Robert Warshow writes that "no convention of the gangster film is more strongly established than this: it is dangerous to be alone."[7] Tom struggles toward this fate throughout the film despite evidence that Bernie would rather court death than live in exile. It is a tenet of the genre which the Coens handle with a measure of gravity; it is perhaps a point that resonates personally with the fraternal auteurs.

While self-conscious bits of the noir and horror genres surface unevenly throughout the film, *Miller's Crossing* is the Coens' most sustained attention to a single generic universe. Its *frisson* results from the Coens' idiosyncratic refractions of the traditional conventions of a form thoroughly familiar to the film's genre-literate audiences. Critic Louis Menand has written, "The true pleasure of a representation does not come from its indistinguishability from the real thing. It comes from its distinguishability."[8] The Coens predicate their work on a presumed shared base of film aesthetic knowledge. Both filmmakers and audience appreciate the distinctions which separate *Miller's Crossing* from the "real thing"; implicitly understood is what is being departed from, and how. The result is a film connected by the most erratic of kite strings to the traditional generic product which inspires it and which artfully expands the realm of generic signification.

Miller's Crossing received sharply mixed reviews from critics bombarded that year with gangster melodramas: Martin Scorsese's *Goodfellas*, Francis Ford Coppola's *Godfather III*, Peter Medak's *The Krays*, Abel Ferrara's *King of New York*, and Phil Joanou's *State of Grace* were among the films of 1990 that fixated on the aberrations of the mobster milieu. In the wake of this onslaught, *Miller's Crossing*, made on the largest budget the Coens had commanded to date—$10 million—died at the box office.

Terrence Rafferty of the *New Yorker* speaks for many when he criticizes *Miller's Crossing* for an emphasis on style which, he feels, fails to compensate for a lack of substance:

> The picture seems to have no life of its own, and the Coens' formal control and meticulously crafted ironies become, after a while, rather depressing. ... This is not so much a gangster movie as an extended, elaborate allusion to one.[9]

Sheila Benson of the *Los Angeles Times* echoes Rafferty's sentiments when she decries the self-conscious formalism that made for an "emotionally remote" film; "its diversions," she writes, "aren't enough to melt its cold, cold heart."[10]

Other critics disagreed. Peter Travers of *Rolling Stone* calls the film "the best picture yet from the Coen brothers."[11] David Denby of *New York* magazine writes that *Miller's Crossing* offers "the elements of a challenging new classicism that demands our appreciation,"[12] while Tim Pulleine of *Sight and Sound* notes in the film "a precision of correspondence between content and form which is all too rare in the cinema today."[13]

Pulleine's apt phrase describes the organic unity which marks nearly all of the Coens' films. In no Coen film is this more apparent than in their follow-up to *Miller's Crossing*, a film literally spawned by *Miller's Crossing*: *Barton Fink*.

CHAPTER 4

Barton Fink

In the autumn of 1987 the Coens were struggling with an untitled script they referred to as *The Bighead* in affectionate deference to its central character, a cerebral gangland strategist. The Coens took a break from writing what would become *Miller's Crossing* in order to nurse a crippling case of writer's block; in three weeks was born the script for *Barton Fink*, a film not incidentally about a writer wrestling with writer's block. A friend with whom the Coen brothers stayed during the period preceding *Barton Fink*'s inception recalls his response to their new script:

> I saw immediately the Coens had overcome their problem in an ingenious way. They had taken their writer's block and made an effigy of it, an effigy named Barton—a hang-necked, rag-stuffed, immolated dummy vaguely resembling themselves—to which they could then also play the angry, ululating mob that paraded it rebelliously through the streets while chanting simple but catchy slogans of humiliation.[1]

Barton Fink, released in 1991, is a standout triumph of originality from filmmakers whose careers have been built on inventiveness. Arriving on the heels of the Coens' most generically secure picture, *Barton Fink* dazzles with a hallucinatory pastiche of inverted conventions and allusions to auteurist texts that evolve too quickly to engender an alignment with any single overarching genre. An audaciously satiric parable of manners, the film chronicles, in sumptuous style, its eponymous hero's devolution toward a clear-sighted madness; the journey is investigated with the Coens' characteristically stylish detachment.

The credit sequence which opens the film barely hints at what will become *Barton Fink*'s mood of stylized visual and aural excess. Elegant lettering is superimposed against a backdrop of faded, tropical-print Art Deco wallpaper. A title tells us that we are in New York City. The year is 1941.

We follow a cat backstage to a Broadway theatrical production where a tuxedoed young man waits tensely in the wings, his concentration fiercely focused upon the performance onstage. The dialogue of the play reveals its instantly recognizable genre: the sort of socially conscious left-wing melodrama for which writers such as Clifford Odets became renowned. The play concludes; it is a resounding success. The wildly applauding audience calls for the play's author to step forward. The young man's appearance is greeted by a standing ovation.

The camera winds its way through crowded tables at a posh restaurant as the young playwright, Barton Fink (John Turturro) is shown to where his party waits. In the face of his companions' enthusiastic congratulations on the play and its glowing reviews, Barton is self-consciously humble as well as clearly contemptuous of his company. He can't, he says, "start listening to the critics" nor kid himself about his own work. "A writer," he says, "writes from his gut," which, he asserts, allows him to differentiate between "what's good" and what's "merely adequate."

Called to the bar to meet with his agent, Barton chides the man for leaving him alone with "those people." His agent has news of some import; Capital Pictures, it seems, is requesting Barton's literary services. Barton seems initially confused by their lucrative offer. His profession, he says, is "trying to make a difference." He seems baffled then antagonistic toward Hollywood's interest in him.

His place, he says, is in New York, where he is on the brink of "real success": the establishment of a "new living theatre of, and about, and for the common man." To run to Hollywood, he says, would be to cut himself off from the source of his inspiration and from his artistic destiny which, he notes, has little to do with the kind of success leveraged by "fawning critics." With his next breath Barton expresses passionate interest in the opinion of one of these critics. Barton's agent argues that a "brief tenure" in Hollywood would serve to finance a number of his projects. He notes further that "the common man" will survive Barton's sojourn in Hollywood. The shot which concludes the scene eloquently suggests Barton's dilemma. The two men sit facing each other in profile at the bar; a gold-veneered cash register fills the screenspace between them.

A cut to the bluest of ocean waves cresting against a large rock signals Barton's decision and the film's transition to Hollywood. The image dissolves to Barton as he enters his hotel lobby. Though the film has, to this point, been a characteristically Coenesque study in stylized filmspace, Barton's slowly paced introduction to his new home initiates a deepening of this aesthetic. The lobby of the Earle Hotel portends this shift. Its cavernous expanse is a gothic mausoleum of overstuffed plush furniture; poisonously bloated-looking tropical plants glisten through the ancient dust which coats the room. The lobby is claustrophobic despite its size. A high angle shot of Barton's back as he moves toward the front desk seems to capture an almost atmospheric resistance to his passage through space.

A nearly inaudible roar accompanies Barton's ingress; this slight sound is soon superseded by the continuously reverberating ring of the bell that Barton activates. Footsteps are heard. An ossified bellboy emerges from a trap door in the floor. He silences the bell and welcomes Barton to the hotel with a well-rehearsed short speech. His name is Chet (Steve Buscemi), and he is anxious to be helpful.

Barton takes a creaking elevator to his floor. The corridor he must negotiate is surreally elongated; lighting fixtures positioned regularly along the walls emphasize a distant vanishing point. Barton enters his room, and the door swings shut behind him with a hydraulic whir.

Barton makes himself at home, carefully distributing his few possessions about the room and attempting to force a reluctant window open. Reverently he places his typewriter on the desk. He notices hotel stationery embossed with an ominous slogan: "Hotel Earle—A day or a lifetime." The pencil which rests upon the writing paper is broken, a sly foreshadowing of Barton's tribulations to come. Barton is transfixed by the cheap picture over his desk: a bathing-suited beauty sits under an umbrella as she looks out to sea, her back to the viewer. The camera dollies forward toward the image while the soundtrack hosts the crashing of ocean waves and the cries of seagulls, vacuous sounds which manage to imply more than a literal support of the image.

A low overhead shot of Barton's head as it hits his pillow notes his attention to the rotted ceiling above his bed. A high overhead shot follows. The camera peers down at Barton as he lies sleepless. The image begins to spin while the high-pitched whine of a dentist's drill or an extremely large mosquito inflames the audiotrack.

Barton is escorted to Jack Lipnick's (Michael Lerner) office (a study in minimalist Art Deco ostentation) the following morning by Lou (Jon Polito), Lipnick's underling. Lipnick, head of Capital Pictures, enfolds Barton in a hearty bear hug while he delivers a high-volume, high-velocity, vehemently effusive welcoming monologue. Alarmed at the sight of Barton's blemished face, he orders Lou to explain. Barton tells Lipnick that he's been the victim of a mosquito. Lipnick asks about Barton's hotel and appears to appreciate the writer's wish to avoid the glitz of a "Hollywood" establishment. Lipnick tells him that whatever he wants is fine. The writer, he says, "is king" at Capital Pictures.

If, as Roger Ebert has noted, the Coens seem persistently drawn to images of crass, venal men behind desks, Lipnick must surely be the apotheosis of this syndrome. A scathingly sharp-edged parody of studio-era moguls, he delivers a delirious diatribe during which he deconstructs the dizzying array of illusions upon which his life is based. As the demented tyrant winds toward a conclusion to his rant, the rocking sound of his upset ashtray provides endgame punctuation: we hear an untethered mind. This aural metaphor is an early manifestation of what will be *Barton Fink*'s dominant aesthetic strategy. Throughout the film the Coens will use stylized sounds and images to project internal states.

Barton seems stunned by his initial encounter with his new boss, nearly immobilized by the discussion of his task. His assignment is to pen a Wallace Beery wrestling picture replete with "that Barton Fink feeling." As Lipnick puts it, "We all want it to have that Barton Fink feeling. I mean, I guess we all have that Barton Fink feeling, but you're Barton Fink—I assume you have it in spades." Though Barton fails his very first test— when asked if the wrestler's life should be complicated by "an orphan or a dame," Barton transgressively offers to include them both—Lipnick expresses his profound confidence in Barton before dismissing him. A shell-shocked Barton is elbowed from the room by Lou. "We're all expecting great things," warns Lipnick as the door closes with an exaggerated whipping sound upon Barton's panicked face.

The camera glides down the eerie corridor outside Barton's room; the sound of his typewriter competes with a roaring noise that is unsettlingly incongruous with the narrow interior space it describes. Shoes placed outside each door embellish the image's murky malignity. These tracking shots are reminiscent of Stanley Kubrick's signature tracking style and especially recall such work in his 1980 film, *The Shining*, which is similarly concerned with mapping the malevolent contours of an old hotel.

In his room Barton is typing his script. Its opening lines reveal that Barton is revisiting familiar ground, situating his scenario in a New York Lower Eastside tenement building. Barton stops typing, distracted by the sound of a ghostlike sobbing/laughing emanating from the room next door. He opens his door; the sound is akin to that of mechanical gears shifting within a punctured vacuum.

The corridor exudes its characteristic white-noise roar; the sound of sobbing/laughing continues. Barton returns to his room. His door creaks slowly closed and, surreally, the voices crescendo madly before they are cut off by the door's closure. The voices echo inside Barton's room. He calls Chet at the front desk and complains of these auditory intrusions. Seconds after Barton hangs up his phone, the phone rings next door; Barton stares at the wall through which he can hear his neighbor respond to the complaint. The camera pans from the wall to the door, following Barton's neighbor's unseen but audible path. There is a loud knock on Barton's door.

Barton opens his door, initiating a sound effect which is regularly deployed throughout the film. The door of his motel room will consistently open and close upon a just audible whining roar, as though hell's own inferno rages just beyond the limit of our ability to perceive it. His neighbor is slumped against its frame, looking peeved. Charlie Meadows (John Goodman) introduces himself following Barton's nervous explanation of his call to Chet. Meadows barges past Barton into his room after procuring a bottle of liquor, which he proposes to share with Barton in order to apologize for the inconvenience he has caused. Unable to discourage Meadows' blustery bonhomie, Barton acquiesces.

Meadows is interested in Barton's work. Questioned about his own, the man tells Barton that "you might say I sell peace of mind." Time will prove the line a macabre pun. Meadows says that he sells insurance and treats Barton to his philosophical views on the subject. Learning that Barton writes for the movies, Meadows apologizes for his patronization; the irony is that Barton barely tolerates Meadows' hearty and overly familiar manner of speaking. Barton displays his first sign of true interest when the opportunity arises to discuss his own career. He is condescending to Meadows.

Onto this modest salesman, Barton casually projects the qualities of "the common man," a construct with which Fink is aesthetically obsessed (his plays document, in the words of one storyworld critic, those "whose brute struggle for existence cannot quite quell their longing for something higher"). Barton tells his neighbor that his subject consists of "people like you ... the average working stiff—the common man." "Ain't that a kick in the head," responds Meadows. (References to the word "head" or a closely related word [such as "mind"] occur, according to one critic, seventy-seven times in *Barton Fink*.[2])

Barton warms to his subject. In one of the film's wittiest passages, he describes his artistic ambitions. "There's a few people in New York— hopefully our numbers are growing—who feel we have an opportunity now to forge something real out of everyday experience." Barton is comically blind to the absurdity of his words. Enthused, Barton delivers a passionate

Barton (John Turturro) battles writer's block in *Barton Fink*.

speech on the merits of his vision for a new mode of theatre in America; in the full throes of his oratory bliss he fails to bestow any attention whatsoever on his companion's attempts to join the conversation. Interrupting Meadows, he rails against artists who "insulate themselves from the common man," causing their work to "regress into empty formalism." (A charge with which the Coens are not unacquainted; Barton's pronouncement is amusingly concurrent with those of some of the filmmakers' more hostile critics.) He tells Meadows that he can help his work by "just being yourself." Barton is oblivious to the irony of his encounter with his neighbor, an average working stiff whose attempts to speak he has repeatedly ignored. Though Barton has invested in the abstraction of "the common man" every manner of nobility and proud purpose, his reverence toward this fantasy demographic does not extend to actual living persons such as Charlie Meadows. With a cheery flourish Meadows leaves. "I could tell you stories," he says, exiting on the line Barton has several times stepped on.

Ensconced once again in front of his typewriter, Barton is doubly distracted. The picture of the beach girl above his desk seems to exert an irresistible siren call. More disturbing is the wallpaper over his bed; it is peeling away from the wall, oozing a viscous goo in the process. Barton investigates his situation with the same open-mouthed passivity which has thus far characterized his response to the demands of his new life. The camera recedes in a dizzying fashion from Barton's face. It is a kinetic metaphor for Barton's increasing disorientation as he becomes aware of the surreally heightened sound of insects, joined by the equally hyperbolic creaking noises generated, presumably, by other hotel guests.

Fink meets with the producer of his wrestling picture, Ben Geisler (Tony Shalhoub). When Barton confides his "blocked" condition, Geisler advises him to consult with another writer. Barton asks for a reference. "Jesus," breathes Geisler, his eyes roaming around the studio commissary, "throw a rock in here and you'll hit one. Do me a favor, Fink," the man adds, "throw it hard."

In the commissary men's room Barton is startled by the sound of a man being violently ill in a nearby stall. Most unusual, the man has taken the care to protect his knees from the bathroom floor with a delicately colored handkerchief. The man who emerges from the stall introduces himself as Bill Mayhew (John Mahoney). It takes Barton a moment or two to recognize the name; when he does he enthusiastically pronounces W.P. Mayhew "the finest novelist of our time" and expresses surprise to find Mayhew in Hollywood. This alcoholic southern literary luminary, a character who resembles William Faulkner to the same extent that Barton does

Odets, tells Barton that he is one of many writers who have "made their way out here to the great salt lick. That's probably why all of us have such a powerful thirst," he explains before downing a copious amount of whiskey from the flask he produces.

Barton asks for Mayhew's advice concerning his difficulty getting started on his writing assignment. Mayhew answers him kindly in a poetic, eloquent drawl which belies the underlying bitterness of his attitude toward his current mode of employment. Sarcastically dismissing himself as a failure at writing for the pictures, he nevertheless invites Barton to his bungalow where, he dryly suggests, they may discuss "wrastlin' scenarios and other things literary." This appointment is postponed until later in order to accommodate Mayhew's drinking schedule.

Barton arrives at Mayhew's bungalow later that day but hesitates at the door when he registers what sounds like a drunken brawl taking place inside. Audrey Taylor (Judy Davis), Mayhew's personal secretary, responds to Barton's knock. She tells Barton that Mayhew is indisposed; Mayhew himself may be heard raving loudly from the room beyond. Audrey apologizes several times to Barton. She tells him that Mayhew drinks when he can't write, and as Mayhew's slurred rant intensifies, she asks Barton not to judge them though their situation may "look funny." Barton seems deeply affected by the hand she places briefly on his shoulder. He asks to see her. She tells him that she'd like the three of them to get together. She is not only Mayhew's secretary, she tells him; they are in love.

Back in his hotel room Barton unwraps Chet's solution to his wallpaper problem: a small box of thumbtacks which Barton gamely attempts to apply to the viscid sheets which now drape halfway down the wall above his bed. The wallpaper's repulsively drenched surface notwithstanding, Barton presses his ear against the wall when he hears the ambiguous cries of a woman emanating from the room next door. An overhead shot of Barton's stance emphasizes Barton's private lapse of decorum.

Barton's attention is claimed by his typewriter, which looms reproachfully on his desk, surrounded by the debris of Barton's failed efforts. The camera conveys the extent to which Barton is stymied. It zooms toward the blank space of the page he has been working on since arrival. Its textured whiteness fills the frame, becoming our entire world as it has Barton's. Barton's reverie is interrupted by the jovial Meadows, whose appearance is greeted by Barton with something that approaches relief. They discuss Meadow's ear infection which, like the walls, is oozing a white sticky substance. "Can't trade my head in for a new one," laughs Meadows. Like most of Meadows' seemingly banal conversational tropes, this phrase will acquire a chilling subtext during the course of the film.

Meadows engages Barton in a discussion of his love life, a topic with which Barton is uncomfortable. He blames his solitary existence on his work; it would be unfair, he suggests, to involve a wife or girlfriend in such a driven life as his own. Meadows commiserates. He asks Barton about his family; Barton tells him about his parents and uncle in Brooklyn. Meadows' own family, he says, raising his eyes heavenward, have passed on.

Meadows is once again prevented from regaling Barton with stories of his life, interrupted as he is by Barton who waxes philosophic concerning the relative ease of Meadows' simple existence and the taxing complexity of his own. His job, he says, is "to plumb the depths, so to speak. Dredge up something from inside, something honest. I got to tell you— the life of the mind; there's no road map for that territory." Barton speaks of his pain, a pain, he says, about which most people know nothing. He patronizingly suggests that this kind of talk must bore Meadows, a charge which Meadows vehemently denies.

Hearing that Barton knows next to nothing about wrestling, Meadows suggests that Barton acquaint himself with his subject. Meadows then demonstrates some wrestling techniques. Maneuvering Barton into a hold position, he effortlessly flips him over and pins him to the floor. Meadows is apologetic for hurting Barton, though Barton assures him that the exercise was helpful. The scene ends after Meadows makes a noisy exit, and the camera moves in toward the bathing beauty picture; the sound of ocean waves wafts lightly over Barton's head.

The following scene opens with Mayhew's inscription to Barton on the flyleaf of one of his novels; it refers to what Mayhew calls Barton's "sojourn among the Philistines." Mayhew, Barton, and Audrey feast on a picnic lunch of fried chicken and discuss "things literary." Mayhew snipes at Audrey, whose face registers a blend of indulgence and resentment. Mayhew opines that the act of writing generates peace. Barton disagrees; his open contradiction of Mayhew's idea causes Audrey to startle. He delivers a short speech on the "great inner pain," the result of social conscience or private torment, to which his writing is indebted and which he feels is a prerequisite for "good work." Audrey is visibly impressed by Barton, drawn to his account of sacrifice and suffering.

Mayhew describes his anguish at being unable to write in highly graphic terms. In his elegantly modulated voice he confides that this state causes him to "want to rip my head off and run screaming through the streets with my balls in a fruit picker's pail." Mayhew hoists his whiskey bottle to his lips, allowing that it sometimes "helps"; this assessment elicits twin negations from Audrey and Barton. His patience obviously wearing thin, Mayhew begins a story to which Audrey is compelled to put a quick stop. Her transparent attempt to then mollify Mayhew arrives in the form of a literary compliment, a strategy which further irritates the great author.

Barton tells Mayhew that he feels he is wasting his gift on drink and cutting himself off from all that is meaningful in his life. Mayhew disagrees with him in colorful terms. The conversation turns to Mayhew and Audrey's relationship. Barton makes clear his sympathy for Audrey and his admiration for her tolerant attitude toward Mayhew. Mayhew wanders from their table to weave among the trees, singing drunkenly. Audrey goes to him, and Mayhew strikes her in the face.

Barton comforts a crying Audrey but is astounded by her reaction to Mayhew's abuse. She feels sorry for him. She tells Barton that Mayhew's drinking is related to his feelings for Estelle, his "disturbed" wife still living in the South. A long shot of Mayhew details his drunken progress down a roadway where he causes an oncoming vehicle to swerve in order to avoid him. Audrey tells Barton that eventually he will sober up and return, apologetic. She hints that there are reasons why she empathizes with Mayhew that are beyond Barton's understanding.

An overhead shot spirals down toward Barton's face as he lies prone on his bed; the insectile whine that accompanies this camera movement completes the suggestion that our point of view has been a mosquito's. Barton slaps his hand at the insect, waking himself, and glances wildly at the disintegrating ceiling above before his disorientation fades.

He goes to his desk and stares morosely at the single paragraph he has typed, words which represent the sum of his productivity since arriving in Hollywood. He slips on the shoes which rest underneath his desk; his feet swim in them. He types a sentence before Meadows enters his room, holding a pair of shoes aloft. They exchange shoes. They have been accidentally switched by Chet, whose job it is to polish shoes left in the corridor by hotel residents. Barton invites Meadows in.

Meadows complains of the "cruelty" of housewives uninterested in purchasing the peace of mind he offers them and who feel entitled to comment negatively upon his physique. Barton commiserates with him. Meadows confides an altercation with a local doctor over his ear infection. He then asks Barton, "How goes the life of the mind?" Barton confesses a lack of progress on his script. Meadows segues into a discussion of "the lovebirds next door" and the amount of noise they make. He twists his face as if in pain, saying, "It seems like I hear everything that goes on in this dump." He blames it on the pipes.

Meadows expresses great optimism regarding Barton's ability to "lick this picture business." "You got a head on your shoulders," he says cheerfully, "and what is it they say? Where there's a head there's hope." Barton corrects Meadows' macabre miswording of the aphorism, a feat which appears to further fuel Meadows' admiration. They exchange glowing predictions for each other's prospects.

Meadows tells Barton that he is leaving town for a few days, going, in fact, to Barton's hometown of New York City. Barton seems honestly saddened by the news. Meadows says that he must make the trip because "things are all balled up at the head office" but assures Barton that he will certainly return to Los Angeles where he maintains a room at the Earle. Barton gives Meadows the names and addresses of his parents and uncle. New York, he tells him, can be cruel to strangers, and he hopes that Meadows will avail himself of a home-cooked meal at his relatives'. As he passes the information to the salesman, a sheet of wallpaper peels noisily away from the wall in Barton's room. "Your room does that, too," intones Meadows.

Barton positions himself at his typewriter; an overhead shot emphasizes his distress as he struggles for an idea with which to proceed. The camera moves toward Barton's face as he listens to the sounds of movement from within the hotel—heavy bumps and footsteps. A match cut from the textured paleness of his ceiling to a close-up of the page a secretary is typing follows; Barton waits in Geisler's office for his appointment with his producer.

Barton is greeted with a rough inquiry regarding the state of his facial skin. When he tells Geisler that it is nothing, just mosquito bites, the man is incredulous and insists that there are no mosquitoes in the city. Geisler moves on to matters more germane to his self-interests. Shalhoub delivers a screamingly funny performance in the scene which follows. Geisler is upset at both Barton's lack of progress and his choice of mentor (Geisler is succinct in his description of the great Mayhew, bellowing the word "souse" as many times as a single breath will allow). He tells Barton that he has committed a grave error: he has made Lipnick *like* him. Lipnick has therefore "taken a interest" in his career. "Never," intones Geisler, "make Lipnick like you. Never!" When Barton says he doesn't understand, Geisler nearly leaps across his desk during an abbreviated lunge at the disconcerted author. He tells Barton that because he has covered for him, they are now both vulnerable to Lipnick's displeasure. Barton is to visit Lipnick the next day and discuss his progress on the Beery picture. When Barton protests that he can't possibly write anything by this deadline, Geisler says, "Who says write? Jesus, Jack can't read … you got to tell it to him. Tell him something, for Christ's sake." Barton is now nearly paralyzed with fear. Geisler arranges for him to view some of the dailies of a wrestling picture in production. He gives Barton Lipnick's address and tells him to traffic in "broad strokes" during his pitch. "Don't cross me, Fink," Geisler warns, searching Barton's ravaged, stricken face.

The blackscreen which follows introduces the snippets of the wrestling picture that Barton looks to for inspiration. The rushes of *Devil on the Canvas* are hilarious, consisting of a very large man in tights rushing the camera and screaming, "I will destroy him." This same gentleman also grapples with an equally ample colleague on the mat, producing agonized vocalizations and impact effects which seem to grow more surreally intense as Barton watches, open-mouthed and slack-jawed with horror. Barton's glasses reflect the screen's activity, an effect which emphasizes his stupefaction as he contemplates the genre to which he has indebted his literary talents.

Barton paces his hotel room in distress, having succeeded in committing two words to paper since his visit to the studio. Desperate, he calls Audrey and pleads for her help; Mayhew's drunken raging can be heard in the background. Audrey promises to try and slip away from Mayhew if he passes out. She dares not visit Barton if Mayhew remains conscious, however, as Mayhew considers Barton "a buffoon" and is, in any case, prone to jealousy.

Audrey arrives and attempts to soothe the distraught Barton. Barton tells her he must have a three-act scenario by morning and asks about Mayhew's contributions to the wrestling genre. Audrey describes the plot outlines Mayhew generally adheres to. Comforting Barton, Audrey tells him not to worry, that she will help him as she has helped Mayhew so many times. Confronted by Barton, Audrey admits that she herself has written not only Mayhew's filmscripts but various novels as well, though, she insists, "Bill was always the 'author' so to speak." Barton explodes in outrage upon learning that Audrey has ghostwritten much of Mayhew's work but must limit the length of his diatribe so that he may employ Audrey to similar purpose.

Audrey asks Barton not to judge or condescend to Mayhew; she tells him that her most important function is to "understand" and "appreciate" Mayhew. As she speaks she caresses Barton lightly and offers him the same. They kiss and recline on the bed where Audrey gently removes his glasses. The camera pans slowly from the bed across the room. The shot glides laterally to the sounds of their lovemaking, then moves into the bathroom, into the sink, and, with a *Psycho*-esque flourish, down the drain of the sink and into the encrusted pipeway of the plumbing below. The sounds of Audrey's sighs merge with a demonic cacophony of voices blended with the sound of running water. It is a tour-de-force manifestation of Meadows' earlier remark concerning the hotel's pipes' ability to transmit sound.

Barton awakes and is graced with a view of his stained ceiling and of the loud mosquito executing figure eights below it. Turning his head he sees Audrey's naked back. He watches a mosquito bite her; the image is highly magnified as the insect penetrates Audrey's skin. Barton slaps at the bug and a splotch of blood appears. Audrey remains still. Barton is mystified. Blood begins to seep from beneath her body. Barton turns her toward him. She is dead and covered with blood. Barton screams.

The camera focuses on the far wall of Barton's room, locating the source of noise which emanates from the other side, and pans to trace its path to Barton's door. Meadows knocks loudly and calls Barton's name. Hyperventilating, Barton leaps out of bed and runs to the door, where, with a jumble of contradictory phrases, he assures Meadows that all is well. He shuts the door on Meadows and staggers back into the room. He sits down at his desk; small whimpering sounds escape his lips. He checks the corridor for activity, interrupting Chet as he collects shoes for polishing. When Chet is gone Barton goes next door to Meadows' room. He asks to be let in; Meadows suggests Barton's room instead. Barton asks Meadows for his support and company while he calls the police, and he tells Meadows that he is not responsible for what he is about to see. Meadows enters the room and vomits at the sight of Audrey bloodily dead in Barton's bed.

Meadows convinces a blubbering and terrified Barton not to call the police. "You're in pictures, Barton," Meadows explains. "Even if they cleared you eventually, this would ruin you," he says, evoking the specter of countless Arbuckle-esque Hollywood scandals. Meadows directs Barton to wait in the bathroom while he attends to Audrey. Barton listens as Meadows begins work. The screen goes dark when Barton passes out cold after watching Meadows carry Audrey's body past the bathroom to the door.

Meadows slaps Barton's face hard several times to revive him. When Barton asks where Audrey is, Meadows gets very excited; he directs Barton to put the incident out of his mind and carry on as if nothing unusual has occurred. Looking at his watch, Barton notes he has fifteen minutes before his meeting with Lipnick.

Lipnick greets Barton effusively from the lawn chair that protects his bulk from the rococo garden that surrounds a large swimming pool. Lipnick orders Lou to retrieve the whiskey Barton has dazedly requested. He then launches into an inquiry concerning the state of Barton's work. Asked to synopsize his story "in broad strokes," Barton begins, then falters. He asks Lipnick if he can be honest with him. The question prompts a very amusing, rambling meditation on the incompatibility of such a virtue with the motion picture industry, though, Lipnick hastens to add, as writers are generally removed from the sort of corrupt environment with which he himself is forced to contend, Barton should feel free to indulge any honest impulses.

Barton seems stunned by Lipnick's short monologue. He drinks his early morning whiskey in a single long draught before he delivers his lie. "To be honest," Barton says, "I'm never really comfortable discussing work in progress. I got it all worked out in my head. But sometimes if forced into words prematurely ..." Barton's words trail off in this vein as Lipnick stares at him. With a barely discernible nod, he signals Lou to take over. Lou admonishes Barton for his attitude and tells him that as a contract employee of the studio, the contents of his head belong to Capital Pictures. Lou urges Barton to reconsider his answer.

Lou and Barton look to Lipnick. Lipnick explodes with an antisemitic torrent of verbal abuse. The diatribe is directed, however, not at Barton but at Lou, who he proceeds to berate and humiliate. In a final burst of venom, Lipnick fires Lou when he refuses to lick Barton's shoes in tribute to the man's creative artistry. Barton is appalled and tries to persuade Lipnick to rehire his disgraced underling. Lipnick refuses. He ecstatically celebrates Barton's talent and temperament, bowing to kiss the soles of his shoes—a symbol, he says, of Capital Pictures' apology and respect.

This scene featuring Barton, Lou, and Lipnick is both outrageously funny and disturbing, due largely to Michael Lerner's maniacal performance as Lipnick. John Turturro shines in this scene as well. Turturro's role in the film is largely reactive, which sometimes obscures the delicacy with which he negotiates his portrayal of the deluded writer. Barton's response to this fresh hell is brilliantly acted: equal parts of self-interest, horror, and condescension.

Back in his room, Barton stares open-mouthed at his typewriter. A knock at his door rouses him from his stupor. Meadows is admitted, dressed in his salesman's suit and carrying a suitcase and a paper-wrapped, string-tied box. Meadows is leaving for his trip. He tells Barton that "everything has been taken care of." Barton cries in Meadows' arms. He tells Meadows that he is the only person that he can talk to in Los Angeles; he also moans that he believes he is losing his mind. Meadows tells him that he must pull himself together and endure until he returns from his trip. "We gotta keep our heads," says Meadows. Meadows asks Barton to keep the box for him until he returns. It contains, he says, "everything that he wants to keep from a lifetime." Meadows thinks maybe the box will inspire Barton to finish his work; he encourages the writer to model his protagonist after himself. Barton is grateful for Meadows' interest. As

Barton walks Meadows to the door, they contemplate a strip of wallpaper that has fallen halfway down the wall. Meadows promises to return and disappears into the corridor's maw. Barton sits on the edge of his bloodstained mattress and weeps. The noise he makes is reminiscent of the sounds he has heard through the walls of his room since his arrival. The camera dollies slowly away from Barton; a dissolve to the corridor outside his room conveys how clearly the sounds of his anguish carry.

Somewhat recovered, Barton sits in front of his typewriter and contemplates the Gideon's Bible in his desk drawer. Opening the book at random, he reads a passage from the book of Daniel—"the king's dream." Printed words fill the frame; the alert viewer will note that the king's name is Nebuchandnezzar, the name of the novel W. P. Mayhew has inscribed and given to Barton (the spelling is slightly different). The words "ye shall be cut in pieces" are prominently positioned. Barton turns to the book of Genesis. There he begins to read chapter one. The chapter's first two lines consist of the only written work Barton has accomplished in Los Angeles (words which probably open his celebrated play as well): *Fade in on a tenement building in Manhattan's Lower East Side. Faint traffic noise is audible, as is the cry of the fishmongers.* Barton closes the Bible, his face immobile with shock. The telephone rings.

Barton is in an elevator; its downward plunge is a kinetic reference to the fiery nether region Barton is dimly beginning to recognize as home. The creaking sounds of cables and pulleys blend with another obscure noise. This sound is revealed to be the heavily labored intake of oxygen by Pete (the wonderful Harry Bugin), the elevator's demi-corpse of an operator. Barton asks Pete if he's ever read the Bible. "*Holy* Bible?" asks Pete. With a succinct two words, he manages to evoke a thousand questions concerning the dark night of his particular soul.

Barton trudges through the hotel lobby toward the two men who pace and smoke within its murky depths. They introduce themselves as detectives. They have some "routine" questions for him, which they deliver in the syncopated wisecracking rhythms of noir detective-speak. They show Barton a picture of Meadows; Barton's neighbor leers dementedly at the camera in what is clearly a police photo. They tell him the man he knows as Charlie Meadows is actually named Karl Mundt, aka "Madman" Mundt. The detectives tell Barton that his confidante likes to "ventilate people with a shotgun and then cut their heads off." They enlighten him further. In colorful terms they describe Mundt's latest victims, an ear, nose, and throat doctor and a woman we understand to be Audrey. The detectives find Barton's contributions singularly unhelpful to their investigation and depart with an ethnic slur and a gesture of disrespect.

Meadows/Mundt's mysterious box is centered in the frame as Barton slowly approaches. This box has an arresting physical appearance: it is nothing so much as an artist's abstract conception of such an item made corporeal. Barton gingerly lifts the beige stuccoed package, shakes it, and inspects it closely before placing it on his desk, behind his typewriter. It appears to inspire Barton in the way Meadows/Mundt had hoped. Barton begins to type steadily. Time passes; a typing Barton ignores the ring of his telephone. He improvises earplugs in order to avoid such future distractions and continues typing. Tucked in the frame of the bathing beauty picture is a photograph of Meadows/Mundt. The box and the photograph seem to be talismans; under their malevolent influence Barton is finally able to produce a script, somehow galvanized by the trauma these items represent. A sound montage of the voices in Barton's head as he works gives us some idea of his writing.

Barton telephones his agent in the middle of the night in order to proclaim that his oeuvre in progress is "big … important … this may be the most important work I've ever done." His agent thinks Barton sounds a little odd. Barton angrily decries the man's lack of support and hangs up. He continues to type. He finishes the script, removes his earplugs, and showers.

Barton celebrates by going dancing. The crowded dance hall is marked by a vintage cartoon aesthetic; brightly clothed revelers move frenetically to the strains of a swing band amidst a swirl of color and motion. Nobody dances more exuberantly than Barton himself; his exaggerated execution of the forties choreography is grotesque.

A sailor attempts to cut in. Barton resists; his face is feverishly animated. A crowd of military personnel and civilians gather. "I'm a creator!" Barton shrieks. "This," he says pointing to his head, "is how I serve the common man!" A sailor punches him, and Barton falls into the arms of a soldier, initiating a brawl between the two military factions. Barton watches from his position on the floor. Canted angles and slow-motion photography convey Barton's altered state of subjectivity; the camera weaves and rolls through the action toward the fluted end of a trumpet, where it seems to disappear into the instrument's sonorous depths.

The big band sound overlaps into the next shot; the camera languidly tracks down the by now familiar corridor of the Hotel Earle. Barton approaches his door somewhat unsteadily, enveloped by the vacuous roaring sound with which we have come to associate the hotel's interior space. Inside there are voices. Barton enters his room to find the detectives reading his script. Derisively wisecracking, the policemen provide Barton with a grisly account of recent events: W. P. Mayhew has been found headless.

The detectives have several questions. They are interested in Barton's relationship to Mayhew and Audrey and even more curious about his bloodstained mattress. They suggest Barton and Meadows/Mundt are both involved in the murders. Barton suggests they leave and come back when the weather cools down and his head feels better. "Charlie's back," Barton tells them. "It's hot—he's back." The elevator bell signals a stop on Barton's floor. Handcuffing Barton to his bed, the policemen go into the corridor to investigate.

The detectives complain of the heat. Smoke is now visible at the end of the long hallway; flames erupt from beneath the metal plates of the open elevator. The men draw their guns. The corridor darkens as Meadows/Mundt shows himself. Attired in full salesman regalia, he saunters toward the sweating duo. The large man comes to a halt. The detectives instruct him to "put the policy case down and your mitts in the air." Meadows/Mundt initially appears to comply; a long shot frames the man between twin jets of flame as he places his case down. Meadows/Mundt removes a shotgun from the case. As a wall of fire leaps to life behind his back, he directs a shotgun blast to the chest of the nearest detective, screaming "Look upon me! I'll show you the life of the mind!" Repeating this line as the flames behind him expand, Meadows/Mundt runs toward the remaining lawman, chasing him down the smoldering corridor. Great balls of fire blossom in his wake as he roars toward the hapless detective. When he stops before his fallen prey, a blinding backlight of fire renders his form a dark shadow; the effect is to flip our attention from figure to field, emphasizing the hellish dreamworld that has so defined our experience of the film.

From his tethered position, Barton watches as Meadows/Mundt pauses to reload his shotgun outside his doorway. The maniac continues toward the prone detective. "Heil Hitler," he says mildly before shooting the screaming man point-blank in the face.

"Barton," says Meadows/Mundt, entering his room. "Brother, is it hot. ... Don't look at me like that," he tells him, "It's just me, Charlie." "I hear it's Mundt," says Barton. "Madman Mundt." "Jesus, people can be cruel," says the killer. "If it's not my build it's my personality."

Meadows/Mundt looks imploringly at Barton. "They say I'm a madman Barton, but I'm not mad at anyone—honestly." His wordplay underscores an intriguing aspect of this character's speech patterns. In the dialogue of Meadows/Mundt is evinced a postmodern prolonged hesitation of words caught between their metaphoric and literal meanings.[3] This lunatic prone to decapitation is fond of phrases such as "peace [piece] of mind," "where there's a head there's hope," "we gotta keep our heads," "I decided to knock off early," and "foul-ups" plaguing "the head office."

Meadows/Mundt explains to the writer that he functions to relieve people of their misery, a misery with which he empathizes sorely. "But Charlie, why me?" asks Barton. "Because you don't listen!" bellows the killer, his face streaming with perspiration and pus. He tells Barton that his pain, his hell, cannot begin to compare with his own. He himself, he explains, is a long-term resident of the hell which Barton visits as "a tourist with a typewriter." Meadows/Mundt elicits an apology from Barton; this macabre interview is conducted against the aural backdrop of the flames which roar beyond the perimeters of the frame.

With a show of inhuman strength, Meadows/Mundt frees Barton from the bed. "I'll be next door if you need me," he says. He also tells Barton that he has "dropped in" on his parents and uncle in New York and that the package he has left with Barton "isn't mine."

Barton grabs the box and his script before exiting. In the corridor, he watches as his neighbor lets himself into his room. He then strides down the hallway toward the elevator. The shot affords us a nightmarish illustration of linear perspective, the image's vanishing point a flaming holocaust.

Outside Lipnick's office, Barton tries without success to reach his parents and uncle by telephone. Ushered into the studio head's inner sanctum, Barton is greeted by Lipnick in the dress uniform of an army colonel. Though his reserve commission has not yet gone through, he has obtained his outfit, he says, from the studio's wardrobe department. He appears to take the country's at-war status quite personally. "The enemy," he snarls, "would love to see me sit this one out."

As Lou hovers in the background, Lipnick tells Barton that his reinstated sycophant has read Barton's script for him. Their critical estimation of the script is that "it won't wash." Lipnick finds Barton's assertion that it is his best work ridiculous. The crazed mogul delivers a near stream-of-consciousness rebuke to Barton, at one point insisting that Barton's opinion counts for little in any case, since "the lunatics are not going to run this particular asylum. So let's put a stop to that rumor," he says, vigorously slapping his desk several times, "right now!" Lipnick's monologue concerning what are to him the obvious pitfalls of putting Wallace Beery "in a fruity movie about suffering" is hilarious.

Lipnick tells Barton that Geisler has been fired as a result of his incompetence. Barton's punishment, explains Lipnick, will be worse. He will remain under contract to Capital Pictures. Everything he writes belongs to them, and they will produce nothing he writes. Lipnick disgorges yet another diatribe. The antisemitic rant details his opinions regarding Barton's hypocrisy and arrogance.

A cut to the same shot that marked Barton's transition to Holly-wood—impossibly blue ocean wave hitting a large rock formation—pre-cedes one of Barton as he walks along the water's edge in his suit. He carries Meadows/Mundt's box, an object that remains richly ambiguous. He sits in the sand, the box beside him. A beautiful young woman approaches him and speaks. She asks Barton about the contents of the package. When Barton tells her that he doesn't know what is inside, she asks him if the box is his; he again answers that he doesn't know. He tells her that she is beautiful and asks her if she is in pictures. "Don't be silly," she replies. Sitting in front of him in the sand, she turns toward the ocean, shading her eyes against the glare of the sun. Perfectly recreated is the picture above Barton's typewriter in the Hotel Earle. Held by Barton's mad vision, we watch as a seagull plunges out of the sky and into the sea; the bathing girl watches, too.

The movie's final credits scroll up against Barton's hotel wallpaper as the camera pans endlessly down, the motion reinforcing the film's orga-nizing metaphor. Barton, it seems, has traded in his tourist's visa for per-manent residency, exercising what has been an option from the beginning. The Hotel Earle has threatened from the outset accommodations for "a day or a lifetime."

In *Barton Fink* the road to the division of hell known as Hollywood is paved with self-delusion. All the characters in the film are defined by the particular fictions they have appropriated, illusions made conspicuous by the self-interests they serve and by the deliriously inflated scope of the traits they incite.

Audrey maintains her belief that Mayhew is a great man whose for-tunes are at low ebb due to the pain he endures on account of the wife he has driven insane; she also believes that her sexual liaisons constitute the ministrations of a worshipping Muse. Audrey facilitates Mayhew's self-destruction; she concedes to Fink that it may look "funny" but implores him to refrain from the judgment which she herself holds admirably at bay.

Charlie Meadows/Karl Mundt has convinced himself that he is an angel of mercy who relieves people of their pain; meanwhile, the madness which constitutes his particular frame of reference percolates out of his head in the form of a drippy ear infection. His final murderous charge is savagely satiric as he comments on Barton's existential lament regarding the life of the mind. In his cheerful "It's just me, Charlie" resides an echo of what philosopher Hannah Arendt has called "the banality of evil."

Jack Lipnick, the venomously autocratic head of the fictitious Cap-ital Pictures, is a metaparody of studio-era moguls (Louis B. Mayer was especially well known for his mercurial disposition.) In his casually anti–Semitic self-hatred and volatile psychopathology are worlds within worlds projected outward. W.P. Mayhew, Barton's fellow literary exile, may be the character most conscious of his own fraudulence. A parodic character who indulges within the film's storyworld in self-parody, he uses alcohol to medicate the consequences of self-knowledge.

No one in the film is more self-deluded than Barton Fink himself. A quirky caricature of artistic self-involvement and intellectual pretension, he speaks not a word of his avowed belief system which he does not subsequently contradict through his behavior, nor does he have an idea in his head that is not unexamined. He is fixated on the language of a particular political vocabulary, as completely unable to imagine the application of these ideas as he is removed from the moral framework that inspires them. *Barton Fink* is at one level an incendiary study of intellect minus soul: Barton's ideologically based megalomania blinds him to his world and deafens him to its stories.

Some of these stories speak truths which take shape within *Barton Fink*'s richly conceived dreamworld. The rise of Hitler's fascism is embodied in the diabolical Meadows/Mundt, whose eagerness to please veils a bloody agenda. The holocaust which ultimately consumes the hotel is potent imagery which, in this context, speaks for itself.

The Coens initiate an interesting deconstruction of the divide between "low" art and "high" art in their attention to Barton's transition from "highbrow art"—New York theatre—to "lowbrow art," movies. Barton tells his neighbor that he is among those who wish to "create a theatre for the masses based on a few simple truths"—a concise definition of forties Hollywood films (it is especially apropos to, in this way, describe the kind of B picture Barton has been hired to write). Foregrounded is the fact that the movies represent exactly what theatre has never been: the kind of accessible mass art to which Barton is so fervently dedicated. That both "high art" and "low art" are dependent on the same mythic forms and illusionary surfaces is suggested in a sequence wherein an expressively mobile camera focuses on Barton's common man/noble savage script, then travels to the picture of the archetypal Hollywood beach beauty shading her eyes as she looks off to sea. The camera then observes the wallpaper as it slickly peels away from the wall. The gritty "reality" of Barton's script, its inclination toward an attempted documentary-like social "truth," is revealed through the camera's kinetic symbolism to reflect no less a mythology than the dreams produced by Hollywood's film factories. Barton's shredding sanity is suggested by the decomposing wallpaper as Lower Eastside tenements and southern California beaches are revealed as screens which are roughly equivalent in their ability to support projected illusion.

Relatedly, this first Coen brothers film to be shot in Hollywood sardonically touches upon the idea of artist-as-commodity. Initially prized as the progenitor of "that Barton Fink feeling," Barton is superfluous a short time later. His signature style has taken on a life of its own, now a thoroughly reproducible product. "I got twenty writers that can get me that Barton Fink feeling!" screams Lipnick before condemning Barton to his sentence of hard labor.

Barton's fate is, of course, a palimpsest for the Coens' sly retrofit of a literary historical legend: the moral and artistic debasement of renowned writers who succumbed to Hollywood's clarion call following the industrywide conversion to sound. Clifford Odets, Nathaniel West, William Faulkner, and F. Scott Fitzgerald are among those writers whose encounters with Hollywood's dream factory have been transmogrified through time and imagination into the stuff of myth and moral fable.

At a basic level, *Barton Fink* is an experiential film. Much of its highly expressive, artfully stylized audiovisual text is Barton Fink's interior subjective state expelled outward—immanent wakeful dream made corporeal.

Barton's hellish hotel, in particular, functions as an audiovisual metaphor for his deteriorating mindset. As in Roman Polanski's *Repulsion* (1965) and *The Tenant* (1976), physical environment is transformed into tropological filmspace. Cinematographer Roger Deakins, production designer Dennis Gassner, and soundmen Allan Byer and Skip Lievsay are prominent among those whose considerable talents were pooled to create a dreamworld rich enough to eclipse the film's human characters. Long after Barton Fink and Charlie Meadows have receded from memory, the tactile and auditory horrors of the Hotel Earle retain a potent hold on the imagination.

Barton Fink borrows the conventions of many genres in turn, an amalgamation of darkest black comedy, psychological thriller, horror film, murder mystery, and the self-reflexive "inside Hollywood" picture. The film is also stylistically excessive enough to intermittently suggest an art-film parody, a critique of the kind of thing Barton himself might make one day should he work his way up the Hollywood food chain.

Barton Fink owes much to Polanski's aforementioned *Repulsion* and *The Tenant,* as well as to other auteurist texts, such as Kubrick's *The Shining* and Alfred Hitchcock's *Psycho* (1960). It also recalls the kind of surrealist excursions for which directors such as Luis Buñuel and David Lynch are renowned.

Barton Fink garnered an unprecedented three prizes at the 1991 Cannes Film Festival. Awarded the prestigious Palm d'Or for best film, the festival also honored Joel Coen as best director and John Turturro as best actor. Its cinematography earned it a Los Angeles Film Critics Award (they also gave Michael Lerner a best supporting actor prize), the National Society of Film Critics Award, and the New York Film Critics Award (they also designated Judy Davis best supporting actress of the year).

While the bulk of critical response to *Barton Fink* has been hugely positive, the film also has its detractors, such as J. Hoberman, who finds it full of "sour formalism, bleak humor, and empty word stylistics." Hoberman also notes the film's debt to the work of Roman Polanski and suggests that "given Polanski's power as chair of the [1991] Cannes jury," this connection "may account for the film's unprecedented three awards."[4] According to John Harkness of *Sight and Sound*, who interviewed a member of the jury shortly after the festival, the decision was unanimous.[5] Stanley Kauffmann, writing for the *New Republic*, denounces not only *Barton Fink's* "gaseous fraudulence" but the Coens' other films as well, which he finds pretentious.[6]

"*Barton Fink*," relates Joel Coen, "was never intended to be a movie that would play in malls in middle America."[7] The film did better in Europe than in the United States, where its lack of mainstream accessibility all but guaranteed its box-office failure; produced for $9 million, it returned barely $5 million. This fact did not deter megaproducer Joel Silver from, in the words of Barton's boss, "taking a interest" in the Coens. Intrigued by *Barton Fink's* resounding critical acclaim, Silver judged the time right to gamble on the Coens, whose work he had admired since *Blood Simple*. The alchemy he proposed would result in the Coens' first big-budget, major studio–financed bid at mainstream acceptance, *The Hudsucker Proxy*.

CHAPTER 5

The Hudsucker Proxy

The Coens began to write *The Hudsucker Proxy* in 1984 during a stay with their good friend Sam Raimi, with whom they collaborated on the script. The project was abandoned before it was completed. Raimi and the Coens were having trouble with the ending, and since the lavishly elaborate sets they envisioned for the film were far beyond what they could imagine funding at the time, the three were content to shelve the script and pursue more viable projects.

Four critically acclaimed films later, the Coens found themselves championed by Joel Silver, heavyweight Hollywood producer (*Die Hard*, *Lethal Weapon*) and perennial fan. Raimi and the Coens finished the script in 1991. The Coens had begun to shop it, but, as Silver relates:

> They ... had a reputation for being weird, off-center, inaccessible. They were having trouble getting the money for this 25 million script—people were stymied by the fact that Joel and Ethan's name was on it.[1]

Silver decided to back *Hudsucker*, reportedly telling the Coens that they "were morons for shelving it" in the first place.[2] His clout, plus the delivery of box-office luminary Paul Newman, helped convince Warner Brothers and PolyGram to share the financial burden of producing the film. In exchange Warner Brothers would receive domestic distribution rights and PolyGram foreign. According to the Coens, *Hudsucker* cost between $25 and $26 million,[3] though various journalistic sources have suggested that it topped out near $40 million.

During the deluge of publicity that attended the film's release, Joel Coen described *Hudsucker* as "a more mainstream movie, in terms of its ambitions" than their previous films.[4] With good reason. Explained Jim Jacks, who executive produced *Raising Arizona*, "They'll always try to make a movie as commercial as it has to be to recoup the investment. ...They've never made a movie so expensive that they had to make it that commercial, until now."[5] The pressures and obligations of major-studio big-budget financing made the Coens sensitive as never before to a crucial question posed by *Entertainment Weekly* soon after the film opened: Will America get the joke?[6]

The joke, if it may be so called, is a complicated one. Taken at face value, the film is quirkily entertaining; however, a more complex reading and true appreciation of the film is available only to the cineliterate viewer to whom the Coens typically address their work. *Hudsucker* represents the deepest enunciation of the aesthetic strategies that mark the Coens' earlier four films; *Hudsucker* is, in fact, a radicalization of these strategies. An ultrastylized pastiche of zanily inflected reconstituted bits of film history, it is their most fabulous creation. Thom Nobel's flawless editing rhythms, Roger Deakins' lustrous cinematography, and Dennis Gassner's evocative production design (the film was shot completely on stage sets) contribute marvelously to the Coens' vision: a fantastical blend of conventions and quotations which ultimately transcend their sources in service to a characteristically idiosyncratic, meticulously realized dreamworld.

The Hudsucker Proxy unfolds in the artfully self-conscious storytelling mode so characteristically Coenesque. The film begins with a lilting voice-over narration and highly stylized images of a snow-flecked urbanscape, a fittingly lyrical introduction to the most synthetic filmspace the Coens have ever supervised. "That's right," purrs the unseen narrator, "New York, ...1958," as though the fairytale-like vision before us could be none other than. The extreme long shot dissolves into images presented by a camera which weaves and glides through the upper reaches of the city's fantastic architecture, mapping its magical topography. We learn that it is New Year's Eve and listen to a poetic rumination on the celebration of this event. The camera slowly winds toward a towered clock centered in the frame. A cut to a close-up of the clock face reveals that the edifice belongs to Hudsucker Industries, whose company motto assures us that "The Future is Now." (Coen fans may recall that *Raising Arizona*'s H. I. attempts the straight and narrow by taking a job with Hudsucker Industries.) The camera pans to reveal a man, who the narrator identifies as Norville Barnes (Tim Robbins), as he climbs out of his top-story office window and flattens himself against the building a minute or two before the adjacent massive Art Deco clock strikes midnight. Barnes, the narrator confides, is the president of Hudsucker Industries. "How'd he get so high?" the voice asks in a rhetorical double entendre. "And why is he feeling so low? Is he really gonna do it? Is Norville really gonna jelly up the sidewalk?" The narrator promises to tell us Norville's story, to catch us up to this moment in time. The clock moves to strike midnight, and Carter Burwell's lushly nostalgic orchestrations crescendo. Modern lettering superimposed against a scrolling starry night sky delivers a credit sequence organized around a stylized H.

A brief blackscreen emphasizes the film's transition to the past. A bus (Muncie–New York line!) pulls into a station, and a suitcase is disgorged. Centered in the frame, the bestickered luggage is a proud testament to an education received at the Muncie College of Business Administration. It is picked up and carried. Because the camera remains on the suitcase, it is not until after it has been rested on a city sidewalk that we glimpse its owner—Norville Barnes, fresh off the bus but looking spiffy in his flannel suit and bow tie. He gazes upward to verify his whereabouts and looks gratified that he has found the Nidus Employment Agency. Curtains part in the window of the agency to reveal an ever-fluctuating job board; Norville smiles with delight. Others join Norville. The job-seeking throng grows smaller as various men respond to posted positions, including "bombardier" and "card shark"; Norville, however, is stymied by the board's stipulations regarding experience. The camera moves in toward Norville's face to record his increasing distress. In the first of many visual tropes which pay homage to Hollywood's classical era, transparent bands of phrases such as "experience required" and "experienced applicants only" spin across the screen from foreground to background in a dissolving montage against Norville's despairing countenance. Alone on the sidewalk as the business day comes to a close, Norville's disappointed retreat is noted by a camera high overhead.

The scene dissolves to the interior of an executive boardroom, a space noteworthy for its wall of floor-to-ceiling windows and its great rectangular Art Deco table, burnished to a high luster. As the speaker on the floor delivers a deliriously upbeat message regarding the financial fortunes of Hudsucker Industries, the camera tracks down the length of the table toward the smiling man at its head.

A cut to Norville as he peruses the want ads at a diner reveals his continuing plight: he has none of the background demanded by prospective employers, who require some experience on the part of applicants who respond to their need for goatherds, goal tenders, and rope braiders. Retrieving some of the tip change he had thought to leave for the waiter, a discouraged Norville leaves. The waiter removes Norville's coffee cup from where Norville had set it on his newspaper; it leaves a damp ring around a Hudsucker Industries ad. The image of the circle will echo throughout the film, a recurring symbol of the film's overall structuring motif. The newspaper peels off the lunch counter as the diner's door chimes peal following Norville's exit. The musical bells emphasize the extraordinary nature of this particular gust of wind.

Meanwhile, back at Hudsucker's board meeting, a fluidly mobile camera observes the head executive's accelerating inattention to the fiscal lecture still in progress and his increasing fascination with the view outside the room's grand windows. The words of the speaker recede and reverberate, the subjective aural experience of this increasingly distracted mogul. Norville is shown walking despondently down a city street; its design is calculated to invoke a studio-era urban set. He is followed by his newspaper, which nips at his heels like a playful dog before Norville picks it up and notices the encircled ad.

In the Hudsucker boardroom, the speaker is finishing up, announcing record profits of all kinds. Our head executive's attention is clearly diverted by his own thoughts. He checks his watch, winds it, and carefully places it on the table in front of him. He clears his throat, and his celebrating colleagues quiet. The ticking of his watch is the only sound that accompanies his elaborately gestured cigar puff. Wordlessly, the man fastidiously neatens his clothing, then gingerly steps up onto the table. He initiates an elaborate routine immediately recognizable as a baroque preamble to some physical feat. His underlings stare at him in wonder. "Mr. Hudsucker," one finally ventures, as Waring Hudsucker (Charles Durning) makes as if to launch himself forward in some fashion. A quick cut to the outside of the Hudsucker building shows Norville about to enter; another cut to Hudsucker's watch reveals that it is several seconds before noon. As Norville enters the building, Hudsucker exits—through the window, in a magnificent swan dive. His fall is pure eye candy, a stylishly cartoonish bluescreen effect angled from both above and below. His descent is greatly attenuated, though seemingly speedy (Hudsucker has the time to dislodge a particle from his eye in a relatively leisurely fashion, as well as to motion pedestrians out of his way). The man lands with a campy, exaggerated splat. A fat lady screams (possibly the same screamer from *Miller's Crossing*'s club scene), and the tower clock strikes noon. The camera rests upon the tower clock face for a moment before dipping to observe the broken plate glass of the company boardroom. One of Hudsucker's executives stares through it before turning back to the assembled businessmen.

The executive proceeds to the head of the table and takes a puff of Hudsucker's cigar before sitting in the dead man's chair. After a short discussion regarding the life and times of Waring Hudsucker, the talk turns to business. It appears that Hudsucker's demise has paved the way for his controlling stock to be made available to the public as of January 1. "Do you mean to say," gulps the man in Hudsucker's chair, "that any slob in a smelly tee shirt will be able to buy Hudsucker stock?!" This man, Sidney Mussberger (Paul Newman), spearheads a plan to prevent the company from falling into the hands of the great unwashed. They have, he says, exactly one month to somehow make "the blue-chip investment of the century look like a round-trip ticket on the Titanic." Once they depress the value of the company's stock, they will be able to themselves purchase enough stock to maintain control. What they need, Mussberger tells his cohorts, is "a new president who will inspire panic in the stockholders." "A proxy!" exclaims one man. "A pawn!" intones another. "Sure, sure," says Mussberger. "Some jerk we can really push around."

Mussberger's line cues the cut to Norville Barnes involved in an attempt to digest the barrage of frenzied directives being delivered at breakneck speed and at high volume by his new boss in the Hudsucker Industries mailroom. The gist of this indoctrination is that little occurs in this gray warren of bustling, frightened-looking people sorting the seemingly endless quantities of packages and envelopes that does not result in someone's pay being docked. The scene is a precisely paced and hilariously choreographed satiric nightmare of first-day-at-a-new-job confusion. As in Fritz Lang's *Metropolis*, the production design of this workspace in the bowels of the Hudsucker building is meant to provide sharp contrast to the executive offices, which tower above the city.

Norville creatively solves his first professional challenge while he makes the acquaintance of an aged coworker (listed in the film credits as "The Ancient Sorter"), who gives him little reason to plan on a quick advancement through the ranks of Hudsucker Industries. Norville shares his Big Idea with him. The man stares uncomprehendingly at the creased piece of paper Norville removes from his shoe: a circle is neatly drawn in its center. "You know," Norville enthuses, "for kids!" The elderly worker (who with a flick of his wrist lodges letters in their respective slots at a distance of some feet with a satisfyingly surreal swooping noise) confides that he has been at his job for forty-eight years but is due a promotion "to parcels" if he's "lucky."

Their conversation is interrupted by a loudspeaker announcement informing the workers that Waring Hudsucker has that afternoon "merged with the infinite." A moment of respectful silence is requested to mark the "corporate loss," a moment which, it is noted immediately afterward, will be deducted from the workers' paychecks.

In an exuberantly funny sequence, the mailroom underworld is disrupted by the notice of a "blue letter." The scene which follows is typical of the Coens' unique brand of visual humor. The camera leaps and swishes in cartoonish pans from canted angle to canted angle; lights flash and alarms ring. Panicked employees scatter in all directions and scurry into hiding places. Norville's curiosity overcomes his initial impulse to flee. As the bearer of the blue letter moves toward him, his aged mentor explains that blue letters contain "confidential communication between the brass ... usually bad news." Consequently, the man continues, "They hate blue letters upstairs." Norville is, naturally, singled out for the job. He is told that the letter is from the late Waring Hudsucker to his right-hand man, Sidney Mussberger, and that the letter must be personally hand delivered. There follows a wonderful sequence wherein Norville terrorizes everyone with whom he comes into contact once they learn his mission. When Buzz the elevator operator (Jim True) spots Norville's blue letter, the elevator expresses to the top floor, and its occupants part like the Red Sea, shrinking from Norville and his letter as he enters the Art Deco splendor of the lobby. After Norville asks directions of a sinister figure scraping Hudsucker's name from the glass of his office door, there is another amusing scene with Mussberger's secretaries, whose heightened reactions to Norville's letter are well served by the audaciously mobile camerawork and exaggerated sound effects that mark the film. The scene's final joke exemplifies the kind of comic visual composition characteristic of *The Hudsucker Proxy*: as Norville leaves Mussberger's anteroom, the door frame through which he passes harbors a campily humorous silent tableau in its lower right-hand corner as one secretary seeks to revive the other in pure vaudevillian pantomime style. The Coens know that we know that they know how campily over the top it all is.

Norville's harried figure enters a strikingly appointed, spacious office; its expansiveness recalls the outsized offices of Leo and Caspar in *Miller's Crossing* and that of Lipnick in *Barton Fink*. Sidney Mussberger's office is similarly configured: a huge area of bare carpet must be traversed in order to approach the man's desk. The space also recalls John Frederson's office in Lang's *Metropolis*, an upper management loftiness that contrasts starkly with the crowded subterranean environs of Norville and his colleagues. Minimally furnished in austere Art Deco style, the room is dominated by the back of the tower clock, half of which forms part of the office's front wall. An auditory complement to the clock is the perpetual-motion striking-balls novelty item on Mussberger's desk, which mimics the tick of a second hand.

Mussberger is on two phone lines simultaneously, browbeating, firing, and threatening employees in his quest for an appropriate patsy or, as he puts it, "a grade-A ding dong." Norville approaches cautiously, performing a short dance of deference and trepidation. Asked to state his business, Norville mentions that he has some mailroom business to transact before he launches into a pitch regarding his pet project. Removing the design from his shoe, he shows Mussberger his circle drawing. In response to the man's quizzical silence, Norville offers his opaque explanation: "You know, for kids!" He continues to expound upon his invention until Mussberger yells, "Wait a minute!" The perpetual motion balls stop dead, as does Norville. Sticking a cigar in Norville's mouth, Mussberger considers the effect. Apparently liking what he sees, he invites Norville to sit in his chair, put his feet up, and chat. In a hilariously inverted interview, Mussberger is disappointed to learn that Norville may not be the complete grade-A ding dong for which he had hoped. He orders Norville out of his office and retrieves his cigar, placing it on a stack of papers that begin to smoke, then ignite.

That Robbins is a gifted physical comedian is in high evidence throughout the film and nowhere more so than in the sequence which follows. In a series of gloriously screwball maneuvers that are largely ignored by Mussberger, Norville succeeds in ridding the office of its small conflagration after surviving said fire's brief attachment to his foot, which gets stuck in a flaming wastebasket. In the process Norville inadvertently ruins "the Bumstead contract" on Mussberger's desk, which the mogul has previously described as the most sensitive document of his career. Mussberger chases the papers out the window. He is saved by Norville, who grips the man by his pants. Triggered is one of the film's most engaging sequences. As Mussberger dangles from his pants cuffs thirty stories or so above street level, he recalls, via flashback (introduced by a classical-era wavy screen), that he rejected his tailor's suggestion that his trousers be sewn with a mighty double stitch. "Damn," mutters the upside-down tyrant, and his pants rip several inches. Fortunately for him, the tailor chose to give him the double stitch anyway, a fact we learn during another flashback. Mussberger's pants hold and, still dangling upside-down, he lights a cigar to celebrate.

The next scene finds Norville the laughing center of attention in the Hudsucker boardroom; laughing harder are the executives that surround him. Uproarious laughter is coupled with a "Pomp and Circumstance"–like musical orchestration on the soundtrack that accompanies the artfully accomplished wordless sequence that follows. Cartoony match cuts, swish pans, and pointedly composed shots chronicle the trajectory of Hudsucker's plummeting stock value and Norville's series of transformative grooming procedures.

A shot through a Venetian-blinded window affords us a distant glimpse of the Hudsucker building's clock tower and serves to further map the fantastic metropolis created by the Coens and their collaborators. We are in the office of the editor in chief of the city paper (John Mahoney), who is chewing out his staff for failing to get the journalistic goods on Hudsucker's new president. He wants to know everything there is to know about the company's widely publicized "idea man" (he likes stories that investigate the "human angle," such as "J. Edgar Hoover: When Will He Marry?"). Enter Amy Archer (Jennifer Jason Leigh), Pulitzer Prize–winning lady reporter. Leigh is marvelous in the role, displaying virtuoso skill at her parodic reproduction of the kinds of performance tics for which Katharine Hepburn, Rosalind Russell, and Barbara Stanwyck were renowned. Amy thinks the man at the helm of Hudsucker Industries is a fake; she is, she says, willing to stake her Pulitzer on it. The declaration settles a bet between two of her colleagues concerning her willingness to endlessly flaunt her achievement. Wagering is a theme woven throughout the film, a motif which serves to insinuate the notions of luck and chance into a film as meticulously orchestrated and structurally neat as clockwork.

A short scene transpires back at Hudsucker Industries. Norville and Mussberger negotiate the building's Art Deco splendor in their nattily cut fifties business suits as they head toward lunch. Norville uses the time to question Mussberger on the company's rapidly declining stock value and to promote his invention, which he says would be highly profitable due to the small capital investment required and the "demographics—baby boom, discretionary income of the burgeoning middle class ..." Mussberger offhandedly okays Norville pitching the idea to the board and is whisked off by his limousine driver to what one assumes is a pricey midday meal.

Norville, on the other hand, finds his lunch in a diner below street level. Two cabbies face the young man as he methodically chews his sandwich. After a short exchange during which they address the impact their food has had on their digestive systems, the cabbies begin to narrate a drama they construct around Amy's entry into the diner and her attentions toward Norville. *The Hudsucker Proxy* is thematically and structurally circular; concentric rings of narrative, stories within stories, are inscribed within this framework. The cabbies begin their narrative rather formally: "Enter the dame; there's one in every story." They wager over what they assume is the object of Amy's stylized performance; though they correctly presume she is out to con Norville, we know that her ambitions far outstrip the cost of the lunch they think she is after. Amy's elaborate machinations are initially for naught. As the cabbies provide a dry voice-over play-by-play, Amy effects a pathetic pantomime calculated to provoke Norville's sympathetic notice. The camera pans to record the oblivious Norville as he performs an elaborately stylized inspection of a tough morsel of sandwich filling. The sequence is perfectly emblematic of the film's brand of visual humor, one that glories in the studied, comical expansion of small details of human behavior. Amy eventually succeeds in securing his attention to the great amusement of the cabbies ("That gag's got whiskers on it!"). Her tale of woe is greeted by Norville with embarrassed evasiveness. Amy must feign a fainting spell before she is able to engage Norville's help. He catches her as she is seemingly about to tumble off her stool.

Norville carries the journalist back to his office, passing and attracting the malevolent attention of Aloysius (Harry Bugin), who is lettering Norville's name and new title onto his door window. Amy never ceases her rapid-fire monologue as Norville stumbles beneath her weight, then deposits her on his sofa. In another of the film's miniature narratives, Amy regales her savior with "her story," as canned, contrived, and italicized a hard-luck tale as has ever been compended. "I arrived in town not ten days ago, full of dreams and aspirations, anxious to make my way in the world," Amy says. "A little naive perhaps but—thank you," she says, accepting a proffered drink from Norville and continuing with scarcely a break in her rhythm, "armed with determination, a solid work ethic, and an indomitable belief in the future." Her scam narrative describes Norville's true story. It also references the Capraesque source material so gleefully refashioned by the Coens in *Hudsucker*. Barbara Stanwyck hoodwinking Henry Fonda in *The Lady Eve* also comes to mind.

While Norville fusses around her, Amy spins her yarn, losing her place once or twice in a manner which comically emphasizes the memorized, fictional aspects of her history. Snooping in Norville's desk she finds nothing save a clue as to his hometown. When she tells Norville that she is from this town, she is startled by his response. In one of the film's funniest sequences, Norville erupts into what proves to be the high school cheer he presumes they share, a bizarre reworking of Notre Dame's "Fight On" pep song. Words cannot do justice to the wacky fervor with which Robbins performs this engagingly goofy routine. Leigh for her part does a masterful job of faking familiarity with the cheer, lagging a second or two behind Robbins in order to anticipate his next word and/or gesture. Thrilled to have met a hometown girl in the big city, Norville suggests he find a job for her at Hudsucker Industries. His call to the mailroom elicits an angry request for the voucher he has neglected to return. Norville decides that perhaps Amy ought to work for him. Their encounter is concluded with a final "Go Eagles!" cry and its accompanying hand signal.

A match cut to Amy in the newsroom finds her reproducing the gesture for a coworker. Amy says Norville is "from Chumpsville." She says that if something funny is going on at Hudsucker Industries, Norville himself is most likely not a part of it, but a "patsy" for some "set-up." The scene is a set-piece for Leigh, who maintains an exquisitely timed staccato stream of verbiage adorned by the stylized gestures of thirties and forties career-girl heroines—simultaneously smoking, typing, and occasionally contributing to the development of a colleague's crossword puzzle.

A quick montage abbreviates the process by which Amy's story leaves her typewriter and finds its way to the front page of the next day's newspaper; such classical-era conventions as a spinning front page hurtling from background to foreground are featured. Amy's story is headlined "Imbecile Heads Hudsucker."

Norville is upset when he reads the article. He calls in Amy, aka Miss Smith, his new secretary. His proposed letter to the editor is a loopily indignant rebuttal to the author of the offending story, who, unbeknownst to him, sits comfortably before him. She is treated to Norville's sketched design of what Norville tells her will be the "sweet baby that puts Hudsucker right back on top. You know," he tells her, "for kids." Asked if an imbecile could have come up with this idea, Amy gazes at the simply drawn circle and is noncommittal.

Norville tells Amy to forget about sending the letter. He guesses, he says, that the reporter was just doing her job. Amy is clearly softening toward Norville and appears to somewhat regret the article and its consequences. Norville goes on, however, to propose an explanation for the reporter's hard angle. He speculates that the writer is "one of these fast-talkin' career gals who thinks she's one of the boys ... probably suffers from one of these complexes they have nowadays ... she's probably very unattractive and bitter about it." He goes on to accurately describe Amy's comportment in the newsroom before concluding that the woman must be a "dried-up, bitter old maid." He then invites her out to dinner and a show—*The King and I*. Amy slaps him hard across the face. "*Oklahoma?*" Norville asks. Amy, in tears, suggests that Norville knows not a thing about the woman he has maligned and storms out, leaving Norville mystified. The comedy of the scene is enhanced by the exaggerated sound effects that are a consistent hallmark of the film's soundtrack.

Amy returns to the office after hours in order to continue her investigation. Finding nothing of interest, she opens a door marked "authorized personnel" to find a Fritz Langian wonderworld, a room which houses the gargantuan mechanical clockworks of Hudsucker Industries. The set is a standout in a film replete with gloriously evocative, visually sumptuous stage sets, a stunning composition of metal, mist, and shadow. Carter Burwell's quasi-religious choral strains provide apt accompaniment.

Peering through a keyhole, Amy glimpses Sidney Mussberger at work in his office. The chiaroscuro shot of Amy's profile surreptitiously watching Mussberger is an arresting one, a neoclassical noir moment suspended within *Hudsucker*'s fairytale-screwball universe. She is suddenly addressed by the voice of the film's early, unseen narrator. Amy wants to know who he is and how he knows her real name. A man emerges from the gloom; "Ole Moses," he says, "knows just about everything, leastways if it concerns Hudsucker." He proves it, too. During the exchange which follows Moses (William Cobbs) demonstrates a thorough grasp of company intrigue. He tells Amy what the board is up to and adds that Norville will surprise everyone in the end with his idea—"You know, for kids!" He knows about Amy's deception as well. His knowledge extends to private conversations between Amy and Norville; he is able to quote Amy herself in order to make a point. Most irksome to Amy, Moses can see into her heart. He asks her why she pretends "to be such a hard old sourpuss" when it makes her so unhappy, and he laughs uproariously at her claim to the contrary. He leaves; he has "gears to see to." Moses is responsible for the building's clockworks. He "keeps the old circle turning," he says, a statement which works on many levels. As will be seen, he's got the whole *Hudsucker* wheel of the world in his hands—past, present, and future.

Back at the newsroom Amy and her boss go head to head over the story she has written based on Moses' analysis of the board's motivation for hiring Norville. Amy angrily denies that she is "trying to take the heat off Norville … gone all soft" on them. Amy and her editor get quite heated on the subject while Smitty (Bruce Campbell), Amy's buddy at the paper, sardonically monitors the scene. When he advises Amy to "go easy, tough guy," Amy abruptly switches gears and softly asks if her suit looks overly masculine. In response, Smitty grabs her derrière and invites her for a highball. Amy slugs the guy, hard, leaving the two men astonished as she storms out.

A shot of Hudsucker Industries' very formal invitation to its annual fancy-dress Christmas gala fills the screen. We then transition to the ball in progress, where Norville sits trapped on a sofa between two matrons, listening to their quasi–British-accented banter while he watches his date, Amy, flirt on the dance floor. Mussberger rescues Norville in order to introduce him to some of Hudsucker's biggest stockholders. Norville's earnest efforts to impress are met with a marked lack of success; one notable

Norville (Tim Robbins) demonstrates his new product idea in *The Hudsucker Proxy*. "You know, for kids!"

exchange culminates in a knockout punch to his jaw. The bright lights which follow could be Norville's subjective reality as a result of this assault; instead, they introduce singing sensation Vic Tenetta. Peter Gallagher delivers a deliciously vampy performance in a role roughly two parts Dean Martin to one part Elvis.

Amy finds Norville alone out on a balcony much occupied with an ice pack. At Norville's suggestion that "people are pretty hot over this imbecile story," Amy looks chagrined and tells him that she is sorry. Norville doesn't understand; he says she is the one person who has stood by him. Amy attempts to explain. "I'm not really a secretary," she tells Norville, who reassures her that her deficiencies "in the secretarial arts" should not cause her any anxiety. In fact, he tells her, though he puts up a good front, he has a lot to learn about being president. Amy melts. She tells him that she believes in him or, at least, in his intentions. Amy warns him about trusting people too much, a warning which subsides into a mumble when she realizes that she is one of the people he trusts that he ought not. In the banter which follows, Leigh's Hepburnisms reach their apotheosis, a fitting tribute to the classic versions of the kinds of scenes the Coens skewer with this one. Norville waxes pseudometaphysical in sweetly nutty speculation concerning reincarnation, a tenet he attributes to both "Hindus and beatniks," while Amy wonders whether in a former life she might have been "a fast-talkin' career gal who thought she was one of the boys." Norville demurs, substituting a suitably romantic notion for Amy's confession. Hilariously, Norville's idea of a romantic past existence has Amy a gazelle and himself an antelope or an ibex, "snorffling water from a mountain stream, picking the grubs and burrs from one another's coats." Carter Burwell's lavishly orchestrated theme music pushes the scene to the edge of parody. Their interlude concludes with Norville's talk of karma, a "great wheel that gives us all what we deserve." His words will, of course, prove prescient. Norville presents his ideas to Hudsucker's board the following day, and he asks Amy to give him a kiss for luck. Their initial chaste peck evolves into a romantic swoon à la *Gone with the Wind*, complete with silhouetted profiles and swelling music.

Norville introduces his reinvention of the wheel for the board; standing before a table of solemn businessmen, he demonstrates his new product idea. "You know, for kids!" Norville's hips swivel and gyrate inside a thin plastic hollow ring filled with a small amount of sand, and the hula hoop is born. The board members gaze at Norville with slack-jawed wonder (surely the Coens' favorite facial expression) before commencing a comic inquisition concerning the nature and properties of the hoop. Questions such as "What if you tire before it's done?" and "How do you know when you're finished?" are proposed. Sidney Mussberger pronounces the product brilliant. It is, he tells the board, just what Hudsucker needs. He foresees, he says, an enormous demand for the thing. He congratulates Norville for his genius and tells him that he will recommend to the board that "the dingus" be mass produced with all deliberate speed. He makes it a point, however, that the final say-so rests with Norville, who enthusiastically registers his thumbs-up.

In a wonderful short sequence, the Coens' flying camera documents the process by which the "extruded plastic dingus" evolves from boardroom decision to delivered product. Classical-era film tropes mix with postmodern irony to depict a gloriously whimsical fantasy of corporate protocol.

The Coens' first four films contain signature tour-de-force wordless sequences that seem to encapsulate the tone and feel of each: *Blood Simple*'s burial sequence, *Raising Arizona*'s prison breakout, *Miller's Crossing*'s assassination attempt, *Barton Fink*'s writer's block time-out-of-mind. In *The Hudsucker Proxy*, the Coens top themselves. The film's near-wordless montage chronicling the hula hoop's dramatic rise in popularity among schoolkids and its impact on anxious innovator Norville and his now-ardent supporter Amy, is a hugely entertaining mininarrative driven by likable performances, impeccable pacing, fresh camerawork, and an oddly affecting magic realism.

The sequence begins with a close-up of a poster for the toy Norville has so long envisioned; Hudsucker's "creative bullpen" has named the product the hula hoop. The poster adorns the window of a toy shop, and when its proprietor emerges he looks pleased and hopeful. At Norville's office he and Amy monitor the stock market. The news is not good. Back at the toy store the camera slowly moves in toward the toy store owner, now slumped against one of his windows, smoking in a slightly discouraged manner as pedestrians pass by his shop with nary so much as a glance inside. A cut to Norville's office finds the pair pacing and fretting over Hudsucker stock value. A cut back to the storefront poster reveals rapid decreases in the advertised price of Norville's brainchild; eventually the toy is promoted as a giveaway item. Finally, the disgusted toystore owner throws his brightly colored hula hoops into his alley—he has been unable to *give* them away. One of the hoops rolls out of the alley. It stops traffic while crossing a busy intersection and twirls down a sidewalk before it neatly turns a corner. It rolls directly toward a little boy dressed in classic school-skipping attire: a striped tee shirt, jeans, and red sneakers. Like an affectionate pet, the hoop circles the boy before brushing up against him and falling flat at his feet. The boy squints at it, curious. An overhead shot of the child peering at the hoop recalls Norville's simple line drawings of the toy. The local elementary school lets out for the day; well-dressed children stream from its doors, screaming. The little boy steps into the hoop's center. The boy begins to hula hoop with an adorably deliberate forward-backward motion, stamping his foot in time with the motion of the toy. The school children surge toward him en masse. The boy is filmed in slow motion to emphasize the wonder with which the school children gaze upon his activity. Their mouths are comically agape with an astonishment and puzzlement that increases with the boy's creative variations on the means by which one may successfully sustain the hoop's motion. As one, the children turn around and race toward the toy store. They flood through the store's doors, prompting one of the two spoken words of the sequence: the nonplussed storekeeper says, "Wow!" The price stickers on the hula hoop poster out front climb to an all-time high. Back at Norville's office, Amy, monitoring the ticker tape machine, reads its latest output and claps her hands with joy; Hudsucker stock has gone up. "Norville!" she exclaims happily. Norville's despair is transformed before our eyes to ecstasy.

In a tongue-in-cheek allusion to *Citizen Kane*'s "News on the March" newsreel, which was itself a parody of "The March of Time" series produced in the United States between 1935 and 1951, we are confronted by a black-and-white newsreel called "Tidbits of Time." The sequence, one more example of a self-contained narrative that nestles within the film's larger narrative, is a droll communiqué that profiles "the brainy inventor of America's craziest craze" and the fad he has inspired, which is reaping unprecedented profits for Hudsucker Industries. President Eisenhower himself congratulates Norville; he speaks as well, he says, for both Mrs. Eisenhower and the American people.

Norville is appealingly modest during his press conference, sharing the credit for the product's huge success. Inadvertently stumbling into a pun, he amuses the gathered reporters. We cut to Amy on the subway as she reads the newspaper's glowing account of Norville's achievement; she is delighted.

More newsreel excerpts follow. A heavily German-accented scientist delivers a zany pseudoscientific explanation of the hula hoop's motion; high-society types are shown hula hooping at a black-tie affair; and a bride and groom are filmed as they exchange vows while gyrating within the popular plastic rings.

Norville is then shown dogged by a press now grown weary of his oft-repeated responses to their queries. Amy's subway newspaper reveals their cooling attitude toward him. We cut to Norville as he is elaborately barbered while fielding still more questions from a throng of journalists. Norville's private life has become a topic of society page speculation. Asked about rumors which link him to fashion model Za-Za (Anna Nicole), Norville replies demurely that they are just dear friends; as the camera zooms toward the model reclining in an adjacent barber chair, the soundtrack registers the audio equivalent of popped eyeballs. The impromptu interview concludes with the "Idea Man's" latest—silly modifications of his celebrated plastic dingus. A quick cut to Amy once again reading about Norville on the subway reveals her concern.

Back at Hudsucker Industries, Sidney Mussberger finishes up a boardroom massage as he and his cohorts contemplate the unlucky consequences of Mussberger's strategic manipulations involving their Hudsucker stock. It seems that he has sold it all, hoping to further depress its value by simulating a panic whereupon it could all be bought back plus more at a reduced price. Norville's extruded plastic dingus has instead made their lost stock more valuable than ever. Had they held onto it, moans one executive, crying, they'd all be millionaires. Mussberger offers his characteristic "sure, sure" in response and tells the man to pull himself together. In a funny visual bit, the distraught executive opts instead to leave the boardroom in the same manner as Waring Hudsucker. He clambers atop the glossy board table, clumsily runs its length, and hurls himself against the window. With a loud thunk, the man lands on the glass, where he remains suspended for a second or two, his features squashed, his limbs comically extended. As his open-mouthed colleagues watch, the man slides slowly to the floor, frozen in his quasi-suicidal stance. This descent is accompanied by the sound of squeegeed glass, and we hear rather than see the man's ignoble drop to the floor. Mussberger has, presciently it seems, installed plexiglas in the window frame.

Mussberger gets down to business then, offering the board a thumbnail sketch of his plan to save them all. Invoking the film's central metaphor, he tells them that "the wheel turns, the music plays, and our spin ain't over yet." He proposes to ruin Norville, to orchestrate "shame, dishonor, ignominy, disgrace."

A cut to Norville's office finds the young man in the final stages of his metamorphosis from earnest small-town idealist to arrogant image-conscious mogul-about-town. A string quartet accompanies the efforts of an artist, dutifully bereted and goateed, to sculpt a block of stone. Norville, it must be presumed, hopes that the aura generated by these creative types will help him produce his next big idea. A masseuse and a manicurist attend Norville as he cogitates. A bulky flunky reads newspaper comics, his role less clear than the other members of Norville's new entourage, though no less comical. Amy bursts into the office. Disdainful of Norville's human accessories, she spares them no more than a quick glance before she expresses her outrage over the board's decision to fire a large percentage of Hudsucker's workforce. Upon learning that Norville has had a part in this plan, she lets loose a tirade replete with both moral indignation and hurt outrage at having been, as she puts it, "dumped." Clearing the room of all but the comic-reading flunky (he remains to be kicked in the shins during her dramatic exit), Amy delivers a hilariously heartfelt diatribe on Norville's lost ideals. "Don't you remember how you used to feel about the hoop? You told me you were going to bring a smile to the hips of everyone in America, regardless of race, creed, or color. Finally there would be a thingamajig that would bring everyone together—even if it kept them apart, spatially." Leigh's italicized hand gestures reach their zenith during this speech. They appear to have lives of their own, or rather, lives reincarnated from the sources Leigh's performance references throughout the film. Amy tenders her resignation and flees, leaving behind a dumbstruck Norville. Her exit follows a declaration of love and a swift kick to the flunky's knee.

A white-out screen initiates a dream sequence. In it Norville cavorts with a Rita Hayworthesque dancer adorned with chiffon and diamonds. To the operatic strains of *Carmen* the woman beguiles Norville as they both execute maneuvers strangely reminiscent of his high school cheer. Norville's performance is pure farce. His slinky partner's is only slightly less so; Norville's dream seductress flutters and stomps across his mindscape in a fashion calculated to mock the countless screen presentations upon which Norville would have unconsciously based his erotic fantasy.

The dream begins to break down as Norville responds to a beckoning from the world beyond. Norville is awakened by Buzz, the elevator boy, who wishes to share a product idea. Pointing to an easel upon which a picture of a circle rests, Buzz explains. "You know, for drinks!" he enthuses. He demonstrates a flexible straw that he calls "The Buzz Sucker." Norville makes a show of mocking the idea and goes further: he fires Buzz for his efforts. Buzz falls to his knees. Begging and crying, he kisses Norville's shoes and ankles in an ecstasy of remorse, pleading for his job. "I'm praying to you!" he cries, a line used to great effect by Bernie in *Miller's Crossing*. Norville remains unmoved by Buzz's fervent pleas for forgiveness. Buzz crawls out of the room crying.

Meanwhile, Mussberger muses in a darkened office over the information his henchman Aloysius has brought him. Amy's true identity has been uncovered. "This is ... useful," Mussberger muses while the camera affords us a long shot of his cavernous office, as bare as the soul of the man himself.

Norville arrives at Hudsucker's boardroom fresh from the golf course where, he says, he has been battling the back nine. He has been summoned there by Mussberger, who has some bad news for Norville. Buzz, it seems, has complained to Mussberger that Norville stole his idea for the hoop. But the real problem, explains Mussberger, is that Norville has been duped by Amy, whose paper plans on running the story. Norville's error in judgment, Mussberger says, will compel the board to fire him when they meet after the new year. He is finished, Mussberger says, washed out. "And when you're dead you stay dead. ... If you don't believe me, ask Waring Hudsucker." The line is a playful one for those familiar with the Coens' work, in which the dead quite often do rise, in one fashion or another.

A cut to the office of Amy's editor leads to a scene as replete with jumpy energy as the previous scene was lugubrious with the weight of smooth-talking Mussberger's oozing false sympathy. Amy's paper means to run the story despite her protestations that it is untrue. Mussberger, it seems, has provided off-the-record insider corroboration. Amy is accused of having gone "soft on the Dummy from Dubuque." "Muncie," Amy murmurs. "Whatever!" her editor snaps. He crows over his scoop, while Smitty, Amy's former chum, revels in his new role as journalistic top dog. "Can't you see you're being used?" Amy croons. Leigh's rendition of pre-Method-era screen heroine earnestness is a triumph of style over substance. Amy resigns from the paper, this time delivering a resounding slap to Smitty's smug mug as she leaves.

The next sequence pays hilarious tribute to the spate of postwar films that reflected the public's increasing faith in the field of psychiatry following the successful treatment of many World War II veterans. Especially common was the use of the stereotyped European psychiatrist as a mechanism for exposition. *Hudsucker*'s psychiatrist is vintage Viennese. His-none-too technical evaluation of Norville Barnes ("blue and mopey" and "nuts") is accompanied by a film which the board watches, *Citizen Kane*–style, from a darkened room bisected by a dust-mote-illuminating projection beam. This short film-within-a-film gleefully parodies various generic tropes, from prison movies to horror films. The doctor's diagnosis, delivered with the aid of a chart titled "Psycho-mentality of Patient," is that Norville is a "manic depressive paranoid type B, with acute schizoid tendencies" who will eventually "erupt, posing a threat to himself and others." His prescription: forced incarceration in a mental institution. Hudsucker's board of directors applauds.

New Year's Eve finds Norville sloppily drunk at Amy's subterranean beatnik poetry bar. Norville is unhappy to find himself unable to continue his drinking at this establishment, which serves juice and coffee. "Martinis are for squares," the harried bartender tells him, after calling Amy to come retrieve her friend. Amy arrives much distressed at Norville's condition. Amy apologizes for her deception and begs his forgiveness. When Amy asks for a second chance, Norville drunkenly repeats Mussberger's Machiavellian musings. Norville is beyond hope. Amy attempts to convince "Norville Barnes the Quitter" to "fight on." To this end she executes a subdued but heartfelt Muncie High cheer. Norville is unmoved. "How could *you* lie to me? You, a Muncie girl?" he says despairingly. This last evidence of Norville's sweet dimness moves Amy to tears.

As Norville emerges from the bar, he collides with a newspaper boy hawking headlines that read "Muncie Mental Case: Hud Chief to Tend Daisies." The boy screams out that Norville has been unmasked as a thief and "a moron after all."

The newsboy's voice echoes in Norville's mind; other voices follow with equally disparaging evaluations. They ring in Norville's ears, while the floating images of their speakers' faces grace the screen in a kitschy tribute to classical-era projected mindscapes. President Eisenhower joins the chorus of condemnation—this voice is accompanied by twin images of a waving American flag.

A cut to Hudsucker's boardroom finds Mussberger presiding over a somber New Year's celebration. The businessmen wear party hats that resemble dunce caps as they toast his news that Norville is headed for "the booby hatch," a development sure to send Wall Street into a tailspin. The scene is capped by a Busby Berkeley–style overhead shot that transforms the amber light of the lit table into a rather lovely horizontal abstraction.

Norville lurches through the snow. He bumps into Buzz, who's convinced by now that he is indeed the sinned-against inventor of Norville's hoop. At his girlfriend's urging (the same beauty with whom Norville was linked in better times), Buzz punches Norville to the ground. A crowd of party revelers circle him. Recognizing him, somebody proposes that they call a policeman. When Norville rises and drunkenly trips toward the group, they shrink back in fear and revulsion. Norville flees the scene. Buzz leads the gaggle of partygoers in hot pursuit. In a sequence that draws upon both noir and horror visual idioms, Norville runs through streets and alleyways followed by the yelling mob. A van marked "Sunnyvale" pulls up. Finally, two men dressed in white and carrying a butterfly net and a straitjacket join the chase.

Norville eludes the pack. He stumbles, falling flat onto the sidewalk with the kind of metallic sound effect that consistently graces the film's audiotrack. The image revolves forty-five degrees, and Norville gazes up into the sky from which fat snowflakes lazily drift between the exaggerated geometric shapes of office buildings. He enters the lobby of the Hudsucker building, where he is confronted by his bronze likeness in the lobby, revealed from beneath its filmy white cover by a magical swirl of wind. Beneath the scrutiny of an overhead shot Norville hunches his head into his shoulders, as if to withdraw from this reminder of how far he has fallen.

Meanwhile, Sidney J. Mussberger plots from behind the desk of his darkened office. The camera peers over his shoulder to look at his work. He has rejected "Mussberger Industries" and "Hudberger Industries" to settle on "Sidsucker Industries." One can certainly see why.

Norville must maneuver around Mussberger's evil henchman to enter his office; the sinister figure is busy painting Mussberger's name above the title of president on Norville's door.

A long shot reveals that it is close to midnight in the fantastical city that hosts Hudsucker Industries' magnificent tower clock. Norville dons his old mailroom apron. He climbs out onto the ledge outside his window. Feeling his way gingerly along the ledge, he looks down; the street below seems an impossible distance away. Behind him a noise indicates that some-one has entered his office. The lights in the office go dark. Norville moves as if to retrace his steps back inside. An arm reaches out and closes the window. Norville loses his footing and falls, catching the edge of the ledge with his fingertips at the last moment. Mussberger's dastardly sidekick appears behind the now-closed window. The clock strikes midnight. Nor-ville hangs off the ledge, in a spectacular Hitchcockian matte pose. Nor-ville yells, beginning to slip; the man behind the window remains still, watching. His breath fogs the window slightly, which blurs his face in a most sinister fashion. Norville falls in a gloriously long and goofy bur-lesque of Hitchcock's *Vertigo*; the action is intercut with shots of Muss-berger gloating, his sidekick watching, and the big clock ticking. The musical score builds to a crescendo as Norville descends yelling. Abruptly, both Norville and the music stop, Norville in midair, many feet off the ground. He dangles, upside down, comically nonplussed. Snowflakes con-tinue to float downward. A shot of Hudsucker's tower clock reveals the source of a rhythmic thudding: it is the sound of the second hand's progress somehow impeded. A cut to the clock's gear works shows a broom han-dle obstructing the clock's innards. The film's narrator, Moses, turns and addresses the camera. "Strictly speaking," he confides, "I'm never sup-posed to do this. But have you got a better idea?" Coen fans will likely find the filmmakers' literalization of *deus ex machina* a fine idea.

Time has, for the moment, stopped. Norville wriggles in space, peer-ing at a bright light amidst the falling snow and squinting at a muffled sound. The light is resolved into a figure, an angel with a neon halo, who drifts past Mussberger's window on his way down. Mussberger is frozen in time, his expression one of confident gloating.

The angel proves to be the source of the noise—he is singing "She'll Be Coming Around the Mountain When She Comes." It is Waring Hud-sucker. As he sings he accompanies himself on a tiny white ukulele. He halts his descent when he is abreast of Norville. Close up, his animated halo spins in a motion not unlike that of Norville's hoop. Hudsucker informs Norville that "they're all wearing them upstairs. It's a fad," he says dismissively.

Hudsucker is aware of Norville's recent trials and is sympathetic (though he calls him Norman and an imbecile). He counsels Norville to read the blue letter he wrote, which remains undelivered.

A cut to the clock's fuse box reveals that there is another character impervious to the flow of time. Mussberger's evil henchman, Aloysius, is anxious to fix the clock.

Meanwhile, Norville reads the letter. As Norville gets beyond what

Hudsucker calls "standard resignation boiler plate" (he is joining "the organization upstairs, an exciting new beginning"), Aloysius determines that there is nothing wrong with the clock's fuse box. His look upward toward the tower spells trouble.

Norville reads on while Hudsucker moves his lips. The letter is full of regrets over which Hudsucker weeps. Norville skips to the next part at Hudsucker's request, a poetic treatise on the relationship between life and business and on the circumstances which he feels should govern the reign of the company president to succeed him. Cross-cutting to the Hudsucker clock tower, we find Moses and Aloysius coming face to face. Norville continues to peruse Hudsucker's last testament, comically misreading and juxtaposing the words "fail and fall," which are, in the film, interchangeable after all. In order to afford the new president of his erstwhile company the opportunity to fall ("fail," reads Norville) and rise again, Hudsucker has bequeathed his stock to the person appointed to that office. "That'll show the bastards!" bellows the angelic Hudsucker. As Norville finishes Hudsucker's inspirational ode to second chances, Good and Evil are squaring off on a high catwalk in the tower clockworks. The two begin by assuming a boxing stance. When Moses knocks his opponent's dentures out, Aloysius pulls out the sharp chisel with which we have seen him sinisterly erasing names from office doors. Moses is forced to defend himself with his broom. He knocks his foe off the catwalk but, in doing so, frees the clockwork gears. Time begins again. Norville plunges toward the ground, stopping inches from it. A cut to the clockworks shows Aloysius' dentures temporarily blocking the gears. When time resumes, Norville tumbles harmlessly onto the sidewalk. He runs off joyfully, with Hudsucker's admonition to deliver the letter in the morning ringing in his ears.

Norville races along stylized city streets. Returning to the bar where he last saw Amy, he fights his way through the celebrating crowd to where she sits weeping into a handkerchief. Amy sees at once that Norville has recovered his equilibrium, such as it is, and after an exchange of "Go Eagles" handsigns and a steamy kiss, they are reconciled.

The scene dissolves into a shot of the blue letter lying on the boardroom table at Mussberger's customary spot. A cigar lies in an ashtray next to the letter, upon which has been placed a key and a watch. The camera pivots to reveal Hudsucker's boardroom executives crowded around the huge open window at the foot of the table. Moses narrates in his role as omniscient storyteller. The new year has brought with it the news that Norville owns the company, and Mussberger is handling it not at all well. As his colleagues and hired-gun psychiatrist watch, Mussberger cowers out on the ledge while men with butterfly nets move precariously toward him. Moses tells us that he ends up in "the booby hatch," and we watch as Mussberger is led away, suffering precisely the same fate he had attempted to engineer for Norville.

Norville, we are told, goes on to "rule with wisdom and compassion," and he continues to innovate new ideas. As we watch, Norville unveils his latest extruded plastic dingus, "you know, for kids." With a flourish he displays a bright red frisbee to the board. The camera sails out of the room with the flying disk. As the film's theme music swells and the screen fills with the image of Hudsucker Industries' round clock face, *Hudsucker*'s unifying metaphor, Moses brings to a close "the story of how Norville Barnes climbed way up to the forty-fourth floor of the Hudsucker building, and then fell all the way down but didn't quite squish himself." Moses tells us that he knows of "a man who jumped from the forty-fifth floor ... but," laughs Moses, "that's another story." Thus ends 360 degrees of inspired fun.

The Hudsucker Proxy is a megapastiche, a pop cultural cannibalization of more vintage source materials than can be counted. A radical example of Robert Venturi's "difficult whole,"[7] the film approaches, paradoxically, the quality of a distilled essence, of a pharmaceutical-strength Hollywood ether dream.

The Hudsucker Proxy is "difficult" in the extreme. The idealistic films of Frank Capra of the thirties and forties, such as *Mr. Deeds Goes to Town* (1936) and *Mr. Smith Goes to Washington* (1939) are referenced and mixed with the generic conventions of the screwball comedies perfected by directors such as Howard Hawks and Preston Sturges. Newspaper pictures contribute to *Hudsucker*'s generic collage, with Hawks' *His Girl Friday* (1940) and Capra's *Meet John Doe* (1941) functioning as near-explicit intertextual references. Other prominent stars in the Coens' generic constellation include the career-girl women's pictures of the thirties and forties; corporate rat-race films such as *Room at the Top* (1959), *Executive Suite* (1954), and *The Man in the Gray Flannel Suit* (1956); and the fantasies and filmed fairytales so popular in the politically conservative fifties and early sixties.

Fragments of individual films abound. The design of Hudsucker Industries' clockworks area is indebted to Lang's *Metropolis* (1926), as is the stark contrast between the grounded blue-collar workers and the towered management. The film's angel-and-suicide nonlinear time motif is a liberal reworking of Capra's *It's a Wonderful Life* (1946), and enough is borrowed from *Executive Suite* that *Hudsucker* might be called a bizarrely refracted version of it. From the subtlety of the one-monkey-in–one-monkey-out routine from *Sunset Boulevard* (1950; William Holden enters as Gloria Swanson's dead pet monkey exits; Tim Robbins enters as Charles Durning flings himself out a window), to the outrageously broad stylizations performed by Jennifer Jason Leigh as she channels Hepburn, Russell, and Stanwyck, the film is a compendium of quotations.

Hudsucker's characters emanate from the discontinuous dreamworlds which fuel the film. They are abstractions of ideas of characters: the roles and performances upon which they are based are themselves stylized stereotypes. Like their italicized surroundings, *Hudsucker*'s characters are purely aesthetic constructs; as such, they seem to be valued equally. The film's characters are depthless and inhuman, interesting only as formal objects which reference the aesthetic past of Hollywood.

Norville Barnes, for example, is the quintessential Capraesque protagonist: a naïve country soul who struggles to maintain his integrity and individuality while caught in the maw of an institution which is inherently antipathetic to such an endeavor. *Hudsucker*'s leading lady, Jennifer Jason Leigh, displays virtuoso skills at her parodic reproduction of the tough gal, fast-talking, initially-cynical-but-revealed-to-have-a-heart-of-gold career woman featured in countless films. Moses is the most complex creation of the film; he is the Coens' proxy in his role as fairytale narrator and timekeeper. It is this latter status which works on many metaphoric levels, not the least of which is that he, like the Coens, flaunts his authorship of the dreamworld over which he presides.

The Coens' first four films are highly stylized, with characters distinctly unencumbered by extrageneric debts to realism. The actors playing their roles in those films, however, accomplished them as though unaware of their aesthetic significance. *Hudsucker*, by comparison, is redolent with characters who foreground their status as ideas; the actors playing these roles seem to consciously project an abstraction, and they force a similar conscious awareness upon the viewer.

The film's characters, in fact, often helpfully guide the viewer toward a recognition of the motifs they embody. *Hudsucker*, as has been noted, is circular, and contains wheels within wheels, stories within stories. These embedded narratives self-consciously refer to the aesthetic origins of each character, just as the self-contained miniature dramas (such as the story of the hula hoop's rise to fame and the story of Mussberger's tailor's life-saving decision) situate themselves as fictions within larger fictions. Thus Amy details the archetype upon which Norville Barnes is based in her fraudulent autobiography: "full of dreams and aspirations, anxious to make my way in the world, a little naïve perhaps but armed with determination and a solid work ethic ... and unsullied optimism." Norville describes the model for Amy in his diatribe against the woman responsible for his negative newspaper profile (who, unbeknownst to Norville, actually is Amy): "a fast talking career gal who thinks she's one of the boys ... cynical ... bitter." Sidney Mussberger describes the generic form to which he owes his existence: decades-old movies which feature heartless moguls who subscribe to the belief that "business is war ... take no prisoners, get no second chances." Moses overtly acknowledges his role as omniscient narrating agent to Amy.

The Hudsucker Proxy is the most insistent delegate in a progression of films which synthesize the aesthetic past. In virtually every frame of the film may be recognized what theorist Fredric Jameson has termed "the imitation of dead styles, speech through all the masks and voices stored up in the imaginary museum of a new global culture."[8] Jameson identifies this strategic deployment of bricolage as a preeminent feature of postmodernist cinema. He writes, "Our awareness of the pre-existence of other versions ... is now a constitutive and essential part of ... film's structure: we are now, in other words, in 'intertextuality' as a deliberate, built-in feature of the aesthetic effect."[9] Film theorist Patrick Phillips calls the surplus of meaning that results from this strategy the "text's adventure."

Through the agency of a marked authorial presence, which mediates our perception of their playful deployment of conventional generic and stylistic elements, the Coens display a witty inventiveness nonpareil. In their assumption that the "text's adventure" will be ours as well is a measure of faith which has been extended consistently in their work.

Alas, this faith proved particularly misplaced in the case of *The Hudsucker Proxy*. Audiences stayed away en masse, and most critics had problems with the film, which grossed a mere $2.869 million for Warner Brothers in the United States. PolyGram, responsible for foreign distribution, did not lose money on the film, which was much better received overseas.

Reviews were often mixed, lauding the technical achievements of the film (especially Dennis Gassner's outstanding production design, which won 1994's Los Angeles Film Critics Association Award) but decrying its "heartlessness." Todd McCarthy's review for *Variety* is fairly typical. McCarthy writes that "for connoisseurs of filmmaking style and technique, *Hudsucker* is a source of constant delight and occasional thrills." Calling the Coens "among the most imaginative and supple craftsmen of the cinema," he describes the film as "inspired and technically stunning." He also, however, finds the movie "synthetic ... nearly all the characters are constructs rather than human beings with whom the viewer can connect." Ultimately, McCarthy judges *Hudsucker* "a wizardly but artificial synthesis of aspects of vintage fare, leaving a hole in the middle where some emotion and humanity should be."[10] Kenneth Turan of the *Los Angeles Times* agreed.

David Ansen notes that, though the film achieved a brilliant artifice, "there's something hollow at its core." Ansen writes:

> In the past, the Coens took old genres and twisted them into distinctive new shapes. Here they seem as much imprisoned by old movies as inspired. This supremely self-conscious comedy is both delightful and exhausting. But never for a moment do you doubt that it's exactly the movie they wanted to make. Its gleeful, cartoon heartlessness is for real.[11]

Some critics, like John Harkness, writing for *Sight and Sound*, were put off by the film's freewheeling approach toward "jam[ming] together ... items that simply don't mix." He terms *Hudsucker* a "monstrous confluence" and describes "an emptiness at the heart of their work."[12] John Powers minces few words, calling the fifth *cri de Coen* "the most expensive bad art film in motion-picture history." Some of his other choice phrases include "sealed off and inert," "muffled ... miscalculated," and "self-congratulatory." This last evaluation gets to the heart of what Powers seems to most dislike about the film: the Coens' "smirking sense of superiority."[13]

Other writers found mostly good things to say about the film, Peter Travers of *Rolling Stone* going so far as to anticipate and refute

> the usual complaints about cold Coen calculation. That's only true if you're expecting Hallmark. The Coens run from sentiment, not feeling. Though their affection for character and genre is apparent, the Coens don't duplicate old movies. They refract the past through a contemporary lens.

Travers goes on to call *Hudsucker* "triumphantly fresh and witty," a film which illustrates the Coens' feeling for "comedies that aren't afraid of the dark."[14]

Jack Matthews, reviewing the film for *Newsday*, credits the Coens with making "the most inventive, unpredictable, visually interesting films out there today," though he concedes that the film is not mainstream audience fare. "The Coen brothers," he writes, "haven't shown yet that they can, or care to, come up with stories or characters outside of their own movie references."[15]

Kim Newman of *Sight and Sound* disagreed with her colleague

Harkness. She loved the film and praises the Coens as "the most exciting, imaginative and confident movie-makers in America."[16]

Joel and Ethan Coen were typically low-key concerning *Hudsucker*'s expensive failure to attract viewers. "We got spanked," Ethan told Tom Green of *USA Today*.[17] To *Premiere*'s Peter Biskind, Joel expressed appreciation at the treatment they received from Warner Bros., and gratitude that the studio opted not to repossess Ethan's car.[18]

Hudsucker concludes a cycle of sorts, the most strenuous articulation of an aesthetic begun with *Blood Simple*. Their next film, *Fargo* (1996), would represent a successful departure from the Coens' habitually ultra-stylized dreamworlds.

CHAPTER 6

Fargo

Carter Burwell's melancholic Scandinavian-flavored air provides a haunting aural backdrop to *Fargo*'s printed prologue. The text suggests that the film is "a true story," despite name changes made at the request of the survivors. "Out of respect for the dead," it reads, "the rest has been told exactly as it occurred." With a few simple sentences the Coens identify the film form they have chosen to revision, throw down an epistemological gauntlet, and indulge in the sort of wry misdirection that has been the hallmark of their public address.

White-on-black letters fade against what becomes a white screen, though subtle gradations of color afford the space great textural depth. Slowly an image resolves while credits fade in and out. A bird appears, a small dark form that wavers against what we come to see is a snowfall. A car's headlights emerge from the whiteness, their path parallel to a stark line of telephone poles that border the highway. The car sinks from view. It rises again, cresting a small hill. With a flourish of snare drums, the mournful music swells as the car looms larger in the frame. As it moves past the frame we see that it is towing another car. Left in its wake is a monochromatic abstraction of white-on-white screenspace, a snowstorm that appears simultaneously lighter than air and of colossal density. The film's title fades in. The car then races past the camera, which pans slightly to follow its trajectory. A cut to the vehicles as they recede into the whiteness seems the perspective of an observer powerless to impede the flow of events to come.

This opening sequence establishes the stylized "realism" that will mark *Fargo*. Beautifully composed shots are naturalized in the manner of conventional Hollywood-style production methods: the camera appears to capture selected images of a world that exists independent of the film-makers' record of it. Checked in *Fargo* is the Coens' characteristically flamboyant subjective film style. Camerawork is designed to affect a more observational stance; when camerawork does comment upon or become the content of the images it presents, the result is restrained, relatively subtle. Though elements of style that would ordinarily command center stage in a Coen brothers film are subordinated in *Fargo* to the interests of its story, the film achieves a distinctive look that is most arresting. Its artfully ordered and refined "artlessness" yields composed images that are richly metaphoric and, especially in the case of those which depict the natural environment, imbued with a poetic lyricism that links these screenscapes to the Coens' previous, more overtly stylized, imaginary geographies.

White-on-black print reads "Fargo, North Dakota." The image of the doubled cars fades in behind the text. They pull into a parking lot off a deserted snowy street.

A man enters a seedy bar. Country music playing on the jukebox competes with the clatter of billiard balls. The man looks beyond the pool tables to one of the back booths, where two men sit. He approaches their table and identifies himself as Jerry Lundegaard (William H. Macy). The younger of the two men glares at Lundegaard from behind a table littered with empty beer bottles while his companion dozes, open-mouthed, a cigarette hanging from his lip. The younger man is displeased. They have, he says, been waiting an hour for Lundegaard to show. They establish that there has been a mix-up regarding the appointed meeting time, which has been arranged by a go-between, Shep Proudfoot. The younger man, Carl Showalter (Steve Buscemi) asks if Lundegaard has the car. He assures him he does, and Carl indicates that he and his "associate" Gaear Grimsrud (Peter Stormare) are ready to talk business.

Lundegaard is halting, awkward, and naïve, clearly out of his depth. Carl is a talker, curiously interested in the details of the job Lundegaard is, in Carl's words, "tasking [them] to perform." The hulking Gaear is all but completely silent; the single line he utters offers little hint as to the beat of his particular drum. The "mission," as Carl puts it, is discussed. Lundegaard is in some kind of financial difficulty. He wants his own wife kidnapped, he says. His father-in-law is wealthy; he'll get the ransom from him, pay Carl and Gaear half, and keep half for himself. The car he has towed to the bar is to be given to Carl and Gaear as well. It is partial payment toward the faux abduction scheme Lundegaard insists is "real sound … all worked out."

A title locates us in Minneapolis, Minnesota. The sounds of televised sports fade in behind the title, replacing the clink of the exchange of car keys that cap the previous scene. Lundegaard enters his home laden with groceries and calls to his wife, Jean (Kristin Rudrüd). "Dad's here," she says, with a near-breathless mixture of hope and anxiety. Lundegaard finds his father-in-law, Wade (Harve Presnell), in front of his television set. His attempt to converse with the older man is unsuccessful. When Lundegaard learns that his father-in-law is staying for dinner, his discomfort is palpable.

Silence reigns around the dinner table, broken only by the Lundegaards' son Scotty's (Tony Denman) request to be excused. Tellingly, Wade answers before Lundegaard can respond to his son. Wade objects to Scotty's plans for the evening and to his parents' easygoing trustfulness. The short exchange is clearly emblematic of the larger dynamic at work: Wade works hard to keep each member of his extended family under his thumb and holds Lundegaard in special contempt. When his son-in-law asks him about a business deal for which he has sought backing, saying that it "could work out real good for me and Jean and Scotty," Wade's reply indicates the extent to which he declines to conceal his disaffection for the younger man. "Jean and Scotty," Wade says, cutting his eyes to and away from Lundegaard, "never have to worry."

A cut to a car racing past the camera punctuates Wade's remark. A long shot pans slowly to capture the car as it races along the highway, a dark trajectory against snowy flatland. Carl drives while Gaear smokes. In a lilting, obscure accent, Gaear grimly proposes that they stop for pancakes. Carl is sick of pancakes. He wants a shot, a beer, a steak, and sex, "not more fucking pancakes." A look from Gaear leads to a compromise. They will stop first for pancakes, then proceed to a bar outside Brainerd.

Three quick cuts describe the workday environment of Jerry Lundegaard at Wade's Olds dealership. The scene which follows chronicles the endgame of one of Lundegaard's car deals. Lundegaard is in his glass-enclosed sales office, behind his desk. Before him is a highly agitated customer and his wife. Lundegaard is shamefaced yet dogged as he lies and winces his way toward victory; his disgusted customer ultimately accepts the hidden costs of his new car, cursing Lundegaard with each breath. Lundegaard's sharp-eyed glance at his fuming buyer from beneath his sorrowfully furrowed brow ends the scene. William H. Macy brings to such moments more nuance than can be digested in a single viewing; the look is a wonderfully ambiguous hint of what lurks beneath Lundegaard's meek exterior.

A lone car angles toward the camera on a road which darkly bisects an expanse of snowy flatland which extends, one imagines, for untold miles beyond the edges of the frame. As in all Coen works, this unseen world is as much a part of the visual experience of the film as what is before us. The car rushes past a huge Paul Bunyan totem. Brandishing a menacing-looking, outsized ax, he welcomes visitors to Brainerd, his home.

We are in the parking lot of a truck stop called the Blue Ox. A cut to some part of the establishment's interior finds Carl and Gaear in twin beds having noisy sex with a pair of girlish prostitutes. The scene fades to a later one of the two couples as they lounge in their respective beds, bathed in the blue glare of the TV they watch. Ed McMahon's distinctive vocal kitsch blares from the offscreen set.

In the Lundegaards' kitchen, Scotty is in the foreground, eating cereal and watching early morning cartoons. Jean fixes breakfast behind him while delivering a heartfelt lecture regarding Scotty's failure to work to his potential in school. Jean's father calls Lundegaard. Typically brusque with him, Wade tells him that the deal he has proposed is looking "pretty sweet." Wade orders him to meet him at his office later that afternoon. His son-in-law looks happy to comply. Macy's Lundegaard is a taut compression of fearfulness and desire. His features seem both grotesquely animated and inert in this role; beneath the Howdy Doody surface of his face seems to surge a tsunami of repressed emotion.

Lundegaard seeks out Shep (Steven Reevis), the mechanic who put him in touch with Showalter. Shep emphasizes the fact that he can't vouch for the guy Lundegaard describes as his buddy. Shep is unable to help Lundegaard get in touch with the two men; in the wake of his conversation with Wade, Lundegaard feels he may no longer be in need of their services. After some salesman's false jocularity, which Shep notices not at all, Lundegaard leaves, scratching his head in unconscious self-communication: Now what? As he crosses the garage, a radio becomes more audible. In a subtle sound bridge the same song is blasting from Carl and Gaear's car radio as we cut to the vehicle's interior. The song, "These Boots Are Made for Walking," adroitly reflects the film's interest in the complex dynamics of power and subjugation. Steve Buscemi delivers a characteristically mesmerizing performance in the short scene which follows wherein the chatty Carl labors in vain to involve Gaear in conversation. The inscrutable Gaear remains completely indifferent to his companion.

We dissolve from the car's interior to a shot of Lundegaard on the phone in his office. The camera moves slowly forward toward the open vertical blinds that mask the frame to create a visual prison for the man. Macy affords us a glimpse of what it takes to be a professional liar. Lundegaard lives his lies as he sidesteps the caller's questions concerning a phony loan he has succeeded in extracting from the man. Smiling obligingly and gesturing ineffectively in the direction of papers he knows do not exist, Lundegaard is able to successfully fend off discovery. Macy's rubber features are contorted with worry as the scene ends.

A close shot of a television screen reveals a morning show in progress. Jean is curled up with some knitting on the sofa in front of the set and cheerfully allows herself to be entertained by a very old joke. Her attention is suddenly diverted by a sound outside on the deck. A ski-masked man with a crowbar ascends the deck stairs, then peers through the glass sliding door, cupping his hands around his eyes like a five-year-old at a candy store window. Jean is paralyzed with horrified fascination. It is not until the man smashes through the door that she reacts, leaping up from the sofa, screaming, knitting needles flying. She runs toward the front door only to find a large man also wearing a ski mask entering. He grabs her from behind when she turns to run. She bites his hand, and he drops her on the floor. Gaear rolls his mask up. "Unguent," he mutters, as Jean races up the stairs pursued by the smaller intruder, whose voice we recognize as Carl's.

Jean grabs the phone in her bedroom and bolts into the master bathroom, locking the door behind her. She stands sobbing in the middle of the room cradling the phone, dialing for help. Abruptly the telephone is ripped from her grasp by its cord, which has been yanked by the men on the other side of the door. The telephone flies across the room before it lies smashed on the floor, useless. Jean turns toward the window, trying to get it open as the sounds of an attack upon the door fill the room. The camera focuses upon the intruders' crowbar, which has broken through the wood to lodge between the door and its frame. When the men succeed in breaking through, the bathroom is empty, the window open.

Carl runs to the window, peers out, and runs out of the bathroom, dropping the crowbar. Gaear, unhesitating and deliberate, makes for the medicine cabinet, single-mindedly pursuing his own agenda, as usual. Gaear finds the ointment he wants and stands before the medicine cabinet mirror, applying it. He looks up, at the reflection of the shower curtain behind him. He turns around slowly. Suddenly Jean leaps from the bathtub and, draped in the shower curtain, runs out of the bathroom. Gaear watches her placidly as she rushes past him and, still covered in the curtain, lurches through the bedroom. Jean stumbles blindly toward the staircase and falls, thudding painfully against the steps as she descends. She lands in a heap, still shrouded in the shower curtain. Gaear pokes at the form as if to test for life signs, his face expressionless.

Meanwhile, Lundegaard keeps his appointment at his father-in-law's office. He is initially happy to hear that the investment opportunity he has brought to Wade and his money man, Stan Grossman (Larry Grandenburg), has met with their approval. His joy and relief are, however, extremely short-lived; Stan and Wade make it clear that they are willing to pay him a finder's fee for bringing them the deal but are unwilling to fund Lundegaard's involvement. Wade and Stan repeatedly point out that they're not a bank, and Lundegaard is made to understand that his father-in-law cares nothing for the fact that he is his daughter's husband; Wade is all business. They laugh out loud at his request for a loan that means no financial benefit for them. The meeting ends with the idea that Wade and Stan may move independently on Lundegaard's deal.

Throughout the scene Macy's face is a rubber-featured barometer of feeling. From the early smile that stretches an impossible distance across his face to the final despair of a man who has run out of options, Macy brings pathos to an essentially bathetic character.

One of the film's most compelling scenes follows. An aerial view of a snowy parking lot is a geometric black-and-white abstraction. A figure intrudes. It is Lundegaard, trudging heavily in the snow to his car. From the back seat of Lundegaard's car, we watch as he enters the vehicle. He sits behind the wheel and exhales loudly several times, his breath visible in the frigid air. He retrieves a red plastic windshield scraper from the depths of the front seat and, with a kind of resigned grace, exits the car and begins to rhythmically scrape at the film of ice covering his windshield. The motion seems to unleash something deep inside the man. Lundegaard loses control, bashing at the window with his scraper and emitting choking growls of frustration. He throws the scraper to the ground and stamps around furiously before he regains his composure and resumes his task. The sound of the scraping is unnaturally loud. A final shot, high and wide, captures the man at work. At war with elements far more powerful than he, Lundegaard fights methodically on.

He arrives home laden with groceries. Slowly he takes in the damage to his home. The camera lingers on shreds of plastic that still adhere to empty rings in his bathroom, all that remains of his shower curtain. A cut to the curtain itself lying crumpled on the carpet follows. As the camera discovers other evidence of the break-in—broken glass, static on the TV—we hear Lundegaard's voice. He is on the phone to Wade, giving him the bad news. Only when the camera cuts to Lundegaard do we realize that he is not yet on the phone with his father-in-law but rehearsing his lines. The camera observes Lundegaard wryly from a short distance. Its subtle commentary is intensified when Lundegaard forgets to play-act when giving his name to Wade's secretary.

The screen blacks out. It is the night sky, photographed by a camera that angles down to reveal the mammoth Paul Bunyan statue welcoming people to Brainerd. The figure is surreally vivid against the dark. A car shoots past the statue, small in the lower left corner of the frame.

Then we are in the car with Carl, Gaear, and Jean, who is bound, covered, and whimpering in the back seat. "Shut the fuck up," Gaear snarls, "or I'll throw you back into the trunk, you know!" "Jeez, that's more than I've heard you say all week," says Carl. Gaear gives him a withering look.

A police cruiser's siren alerts the men to its presence behind their car. Carl guesses the cruiser has noticed that the car has no tags. As both cars pull over to the side, Carl tells Gaear that he'll take care of the problem. Gaear glares at Carl, clearly unhappy with this turn of events. Carl directs his attention to the back seat. "Keep it still back there, lady, or else we're gonna hafta, you know, shoot ya," he says, like a bad actor in a late night B movie. His offhandedness conveys just how remote he considers the likelihood of violence.

The state trooper is photographed several times at a distance through Carl's rear window; his approach is noted as a reflection in Carl's rearview mirror. In these shots the trooper is faceless, more archetype than human.

The policeman is at Carl's window, directing his flashlight at the two men's faces. The trooper is depersonalized by the camera, which allows us to see only fragments of the man. Carl and the trooper talk about the tag situation. Gaear is increasingly tense. Carl stresses that he is big on "compliance." He tells the trooper that he hopes he can take care of the problem in Brainerd and extends a bribe along with his driver's license. The trooper declines the money and, handing Carl back his wallet, orders him out of the car. As Carl looks helplessly at Gaear, a small whimper is heard. The trooper leans down to investigate and, for the first time, we see the man's face. Another whimper. As the trooper turns toward the sound, Gaear springs into action. He leans across Carl and smashes the trooper's head against the window frame. Holding it there, he reaches into the glove compartment, grabs a gun, and pumps a bullet point-blank into the trooper's head, producing a grotesque geyser of blood. Carl looks on in disbelief, spattered with the policeman's blood. Jean screams, and Gaear screams at her to shut up. He pushes the dead trooper off the car, and the man's body falls backward in a surreal arc. An extreme close-up of Gaear follows. His eyes are dead, his face a blank. Carl's face, on the other hand, is very expressive. Shock, revulsion, and fear play out underneath the pattern of bloodspray. "Whoa, Daddy" is Carl's unlikely reaction. "You'll take care of it," Gaear taunts Carl. "You are smooth, smooth, you know?" he tells him. Gaear instructs Carl to move the trooper off the road.

We observe from a distance as Carl struggles with the trooper's body. The scene is visually reminiscent of a similar one in *Blood Simple* wherein the pesky problem of a recalcitrant corpse is similarly addressed. The sequence which follows strongly recalls *Blood Simple*'s visual aesthetic.

Carl is ineptly attempting to drag the body off the highway when he and Gaear notice headlights coming toward them. The car reaches the crime scene and passes slowly by. Two young people are in the front seat; the pie-faced youth piloting the vehicle gapes comically at the mayhem into which they have blundered. The two seem to come to their senses. The unlucky witnesses take off, tires squealing.

Gaear slides over behind the wheel and, gun in hand, races after the witness car, screeching past Carl and the corpse dangling from his arms. A side view of Gaear as he drives shows him hunched over the wheel with malevolent focus. Jean, still helpless and covered in the back seat of the car, cries with fear.

The pavement disappears beneath the frame as Gaear races toward taillights which get brighter in the dark as he draws close. There is a skidding sound, and the taillights vanish. Gaear is confused until he spies the red brake lights blazing on the capsized witness car, just off the road. Gaear comes to a screeching halt; Jean yells as she is flung off the back seat onto the floor.

Gaear positions his car so that its headlights illuminate the accident site. The driver of the witness car forces his way out of the car and runs, his parka a bright splotch against the dark sky. Gaear moves slowly across the snow near the disabled car, takes careful aim, and shoots the running youth in the back. The witness falls to the snow face forward.

Gaear refocuses his malign attention. Approaching the overturned car, he peers into its depths to discover the second witness folded inside, a teenage girl. They stare for a moment at each other, the girl's chest visibly rising and falling in silent contractions of pain and fear. We watch from her point of view as Gaear takes aim. The camera moves outside the car as Gaear fires into it. The screen blacks out at the gunshot.

The violence in this section of the film is unlike the violence of the other Coen films, where all manner of bizarre events occur in stylized universes very different from our own. In their previous five films, the Coens' aesthetic imposed distance between the cartoon bloodshed of their elaborately imagined dreamworlds and the viewer, whose experience of each film involved, to a greater or lesser degree, a conscious reading of the Coens' mediation. The viewer is afforded no such buffer in *Fargo*. The second and third murders of the postkidnapping sequence are naturalized in a manner atypical for the Coens. They are, as a result, repellent in a way that shocks.

The mournful music that opens the film begins its second half as well. The screen is filled with the image of a painted duck on a small canvas. The camera pans right and plays across other small paintings, carved decoys, brushes, rags, and other related implements. At the far end of the room is a sleeping couple. As the camera closes in on the woman's face the phone rings, and she is instantly awake. She identifies herself as Marge (Frances McDormand), and we are privileged to meet one of the screen's most original and appealing detectives. She will prove to be that rarest of Coen creations: a character with whom the audience can establish an emotional connection. She listens while her husband sleepily drapes an arm around her. The conversation is a short one. Marge utters a series of sympathetically voiced midwestern clichés, promises to be somewhere "in a jiff," and checks her watch for the time.

Her husband, Norm Gunderson (John Carroll Lynch) awakens. She urges him to go back to sleep, but he sweetly insists that Marge needs breakfast and gets up to prepare it. When Marge stands, we see that she is heavily pregnant. "Ah, Norm," she murmurs fondly.

A cut to their breakfast nook finds Marge and Norm finishing the last of their meal. Marge wears a maternity police officer's uniform. She heads out following an exchange of endearments, and the camera lingers to observe Norm as he eats. Marge returns. "Hon," she nearly sings, "prowler needs a jump." Like the Lundegaards, Marge and Norm's accents are pungent, made even more so by the quasi-musical tones of their rhythmic speech.

A quick shot of Marge's prowler as it speeds off toward a vast expanse of still, snowy horizon ends precisely when the car vanishes from view. At the crime scene, Marge gets coffee from an amiable colleague, Lou (Bruce Bohne), an easygoing guy who calls her "Margie" and makes neighborly small talk while pointing out the location of two of the three dead bodies Marge has come to inspect. Marge is surprised at the lack of activity near the overturned car. "Well, it's cold, Margie," the man says.

Marge peeks into the car. "Aw, jeez," she laments, before identifying the wounds. After learning the location of the third body, the dead trooper, Marge neatly organizes the evidence into an accurate account of what has occurred. "Okay," she says. "So we got a trooper pulls someone over, we got a shooting, these folks drive by, there's a high speed pursuit, ends here, and this execution-type deal." "Yah," Lou answers. "I'd be very surprised if our suspect was from Brainerd," Marge says. "Yah," Lou concurs.

Marge surmises that their killer is large from the size of his footprints in the frozen snow. A surprised look crosses Marge's face, and she doubles over. Lou notices, saying: "Ya see something down there, Chief?" Margie explains morning sickness rather than evidence has focused her attention earthward. Lou is sympathetic. After a short discussion concerning the nature and origin of Marge's breakfast, they take a look at the dead trooper.

We cut to the startling image of the dead trooper's frozen, bloodied face in the extreme foreground; Marge scours the area behind him for evidence. She tells Lou that these footprints are different from the others. "This guy's smaller 'n his buddy," she says. "Oh yah," Lou says. "It's a real shame," Marge sighs, after examining the body. "Yah," says Lou. Marge guesses that since the trooper's car lights are switched off, the smaller man waited there, out of the cold, for the larger to return. The talk turns to night-crawlers, and the two leave.

Back in the prowler, Marge asks Lou if he has checked the trooper's citation book. Lou says yes. The last entry, he says, is a tan Ciera, plate number DLR. He figures that the trooper was stopped before he had a chance to complete the tag. "Uh, huh," says Marge noncommittally. Lou tells her he's got the state looking for a Ciera with tags beginning with DLR—no match as of yet. "I'm not sure that I agree with ya a hundred percent on your police work, there, Lou," Marge says in the nicest possible way. "Yah?" asks Lou. Marge tells him that the vehicle probably had dealer plates. "Oh," Lou says, looking stunned. "Jeez." Marge tells Lou a joke to take the sting out of his mistake, and we like them both immensely. As their cruiser races off, we hear Wade's gruff voice. In an ironic sound bridge, he snaps, "Alls I know is, you got a problem you call a professional!"

We cut to the restaurant where Wade, Stan, and Lundegaard are discussing the kidnapping. Lundegaard is trying to convince Wade not to call the police and not to change the terms of the ransom. Wade is cynical and suspicious. The kidnapping of his daughter is being treated as an unusually unsound business deal; Wade disgusts Stan and frightens Lundegaard when he suggests that they offer half a million rather than the requested million.

Stan queries Lundegaard on the next step, and Wade storms off. After paying a preternaturally cheerful cashier for their coffee, Lundegaard joins Stan outside the restaurant while Wade gets the car. Stan is highly solicitous and reassures Lundegaard that he and Wade will get the money together. When Stan asks if Scotty will be all right, Lundegaard swivels his head around with a start. The look on his face tells us that he has not given a single thought as to how his son will be affected by his scheme.

Scotty sits on his bed in his room, clutching a long-outgrown stuffed animal and crying. Lundegaard enters the room. Scotty is worried that something will happen to his mother, that something unforeseen will go wrong. Lundegaard makes use of a string of clichés as he attempts to comfort his son and convinces him that going to the police is a bad idea. Pathetically, he invokes the opinion of Stan Grossman in order to bolster his argument, as though he does not expect his own opinion to carry much weight, even with his own son. Lundegaard leaves Scotty's room after instructing him to lie about his mother's whereabouts. He closes the door behind him. The screen fills with the poster on the back of Scotty's door: a nearly life-sized photograph of the "Accordion King." The poster accentuates Scotty's youth and innocence and somehow sharpens our sense of the boy's anguish.

A distant, high lens focuses our attention on the tan Ciera as it passes through a small copse of trees to pull up in front of a small, low-lying, isolated cabin. Abruptly, the camera closes in tight as Jean is removed from the back seat of the car. She breaks free of Carl's grasp and runs aimlessly forward, blinded by the black hood over her head and hampered by her tied hands. Dressed still in her pajamas and sweater, feet bare, Jean staggers in the snow. Gaear moves as if to retrieve her but is stopped by Carl, who grins as he watches Jean lurch about. Gaear watches without expression. Carl begins to laugh out loud as Jean stumbles and falls. Gaear, still expressionless, goes after her.

We dissolve to Marge as she makes her way through the police station to her office, greeting coworkers and ordering Avon products. She finds Norm waiting for her. He's brought her lunch; she's brought him a bag of night crawlers. As Marge exclaims over the food, we get a close-up of the worms. The slithering tangled mess provides a comic counterpoint to Marge's appreciation of the Arby's meal that Norm has provided. Marge asks how Norm's painting is progressing, a question Lou echoes a few minutes later when he enters Marge's office, narrowly missing a tender exchange between the police chief and her husband. Lou tells Marge that he has discovered that a tan Ciera transported two men to the Blue Ox two nights before. They had company, Lou tells Marge.

In every Coen film is a scene that one especially wishes to remember verbatim. In *Fargo* this scene is between Marge and Carl and Gaear's truckstop hookers. After a short chat concerning their schooling ("Go Bears!" one of the young women interjects sadly, tentatively, as though at that moment conscious of options lost), Marge questions the two about their evening with her suspects. The interview is peppered with many "yahs" and enthusiastic nods, which are often synchronized. Like so many other denizens of the area, the girls' accents are quite broad.

When Marge asks for descriptions of the men, Carl's partner speaks up. "Well, the little guy, he was kinda funny lookin'." "In what way?" Marge asks. "I dunno. Just funny lookin'." "Could you be more specific?"

Marge asks. The girl tells her that he wasn't circumcised. Marge wants to know if he was funny looking apart from that. "Yah," the girl answers. "Like I say," she offers, "he was funny lookin'. More 'n most people, even." The other young woman tells Marge that her client looked like the Marlboro Man. But, she cautions, she may be saying that because he smoked a lot of Marlboros. "You know," she says, "like a subconscious type of thing." Marge acknowledges the strange tricks the mind can play. Then, with the look of one suddenly infused with extra oxygen, the first girl remembers something—they said they were going to the Twin Cities. Marge is appreciative, and the girls smile and nod, delighted to help.

At the cabin, Carl rages over the faulty television set, screaming and smacking the thing with his hands. Gaear watches, his eyes vacant, his mouth slack, and says not a word. Jean sits next to the open stove for warmth. She is tied with her hands behind her back to her chair; her expelled breath is clearly visible as it filters through the hood still worn over her face. The camera tracks in slowly toward each figure in turn, the movement conveying the claustrophobia that reigns inside the small cabin.

A match cut from the cabin television screen to that of another follows. A nature documentary describes the reproductive cycle of the bark beetle. Marge watches from bed while Norm dozes. Marge wakes Norm to tell him she is turning in, and the screen goes black. A ringing telephone is heard. A high shot of Marge and Norm in bed is followed by a close shot of Marge as she answers the phone. The call is from an old friend of Marge's who has seen her on the news talking about the murders.

We transition to the car dealership where we find a distracted Lundegaard in the middle of a sales pitch. A call comes in for him, and we cut to the ringing phone in his office. It is Carl. Lundegaard is initially cheerful for the benefit of anyone who may be watching him through the glass walls of his office. His demeanor undergoes a transformation as he listens to Carl, who demands more money in light of the "circumstances ... acts of God, force majeure ..." Lundegaard is frantic when Carl seems to not know who Jean is, more so when he learns that the triple homicide in Brainerd is connected to his "deal." The camera mercilessly tracks in toward Lundegaard's face as it contorts with fear and panic. The phone rings almost immediately after Lundegaard finishes his conversation with Carl. It is the same man who called Lundegaard earlier in the film, wanting the vehicle identification numbers he has requested so that he may verify that the cars upon which Lundegaard has borrowed actually exist. Anyone watching Lundegaard's agonizingly falsely cheerful facial expressions would know that they do not. Lundegaard stands very still when the conversation ends; his features seem to collapse toward the center of his face. We cut to a shot of Lundegaard from a distance outside his office. Framed within the picture window of his office, we watch as Lundegaard has a tantrum, slamming down the papers on his desk a couple of times. Lundegaard then glances out the window to check whether or not his behavior has been observed.

To the easy listening strains of "Do You Know the Way to San Jose?" we cut to restaurant steam-table food being piled high upon a tray. The tray belongs to Marge, and her husband is not far behind. They amble to a table, where they begin to eat in companionable silence. They are interrupted by one of Marge's men, who has followed up on the phone records of calls made out of the Blue Ox on the night in question. Marge decides to pursue these leads to the Twin Cities.

Marge and Norm eat. We then match cut to Stan Grossman's florid face; he is methodically chewing. He stares unblinking. The focus of his attention is Wade, mulling over the terms of the ransom demand as communicated by Lundegaard. The three men are in Lundegaard's kitchen; an overhead shot shows them sitting around a small table laden with coffee things and cake. A fourth chair holds an oversized briefcase.

Wade comes to a decision. He, not Lundegaard, is going to deliver the million dollars to the kidnappers. Lundegaard protests. He talks about how "nervous" the kidnappers sound, how adamant they were that they only deal with him, how important it is to follow their instructions to the letter. Wade stops him, scolding that Lundegaard isn't "selling … a damn car." Wade says it is his money, and that makes it "his show." He also, he says, doesn't want Lundegaard "mucking it up." "What the heck d'ya mean?" near-whispers Lundegaard. "It's the way we prefer to handle it," says Stan, cutting his eyes sideways. Once again, Lundegaard is out of the loop, cut out of his own shady scheme for precisely the same reason he was cut out of the legitimate business deal he brought to these men. And one more element of the kidnapping spins out of whack.

Marge arrives at her hotel in the Twin Cities area. She checks in with local police and learns the whereabouts of Shep Proudfoot, who has been identified as a result of the Blue Ox phone records. She also gets a recommendation for a lunch spot.

We cut to Carl behind the wheel of the Ciera. He drives into an airport parking lot and targets the snowiest car's plates for theft. Having replaced the Ciera's dealer plates, Carl heads out of the lot. He tells the man at the pay booth that he has changed his mind about wanting to park in the lot. The man is smiling and friendly as he explains that Carl will still have to pay the $4 minimum. The attendant's smile barely falters as Carl explodes into a profane tirade. Carl is especially put out by what he seems to feel is the man's pretense to authority and the man's uniform, the clip-on tie of which he finds especially irksome.

At the car dealership, Lundegaard asks a mechanic where Shep is. The mechanic tells him that Shep is speaking with a cop. Shep and Marge are indeed in the middle of an interview, though it is a one-sided affair. Marge gently pushes Shep to recall who may have phoned him in the middle of the night in question, sweetly reminding him that it is against the terms of his probation to consort with criminals. Also, she notes, in an almost maternal fashion, he's never been involved in anything like a homicide, and wouldn't he like to avoid getting caught up as an accessory to this one? Shep is all but mute, mumbling monosyllables, his face impassive.

Marge next turns her attention to Lundegaard. She finds him in his office, doodling with great concentration. She asks him if he's had any cars stolen lately from his lot, "specifically a tan-color Ciera." Lundegaard just stares at her, rocking in his chair, looking as though he might burst into tears.

Lundegaard steadies himself enough to bring forth a few dim remarks about Brainerd, which Marge addresses good-naturedly before returning to her question. Lundegaard tells her that no vehicles are unaccounted for. "Okey dokey, thanks a bunch," Marge says and makes a smiling exit. Lundegaard watches her leave, then picks up the phone and calls Shep. He is told that Shep has stepped out.

Some time later, we watch Marge as she pauses nervously before entering what looks like a hotel bar. She has changed out of her uniform and into a nice maternity top and slacks. Spotting a man seated alone in a booth, Marge slowly makes her way over. It is Mike, Marge's old school chum. When Mike hugs her hello he seems to hang on for dear life—Marge must eventually break his hold.

They sit opposite each other and exchange pleasantries. When Mike moves to sit next to Marge, his arm around her shoulder, Marge is kind but firm in her request that he move back across the table. Mike is profusely sorry. Over the next few minutes it emerges that Mike married a girl a year behind them in high school and that he is an engineer for Honeywell. He then tells her that his wife has died, after a long battle with cancer. Marge is sympathetic. Mike is very emotional as he talks to Marge. They toast to better times. Mike repeatedly tells Marge how much he has always liked her. Marge is disconcerted by the manic intensity of these declarations. When she suggests they get together another time, Mike nearly yells his opposition. Soon, Mike is weeping. "I've been so lonely," he cries to Marge. "It's okay," Marge says to him softly. He is crying as the scene ends.

We cut to another bar, a glitzy venue where José Feliciano, playing himself, sings and plays guitar onstage. In the audience sits Carl and an escort he has hired for the evening. Carl's attempts to converse with the woman are met with confused suspicion. Next, they are in bed; the woman is on top of Carl verbally browbeating him toward orgasm. Suddenly a hand grabs the woman's shoulder, and she is flung to the floor.

It is Shep Proudfoot, and he is an unhappy man. He throws Carl across the room, and we watch him flip over an overturned sofa. Shep enters the frame and begins to kick viciously at the man concealed by the furniture. He is yelling furiously to Carl to leave his house and about how Carl is going to put him back in prison. His assault on Carl is interrupted by a neighbor angry about the noise. Shep attacks both this man and Carl's hooker as she struggles half-naked down the hallway away from the melee. Shep returns to his apartment, where he resumes bellowing his discontent at Carl. Carl has been trying to get dressed. Shep grabs Carl's own belt and begins to strangle him with it. A close-up of Carl's feet show them off the ground, one boot on and one boot off. In the background, Carl's hooker is screaming. Shep yells obscenities and whips Carl with the belt as the smaller man crawls along the floor, hiding his face and feebly attempting to kick back.

We cut to the lobby pay telephone of a bar. Carl, his face showing the effects of Shep's beating, dials and waits for a moment. Lundegaard picks up on the other end. Carl begins to yell his instructions for the ransom payoff; at Lundegaard's, Wade picks up an extension line and listens. Lundegaard seems to want to tell Carl something of the change in plans, but Carl is in no mood to take note. He yells his orders and, when Lundegaard interrupts, begins a tirade describing the exact manner in which his family will die if he hasn't received the money at the requested location in thirty minutes. As the phone call ends, Wade grabs the case of money and strides purposefully out the door. He spares not a word nor a glance for his distraught son-in-law.

Lundegaard performs a little dance of frustration in the wake of Wade's departure. He has begun to pull on his boots when Scotty calls down. Lundegaard reassures the boy and continues his preparations to leave.

We cut to a close-up of Wade behind the wheel of his car. His face is an amber circle in the darkness of the car's interior, lending a theatrical cast to what turns out to be a rehearsal. "Okay ... here's your damn money, now where's my daughter?" He pulls out a handgun and cracks the barrel. "You godamn punk," he growls.

An exterior shot of a rooftop parking lot locates the tan Ciera parked under some lights, no other cars in sight. Wade's Cadillac pulls onto the roof, stopping a short distance behind the Ciera. Carl gets out of his car. He squints at Wade, who has exited his car with the case of money. "Who the fuck are you?!" he squeals. He repeats his question as Wade advances. "Here's your damn money. Now where's my daughter?" Wade demands forcefully.

Carl looks very unhappy. He tells Wade to drop the money. "No Jean, no money," yells Wade. The exchange is repeated. "Is this a fucking joke here?" yells Carl. He snaps. He pulls a gun out of his pocket and shoots Wade through his down parka at point-blank range. Feathers fly. Wade's face fills the screen before it falls back and away from the camera. Wade moans. As Carl moves toward Wade to retrieve the money, Wade removes his own gun and fires at Carl's head. Carl reels backward, holding his hand to his bloody face, his gun discharging. "You shot me!" Carl mumbles indistinctly. His hand pressed to his bleeding jaw, he shoots Wade six times; the camera repairs to a discreet distance halfway through the rampage. The camera is close again as Carl howls in pain. He kicks Wade several times; the body lies below the frame. He grabs the case of money and shuffles to his car. The camera adjusts its angle to capture the movement, and Wade's prone form enters the foreground. His body is slightly blurred in the image and unnaturally still. Feathers released by the hole in his jacket flutter in the wind. The images embody the artfully disjunctive impulses of the film, which deploys both macabre comedy and realistic violence like dysfunctionally conjoined twins. Carl drives unsteadily off the roof.

A close-up of Lundegaard behind the wheel of his car follows. He is in the parking structure on a lower level. Suddenly Carl's vehicle careens around the corner and passes him in the other direction at full speed. Then, our point of view is Carl's as he pulls up to the attendant on his way out of the lot. The man's cheerful face falls; a reverse shot shows his perspective of the supremely bloody Carl behind the wheel. Carl's profane response to the attendant's request for a ticket is muffled but clearly understood.

Meanwhile, Lundegaard has ascended to the roof. He pulls up beside Wade's car and stops. A reverse shot from just behind Lundegaard's car: Wade's body lies in the snow in the background. After several beats we see Lundegaard lean over; in a moment the trunk of his car swings open wide in the foreground of the shot. The shot is funny and horrible; its storytelling economy is typical Coen brothers.

As Lundegaard approaches the pay booth, our point of view is his. The wooden exit gate has been broken and lies in pieces on the concrete. He turns his head toward the booth. He first sees a foot protruding upward at an awkward angle. The foot is attached to the corpse of the attendant; the body is overturned inside the small space. "Oh jeez," Lundegaard breathes as he drives slowly by, his face a stunned mask half hidden by his parka hood.

Lundegaard arrives home. He sits heavily on the bench in his entryway and leans forward. Scotty yells down to him that Stan Grossman has called, twice. "Okay," Lundegaard is able to muster. When his son asks him if everything is okay, Lundegaard tells him, "Yah." Scotty asks if he is going to call Stan back, which under the circumstances speaks worlds about the politics of Lundegaard's family. Lundegaard tells him that he is going to bed. The screen goes black.

When we fade back in, we are behind the windshield of what turns out to be a police vehicle. The driver is flagged down by a man working with a snow shovel in his driveway. The policeman identifies himself after verifying the name of the man, who has clearly been expecting the officer. He launches into a comically monotonal description of a conversation he had with a stranger while he was bartending at a local hangout. This man was looking for "woman action" to keep him from "going crazy out at the lake." The two got into an altercation during which the stranger boasted about killing "the last guy who thought he was a jerk." (Though, confides the bartender, he didn't use that word.) The policeman asks for a description, "He was a little guy, kinda funny lookin'," says the man. "Uh, huh— in what way?" asks the policeman. "Oh, just in a general kinda way," says the bartender. The conversation ends with a discussion of the cold front on its way in.

We cut to the tan Ciera parked at the side of a highway. Inside the car, Carl clutches a bloody wad of paper to his mutilated jaw. "Jeez Chrsht," he mumbles as he stares into the open case of money on the passenger side of the seat. The million in the case far exceeds his expectations; his and Gaear's deal was for $80,000. He grabs a few bundles and tosses them into the back seat, then closes up the case. He changes the paper covering his wound, an operation that is as difficult to watch as any in the film. (Oddly, one notices that Steve Buscemi, a man described rather consistently in the film as "kinda funny lookin'" has beautiful, almost feminine, long-fingered hands, graceful even as, spattered with blood, they perform a painfully awkward procedure.)

Carl takes the case of money out of the car and runs with it, stumbling, down the embankment. When he reaches a stake-and-wire fence, he begins to dig furiously with a windshield scraper. He buries the money in a shallow grave. Point-of-view shots follow his glance from right to left as he observes the fence line, which runs along the highway as far as the eye can see in both directions. The post at which he has buried the money is identical to hundreds. He sticks the windshield scraper into the snow at his knees for a marker. Scooping snow up to his wound, Carl lurches back to his car, stumbling and falling as he goes. The scene fades.

In Marge's hotel room, she is on the phone with a friend, talking while she packs to return to Brainerd. Marge learns that everything Mike has told her is false. He has, her friend tells her, psychiatric problems. Marge is stunned. "Jeez. Well. That's a surprise," she says. In the next shot she is in her car; her face is sad as she scans the road. She pulls up to a fast-food drive-through order panel. We cut to her eating a sandwich in her car. She drives on. Throughout this sequence Burwell's mournful orchestrations underscore Marge's heart-heaviness. A shot of Marge behind the wheel focuses our attention on her face; we watch as something occurs to her.

The musical score links the previous scene to the next, making clear the temporal proximity of one to the other. Lundegaard is behind his desk, working at creating an unreadable set of numbers to send to the man trying to verify his loan information. Marge appears in his doorway, and Lundegaard is unable to dissuade her from entering and asking questions. Lundegaard's brow is knit, his eyes panicky.

Lundegaard's concern is well founded. Marge has a lot of questions concerning connections among her killers, Shep Proudfoot, the tan Ciera with dealer plates, and the Gustafson dealership which employs Shep. She also wants to know how Lundegaard can be so sure about the fact that he is missing no cars. What, she asks, is the protocol for inventorying the lot, and when was the last time he did it? Lundegaard can no longer hold her off with evasive answers and snaps. Marge is firm, telling him that he's got "no call to get snippy" with her—she's just doing her job. "We're doing all we can," says Lundegaard, touching his mouth and face with the classic gestures of the liar. She then asks to speak to Mr. Gustafson.

This last request galvanizes Lundegaard, as well it might. He explodes, yelling that if "it's so damned important to ya," he'll do a lot count on the spot. He storms off after donning his outdoor gear, leaving Marge behind in his office. Left to her own devices, Marge investigates the paperwork on Lundegaard's desk, a framed picture of Jean, and the ceiling. Suddenly Lundegaard drives by the office window; Marge stares, open-mouthed with astonishment. "Oh for Pete's sake, Pete's sake! He's fleein' the interview, he's fleeing the interview!" she says, as though recalling the phrase from her student days. She grabs the phone, struggles to get an outside line, and calls her local police contact.

We cut to Gaear at the cabin. He is hunched over a TV dinner that he cuts from a tray in front of the television set. He stabs blindly at his food, riveted to the program; a reverse angle shot from behind his massive shoulder shows a soap opera in progress. The woman onscreen is telling her boyfriend that she is pregnant with his child, a revelation which seems to deeply affect Gaear. That Gaear has become a fan of such shows is grotesquely incongruous, monstrous somehow.

His attention is momentarily deflected by Carl's arrival. He turns his head slowly toward Carl, then stares for a moment at Carl's bloody head before returning his attention to the television. Carl's quip, "You should see the other guy," passes unheeded. Carl's eyes are drawn downward. He sees Jean motionless on the floor underneath her overturned chair. He asks Gaear about it. "She started shrieking, you know," he replies, and we are left to imagine why. Carl is not overly interested in Jean's fate.

Carl tells Gaear that he has the money. "All of it, all eighty grand," Carl says. "That's forty for you, forty for me," he says, putting Gaear's money on the TV tray. Carl tells Gaear that he can have his truck—he'll take the Ciera. Gaear wants to split the car. He insists that one should pay the other for half. Despite the fact that Carl has most of a million buried out on the highway, he goes nuts. He wants the car for his pain and suffering and for putting up with Gaear. He waits for an argument but gets only Gaear's characteristic sour look. Carl screams, "Are we square?!" at Gaear a couple of times and then walks out the door, having displayed the gun at his hip. This earns him a nasty glance from Gaear.

We cut to the cabin's exterior. Carl is making his way across the snow, his hand still pressing a wad of paper to his bloody jaw. The camera tracks him. Behind him we see Gaear burst through the front door, pulling on a hood. In his red-mittened hands is an ax, which he buries in Carl's neck before the smaller man can react. Carl's yell is augmented on the soundtrack to echo with a metallic reverberation. The screen blacks out.

Marge pulls to a stop on the road in front of the cabin. Walking toward it, she stops, hearing a motorized whine. She moves toward the source of the sound. Marge pulls out her gun, and there is a quick reverse shot of her back, as though the camera has momentarily lost its nerve and seeks protection behind her.

Marge advances slowly. She pauses, squinting at the scene before her, trying to make sense of what she sees. A big man works over a large power tool, his back to the camera. His body blocks what he is doing, but the surrounding snow is red, as is the spray exhausted by the machine.

Marge moves closer, the camera tracking her progress. Her cry of "Police!" is lost in the noise.

The tall man is forcing what looks like a human body part down into the machine, which expels blood and small red pieces of matter into the snow. Behind the man lies something unspeakable covered by a tarp; only a bit of rubbery-looking pink is showing.

The man doesn't hear Marge. The camera closes in, and we see that the working figure is Gaear. The foot that protrudes from the basin of the huge wood chipper we may presume is Carl's. Gaear ducks out of and into the frame to find a piece of log, which he then uses to jam Carl's leg deeper into the machine. He is still unaware of Marge's presence. Marge yells a couple of times, and finally Gaear's head turns to see the police chief, her gun extended. Marge gestures to the insignia on her hat. Gaear throws the log in his hands at Marge, who ducks it easily. He then turns his back and runs toward the snow-topped lake. It is worth noting that Gaear runs from no one throughout the film, save this one pregnant, middle-aged detective. Marge shoots twice. The second shot brings him down. A long shot of Marge crossing the lake to her suspect dissolves into the view from behind the wheel of Marge's prowler. The horizon is an endless snowy wasteland. Marge glances at Gaear's face reflected in her rearview mirror; behind the police grille it is stone cold, impassive.

Marge talks to herself more than to her prisoner in the sequence which follows. She remembers the dead and mourns their loss "for a little bit of money." Her face is despairing. "There's more to life than a little money, you know." Gaear turns his head, not in response to her words, but to view the large sculpture of Paul Bunyan that guards Brainerd's threshold. The ax that Bunyan shoulders, the deadness of the wooden eyes, and the outsized dimensions of the statue link Gaear to it; he is a nightmare version of the town's mascot.

Sirens are heard in the distance. Marge pulls over. The police vehicles crest the ridge and move in slow motion toward Marge's prowler in a shot that echoes the first of the film. "I just don't understand it," Marge says, as the sirens get louder. Two squad cars and an ambulance pierce the dense texture of snow windswept across snow. The music swells as the image fades to white.

We cut to a high and wide shot of a nondescript roadside motel; a title informs us that we are outside of Bismarck, North Dakota. A jittery camera follows behind policemen as they ignore Lundegaard's attempts to postpone their entry and break into his room. They find him in his underwear, trying to crawl through the bathroom window. Lundegaard wriggles and thrashes about as they haul him out. They must wrestle the man in order to handcuff him, finally, on the motel bed. Throughout this procedure, Lundegaard sobs and cries and screams.

In the film's final moments, we join Marge and Norm in their bedroom.

Marge (Frances McDormand) advances toward a bizarre crime scene in *Fargo*.

The camera moves slowly toward the couple throughout the scene which follows. Norm is propped up in bed watching television; Marge joins him, making herself comfortable with some effort. "They announced it," Norm says. "So?" Marge asks. "Three-cent stamp," Norm tells her with a small smile. Marge is happy that his painting of a mallard duck has been chosen for this honor. Norm downplays his success, but Marge insists on giving his achievement its due. She tells him how proud she is of him, and the couple exchange I love you's while a sweet tinkly music box version of the film's theme music plays. The two gaze at the television screen, and Norm reaches out and rests his hand on Marge's stomach. "Two more months," says Norm. "Two more months," smiles Marge, laying her hand over his. Thus the film manages to end on a traditional Coen note. While the crime story has been neatly concluded, we are left with Marge and Norm's anticipation of childbirth and the changed lives which will follow, with a world of possibility, rather than a closed file.

Though the media attention *Fargo* generated made much of the film's historicity, the assertion that it is "a true story" is, in fact, apocryphal. Ethan Coen's introduction to the film's published screenplay opens with the line, "Speaking of true stories." A lovingly crafted meditation on the complex interplay among time, memory, experience, and perspective follows. The essay concludes with a description of *Fargo*. The film, writes Ethan, "aims to be both homey and exotic, and pretends to be true."[1] In the same way, when interviewed, Joel and Ethan sometimes pretend to be helpful. For example, following a discussion of the brothers' tendency to fictionalize, fudge, and otherwise direct faux facts to the public, the Coens told *Premiere*'s Peter Biskind in the magazine's March 1996 issue that *Fargo* was, indeed, based on a true incident. "We wanted," said Joel, "to try something based on a real story, and tell it in a way that was very pared down." "How close was the script to the actual event?" asked Biskind. "Pretty close," answered Joel.[2]

The Coens managed to dupe a number of critics on this matter of *Fargo*'s "factual" origins before journalists uncovered the ruse soon after the film opened. *Entertainment Weekly*'s Dave Karger offered a jocose explanation for the falsehood, which, he said, "let the director off the hook." "Without that setup," he wrote, "any viewer of the deathly cold, unapologetically violent film—about a botched kidnapping that leads to the deaths of five civilians and a state trooper before a pregnant police chief catches one crook shoving his partner's body into a wood chipper— would think [Joel] Coen was simply insane." Since nothing in their previous work suggests that the Coens enjoy anything that remotely resembles mental health, it seems unlikely the Coens have ever been concerned with *Fargo*'s potential to testify in this matter.

The invalidity of the Coens' claim is, however, inherent in the words that preface the film. In their assertion that the film depicts its story "exactly as it occurred," the Coens comment ironically on the limits of objectivity, while referencing Hollywood's long tradition of subjectifying history. The note also serves to locate the film as a text with links to other generic texts. *Fargo*'s skewed relationship to the crime docudrama and police procedural genres connects it to the Coens' work that precedes it, as do its abrupt shifts of tone. As in their first five films, the violence of some scenes is jarringly at odds with its comic absurdities. Unlike *Blood Simple, Raising Arizona, Miller's Crossing, Barton Fink*, and *The Hudsucker Proxy*, however, the violence of *Fargo* is heart-stoppingly realistic, relatively unmediated by the self-conscious artificiality that marks their previous work.

The motifs noted above relate *Fargo* to its predecessors, as do many more obvious, superficial similarities. The quirkiness of *Fargo*'s characters and the manner in which they struggle to escape the fates which surge toward them at every turn, the film's attention to the music of personal and regional speech rhythms, the focus on dialogue, the flawlessness with which even the most minor ensemble cast members perform their roles, and the sheer translucent beauty of *Fargo*'s images constitute such common threads. Generally, however, *Fargo* represents a significant departure for the Coens.

Miller's Crossing offered tantalizing glimpses of a Coen protagonist with whom audiences could form an emotional attachment; Gabriel Byrne's Tom is intermittently such a figure. Frances McDormand's Marge breaks new ground for the Coens. Initially as bland as the landscapes that define her environment, Marge evolves during *Fargo* to reveal strength of character, kindness of heart, a sense of humor, and an unambiguous moral authority. She is, in other words, the kind of traditional Hollywood protagonist heretofore conspicuously absent in the work of the Coens. It is likely that her presence in the film leavens its less-digestible elements for many viewers. McDormand's Marge may be the single most important reason why *Fargo* has been able to attract a wide audience.

Fargo's film style is also without precedent. The Coens' films prior to *Fargo* are distinguished by their marriage of the subjective dreamworlds that reflect their dual vision, and the historical dreamworlds from which are siphoned the countless images and modalities that the pair cheerfully cannibalize, revision, and retrofit. The films are self-consciously auteuristic products. Their stylized closed universes are patterned by technical choices that consistently foreground their authorship and self-reflexively reference the fictional status of their flamboyantly mediated worlds.

Fargo is, by way of contrast, what Ethan Coen calls their experiment in naturalism.[3] Unlike their previous films, whose nominal locales must be amended by such suffixes as "of the mind," *Fargo*'s transactions take place in locations unadorned by artifice. Storyworld events are related by a relatively self-effacing camera, which allows the viewer to inhabit *Fargo* in a manner heretofore impossible in a Coen film. The film's evocative framing and composition project an authorial subjectivity that is, for the Coens, quite restrained.

Much of the action is set on the Coens' home turf of Minneapolis, Minnesota, an area they have described as "Siberia with family-style restaurants." The Coens' familiarity with the region permeates the film, this knowledge replacing their customary stylized geographies with a layer of meaning that glazes the screen with a patina that reads, just as Ethan Coen intended, at once both homey and exotic. The way the bulkily clad actors move through frozen air, the stark bleakness of horizons wherein sky and snow blur to indistinguishability, the broad accents of midwestern diners as they linger over steaming smorgasbord—such details are imbued with a quirky specificity that allow the Coens their most subtle exercise in mediation.

The Coens' previous films feature storylines that click along toward a startling inevitability with the precision of a digital Rube Goldberg device; they are studies of the relationship between cause and effect as might occur in a universe only the Coens can imagine. In *Fargo*, certain storyworld events are allowed to remain extraneous to the plot. For example, the reunion between Marge and Mike and the revelations that stem from it go nowhere. Interestingly, its randomness feels almost stylized, the sort of thing the Coens might include to signify the entropy that characterizes "real life."

The Coens' version of real life, bizarre by any standard, thrilled audiences; *Fargo* returned more than $25 million in the United States alone against $6.5 million in production costs. Discussing the ironies inherent in the success of the low-budget *Fargo* following the box-office failure of *The Hudsucker Proxy*, William P. Robertson writes:

> It was as though the Coens' cruel and quirky cinematic universe had sprung a leak into their real lives and turned the boys into unwitting characters in one of their own movies: two independent filmmakers intentionally trying to make a commercial movie and it bombs; then turn around, and make an intentionally inaccessible movie, and suddenly they're laughing, slapping backs, and chatting it up with Joan Rivers on E![4]

Fargo was something of a critics' darling in 1996, as shown by the profusion of awards the film garnered in 1997. The Coens were presented with an Oscar in the category of screenplays written directly for the screen, while the same ceremony saw Frances McDormand win an Academy Award for best actress. Nominated were Roger Deakins for his cinematography, Joel and Ethan Coen for best director and best picture, respectively, both brothers for their film editing (under the pseudonym Roderick Jaynes), and William H. Macy for best supporting actor. The brothers won best director at the Cannes Film Festival, while the Australian Film Institute awarded *Fargo* best foreign film. The British Academy Awards honored Joel Coen with the David Lean Award for Direction. The Chicago Film Critics Association bestowed many of its highest honors on *Fargo*'s creators in 1997. Best actress, best director, best screenplay, best picture, and best original score (Carter Burwell) awards were received. The Golden

Satellite Awards judged *Fargo* worthy of best director, best picture, and best actress honors, while Independent Spirit Awards went to Roger Deakins for his cinematography, Frances McDormand and William H. Macy for best female and male leading roles, and to the brothers Coen for best director, best feature, and best screenplay. The list goes on: the Los Angeles Film Critics Association, the National Board of Review, the New York Film Critics Circle, the Writers Guild of America, and the Screen Actors Guild all paid tribute to the Coens' sixth effort.

More stylish than stylized, *Fargo* scored a direct hit with audiences and critics alike. The Coens had proven they could blast past unexpected commercial failure. What, Coen fans wondered, would the brothers of invention create to follow on the heels of unexpected success? The viewing public would have to wait two years for the Coens' next venture, *The Big Lebowski*.

CHAPTER 7

The Big Lebowski

The day following 1997's Academy Awards ceremony, Ethan Coen spoke with his good friend William Preston Robertson. "What're you going to do, you know? I mean if a movie like *Fargo* succeeds then clearly nothing makes sense, and so, you know, you might as well make whatever kind of movie you want and hope for the best."[1] Presumably, it was in this spirit that the Coens decided to follow their 1996 hit with *The Big Lebowski* in 1998.

The Coens wrote the film well before *Fargo*'s release. Written around the same time as *Barton Fink*, the project was conceived as a vehicle for John Goodman. The Coens delayed production of the film until such time as they could coordinate their schedules with those of their chosen crew and cast, several of whom perform roles written expressly for them as well.

Like their other films, *Lebowski* references a generous range of film genres. Ethan Coen notes that, like *Barton Fink*, *Lebowski* is "a kind of weird buddy movie."[2] It is, however, most indebted to the hard-boiled fiction of Raymond Chandler. *Lebowski* comes close to a straight parody of Chandler's central motif: a Byzantine plot line involves a world-weary detective protagonist whose search for the truth leads to encounters with a wide spectrum of colorful characters who span Los Angeles' social strata. One of Chandler's most famous novels, *The Big Sleep*, shares with *Lebowski* several elements. In the Coen film these components are retrofitted to accommodate the filmmakers' characteristically warped take on the material.

The film opens to the melodious strains of a cowboy chorus singing the classic "Tumbling Tumbleweeds" as the camera dollies languorously above what appears to be desert scrubgrass. Production credits over the image accompany the voice of Sam Elliott in a role the script refers to as The Stranger. His voice-over narration is performed with a Western drawl worthy of the bucolic verbiage he rolls off his tongue with obvious relish.

The camera catches up with a rather flawless tumbleweed as it rolls to the edge of a cliff and goes over. The camera cranes up to record the scene below—the unmistakable, bright-light grid pattern of Los Angeles. The Stranger has been introducing *The Big Lebowski*'s protagonist, Jeff Lebowski, who calls himself "The Dude" or, more simply, "Dude." The Stranger confides that "Dude" is a term "no one would self-apply" where he comes from. He chalks it up, however, as just one more oddity in a man he finds generally confounding. Equally mystified by The Dude's home, Los Angeles, The Stranger allows that that is probably why he finds the place so "durned interesting."

Several dissolves chronicle the tumbleweed as it threads through various urban venues on its way to the Pacific Ocean, where it commences to locomote leisurely along the shoreline. The Stranger promises us a story so stupefying that its very existence provides him with the fodder he needs to die a happy man, knowing he has been privileged to encounter such a tale. The events he is about to describe, he says, took place in the early nineties during the Iraqi conflict. The Dude, he says, is "the man for his time and place." While he makes this pronouncement, The Dude (Jeff Bridges), a long-haired individual who sports a tee shirt, shorts, and a bathrobe, stalks a carton of half-and-half at Ralph's Supermarket. The Stranger allows that The Dude is "possibly the laziest man in Los Angeles County, which would place him high in the running for laziest worldwide." A cut to The Dude at the check-out counter reveals that some portion of the half-and-half has been consumed in the store; the clerk eyes The Dude's white froth–rimmed mustache as he writes out his check and listens to a television broadcast of President Bush proclaiming that Saddam Hussein's "aggression will not stand." Sam's narration ends when he confesses he has lost his train of thought; this admission sets a fitting tone for *The Big Lebowski*, a film about a man whose sentences tend to trail away and whose intentions are, at day's end, seldom remembered let alone actualized.

The Stranger concludes his introduction, and the cowboy chorus wraps up its song as The Dude makes his way through the courtyard of his apartment complex, juggling his grocery bag and a bowling ball. He enters his apartment and flips on the light. Revealed behind him is a waiting figure. The Dude pauses on the threshold. A second man, emerging from beyond the edges of the frame, leaps on top of him, yelling.

The Dude is rushed by this man, blond and lank-haired, into the bathroom where his head is repeatedly submerged in the toilet. The intruder screams for money owed; money, he says, Bunny said he would be good for. "Where's the money, Lebowski?" the man yells. "It's down there somewhere. Let me take another look," The Dude replies, in what we will come to recognize as his characteristically laid-back hippie drawl.

The blond tells The Dude that his wife owes money to Jackie Treehorn, therefore he owes money to the same. The first man pees on the living room rug, an act which leaves The Dude much distressed. He tells the intruders that he has been confused with another Lebowski—a wealthy Lebowski with a wife named Bunny. They leave, calling The Dude a loser. "At least I'm housebroken," responds The Dude.

The film's title appears against a blackscreen festooned with neon starbursts. The image wipes up to reveal a set of bowling pins. In one of the film's most interesting sequences, a montage of bowling alley images accompanies the film's credits; Bob Dylan rocks on the soundtrack. Close-up shots of Brunswick mechanisms are juxtaposed with shots of gleaming surfaces: the ball-return depot, wooden lanes, the bowling balls themselves. Bowlers are caught in a slow-motion choreography of performance and celebration. Rental shoes are sprayed with disinfectant.

The music fades, and we watch as Donny (Steve Buscemi) bowls a strike and joins The Dude and Walter (John Goodman), who are sitting and discussing The Dude's recent encounter with the rug-peeing thugs who broke into his home. Walter, a heavyset man with tinted aviator eyeglasses and a vaguely military style of casual dress, agrees with The Dude: the rug, it seems, "tied the room together." Their noisily profane rehash of the event, occasionally peppered by comments from Donny, who is then silenced by the bullyingly critical Walter, leads to a decision. The Dude will find The Big Lebowski, the married-to-Bunny millionaire, and request that he assume financial responsibility for the ruined rug. For, as Walter bellows, borrowing heavily from George Bush's recently televised Gulf War policy statement, "unchecked aggression" requires "drawing a line in the sand."

We cut to an interior scene at The Big Lebowski's mansion where The Dude is treated to a short history of millionaire Jeffrey Lebowski's many achievements. A stunningly sycophantic assistant (Phillip Seymour Hoffman) reviews these accomplishments as he shows The Dude the great man's many plaques and civic awards. The Dude is especially taken with a photo of the Little Lebowski Urban Achievers, "inner-city children of promise ... without the necessary means for a higher education." Lebowski, his assistant tells Dude, is committed to sending them to college. "Think he's got room for one more?" The Dude asks. Actually, it turns out that

The Dude has been to college, but protesting, pot smoking, and bowling took up most of his time. He doesn't, he tells his host, remember much about it all. In a funny bit, The Dude drives Lebowski's assistant crazy by poking and stroking the wall mementos he has been specifically asked not to touch. Hoffman as Brandt, The Big Lebowski's fervently obsequious right-hand man, steals every scene in which he appears and is one of the film's best assets.

Lebowski (David Huddleston) bursts into the room, an aged, well-dressed man in a wheelchair. The Big Lebowski is yet another of the Coens' autocratic fat men who wield power from behind desks in over-sized offices. The Dude does his best to make his case: Lebowski owes him for the rug since the rug's defilement occurred as a result of the thugs mistaking The Dude for Lebowski. Lebowski is unmoved by this line of reasoning. More interested in establishing The Dude's employment record so that he may compare it to his own record of achievement, Lebowski is energetically unreceptive to The Dude's somewhat disjointed argument. "This aggression will not stand, man," The Dude protests. At The Dude's mention of his wife and the money she owes around town, Lebowski explodes. Lebowski's spendthrift wife, the Korean War, his work ethic, and The Dude's lack thereof are featured elements of the diatribe which follows. "Your revolution is over, Mr. Lebowski!" The Big Lebowski screams. "Condolences! The bums lost!" The Dude makes a laconic exit from the Lebowski mansion.

He is met in the gargantuan hallway by Brandt. The Dude tells him that the meeting went well. He has, he says, been instructed to choose a rug from the house for his own.

The Dude is waylaid on the way to his car by Mrs. Lebowski (Tara Reid), deep in the process of applying emerald green nail polish to her diminutive toes. Dismissing her companion, floating semiconscious in the swimming pool, as a nihilist, Bunny propositions The Dude in the crudest possible manner, offering to exchange oral sex for a thousand dollars. Brandt is apoplectic and hustles The Dude away as fast as possible. The Dude, for his part, voices an interest in finding a cash machine.

The following scene finds us back at the bowling alley once more. Donny bowls a strike and fades into the background as Walter shows up, quoting Theodore Hertzl and toting his ex-wife's Pomeranian. A characteristically blue-languaged discussion of this last circumstance ensues. "Over the line!" Walter bellows to Smokey, a member of an opposing team. Smokey and Walter argue over the charge, much to The Dude's disgust. He prefers to let the matter go. Not so Walter, who eventually pulls a gun on Smokey; this fellow is, says Walter, "entering a world of pain." "This is not 'Nam, this is bowling. There are rules," Walter says. Donny sees the weapon and quietly moves away from Walter and The Dude.

Walter loses it. "Am I the only one around here who cares about the rules?!" he yells, pointing his gun at Smokey. The Dude tells him to put the gun away, the police have been called. Walter releases the safety on his gun and holds it to Smokey's head until the man marks his score zero. "Are you happy, you crazy fuck?" asks Smokey. "It's a league game," says Walter quietly.

Out in the parking lot The Dude attempts to convince Walter that pulling a gun in the bowling alley was a bad idea. Smokey is a pacifist, The Dude explains, a conscientious objector in the war. And, says The Dude, the man has emotional problems. "Beyond pacifism?" Walter asks. As they pile into the front seat of The Dude's car, still arguing, a police cruiser pulls up behind them. Two uniformed policemen run into the bowling alley. Walter and The Dude continue to spar.

The screen fills with the image of the purloined Persian rug on The Dude's floor. The camera pans up to The Dude, who is stretching and fixing himself a White Russian. His phone messages provide audio accompaniment: Smokey, apologizing to The Dude for the action he has taken against Walter; Brandt requesting that The Dude get in touch; a bowling league official protesting the drawing of a firearm during league play. The Dude answers a knock at his door. It is a neighbor, there to invite him to his "dance quintet," his "cycle," which is to be performed at "the venue" he wanted. He wishes The Dude to attend and to provide him with "notes." The Dude sweetly agrees, nodding at this man, who looks much less likely than the average human being to be a dancer. He is, we learn, also The Dude's landlord. The Dude is behind on his rent, it seems. The Dude returns to his living room where he performs a bit of T'ai Chi and listens to Brandt leave another message: Lebowski wishes to see him, and the matter does not concern the rug.

The Dude meets with The Big Lebowski, who is in seclusion, gazing pensively into the fireplace of his beautifully appointed study, blanket over his legs. The scene is visually evocative of a similar one in Orson Welles' *The Magnificent Ambersons* (1942). After a rich display of soul-searching anguish, Lebowski tells The Dude that Bunny has been kidnapped. The Dude is shown a ransom note. Lebowski suspects that the culprits are, as The Dude puts it, "the carpet-pissers." Since The Dude is "in a unique position to confirm that suspicion," Lebowski wishes to pay him to be the courier for the ransom.

A flamenco-style guitar riff provides a sound bridge to the next scene. In the bowling alley a purple-clad Jesus Quintana (John Turturro) bowls

The Dude (Jeff Bridges), Walter (John Goodman) and Donny (Steve Buscemi) enjoy their favorite pastime in *The Big Lebowski*.

a strike. The event is filmed in slow motion replete with surreal sound effects; the soundtrack also features the Gypsy Kings' Latin-spiced version of the Eagles' "Hotel California." Quintana's bowling style is kinetically baroque, as is the victory dance and strut he performs for spectators. The Dude, Walter, and Donny are the targeted audience for Quintana's performance. Walter tells his teammates that Quintana is a convicted sex offender who had to inform his Hollywood neighbors of this fact when he moved in; in a quick flashback we see Quintana fulfilling this obligation.

The Dude explains his deal with Lebowski and brandishes the beeper he's been given. He is, he says, to receive $20,000 for his role as courier. The Dude opines that those who defiled his rug are blameless; he thinks the kidnapping is more likely to be a scam of Bunny's. Hearing this sets Walter off. His volatile disposition has already been ignited by the hapless Donny, who has confused Lennon and Lenin in his remarks. ("I am the Walrus," Donny repeats several times, in a helpful non sequitur.) Walter simultaneously accepts The Dude's theory as fact and manages to connect Bunny and her ilk with the Vietnam War. The Dude, exasperated, urges Walter to bowl. They are interrupted by Quintana, who strolls by in order to taunt The Dude and his companions. In colorfully obscene terms, The Dude's team is warned that they will lose the semifinal league match game to Quintana.

Back at home, The Dude dozes on his rug and listens to the 1987 Venice Beach League playoffs on his headset (the B side is marked "Bob," presumably Dylan.) He opens his eyes to find a beautiful woman and two men standing over him. A fist connects with his jaw. The blow coincides with the sound of a ball smashing bowling pins, which emanates from The Dude's tape recorder.

The first of two dream sequences in *The Big Lebowski* is thus initiated. Fireworks explode. The Dude flies high in the air above the night-lit sprawl of Los Angeles. Bob Dylan sings. The Dude spies the woman from his apartment ahead of him, riding magic-carpet style on his rug, and he swims toward her only to find a bowling ball suddenly attached to his hand. In a bluescreen effect similar to the suicide scene in *The Hudsucker Proxy*, The Dude plunges earthward and finds himself miniaturized, standing in a bowling lane with a giant bowling ball bearing down upon him. As a new delightful sequence begins; our point of view has shifted to The Dude's as he peers through the fingerholes of a rolling bowling ball inside of which he is trapped. The ball hits the pins, which go flying upward, thrown against a field of black.

A beeping sound is heard, and a red dot against the black field becomes a blinking light on The Dude's pager, which is going off. The Dude lies on his back on bare floor; the camera spirals overhead as our protagonist struggles toward consciousness.

Back in the now-familiar hallways of the Lebowski mansion, The Dude takes possession of the ransom money and a bulky mobile phone. He also gets a pep talk from Brandt. Bunny's life, he is told several times, is in his hands.

The Dude drives to Walter's security business (what else?) where his friend waits. Walter has a battered leather bag with him as well as an oddly shaped, brown paper-covered package. Walter gets in on the driver's side and shoves the leather bag at The Dude. "Take the ringer," Walter tells him. "The what?!" The Dude inquires. Walter screeches out of the parking lot.

The mystery bag contains Walter's "dirty undies ... laundry, the whites." Walter explains that the laundry will give "the ringer" weight. He tells The Dude that he thinks they ought not settle "for a measly fucking twenty grand ... when we can keep the entire million." The Dude gets excited over Walter's use of the word "we" and more agitated at what seems to be Walter's plan. "This isn't a fucking game!" The Dude exclaims. Walter tells him that it is a game and reminds The Dude of his theory that Bunny has kidnapped herself. The Dude begins to protest but is interrupted by the ringing of the mobile phone. The kidnappers are making contact.

The call does not go well. The Dude lets on that he is not alone, plus Walter screams at him midconversation, causing the caller to hang up. The Dude is upset about this. "Her life was in our hands!" he screeches. Walter tells him he's being "very unDude." He assures The Dude that the kidnappers will call back. "They're amateurs," says Walter derisively more than once. The kidnappers do call back with directions to the drop-off point. While they navigate toward the designated spot, Walter describes his plan to recover the girl and keep the money. "When we make the hand-off," Walter smirks, "I grab one of them and beat it out of 'em." The Dude is singularly unimpressed. Walter insists that the beauty of the plan is its simplicity. "Once a plan gets too complex, everything can go wrong," he explains, paraphrasing the detective in *Blood Simple*. "There's one thing I learned in 'Nam," Walter begins. He is interrupted by the mobile phone. It is the kidnappers again, with further instructions.

"What'd he say—where's the hand-off?" Walter asks. The Dude answers with his favorite expletive. There is, he explains, no hand-off. They are to throw the money out of the moving car. "No, we can't do that Dude," Walter murmurs. "That fucks up our plan."

The Dude tells Walter to forget about his beautifully simple plan involving the ringer. Grabbing the briefcase Lebowski has given him, he prepares himself as the car nears the designated drop-off point. There is a brief scuffle in the front seat of the car as Walter overpowers The Dude and sends the ringer sailing out the window. Walter gives some quick instructions to The Dude, who is swearing and sputtering with outrage. It seems that Walter's mysterious wrapped package contains an Uzi machine gun.

After giving The Dude a brief outline of his plan to assault Bunny's kidnappers, he urges The Dude to take the wheel. The large man bails out of The Dude's moving car. Walter and the gun hit the pavement separately. The machine gun begins firing, shooting up the back end of The Dude's car while inside the car, our protagonist struggles to avoid being knocked senseless by the heavy metal briefcase of ransom money careening around the car's interior. The Dude is working hard to get behind the wheel and retain control of the vehicle, but he is undone by the machine-gun fire. He is unable to keep the car from slamming into a utility pole. Behind him, back at the drop-off point, three figures on motorcycles emerge from their hiding place and take off in the opposite direction. The scene brings to mind the Coens' related use of an uncontrollable machine gun in *Miller's Crossing*.

The Dude staggers from the car and commences to run with the brief-case toward the disappearing kidnappers. "We have it!" he screams, hold-ing the case aloft. Walter is philosophical. "Aw fuck it, Dude," he says. "Let's go bowling."

A cut to the brightly lit and busy bowling alley finds Walter cen-tered in the frame. As he begins the baroquely choreographed prelude to his roll, a high, wide camera prowls down and forward toward The Dude, who sits on the bench. He stares despondently off into space, the mobile phone cradled on his lap. The phone rings and rings unheeded.

As the camera closes in on The Dude, Walter returns. Dude asks, in the relentlessly profane lexicon he and Walter regularly employ, what they are going to tell Lebowski. Walter at first affects not to know to whom The Dude refers, then asks what the problem is. The Dude is so exasper-ated by this question he can barely form a response. He manages to sput-ter his fear that the death of Bunny Lebowski will be the consequence of their failure to deliver the money. Walter, however, holds fast to the notion that Bunny has kidnapped herself.

"They posted the next round for the tournament," Donny says, rush-ing over. Walter begins a reflexive "shut the fuck up" until he realizes that he is interested in this information. He is not happy with what he hears. He is, in fact, furious that their next round is scheduled for Saturday. He is, he screams, Shomer Shabbos, observant of the Jewish Sabbath. Mean-while, The Dude is growing increasingly distraught. "They're going to kill that poor woman, man! What am I going to tell Lebowski?!" he agonizes. Walter dismissively opines that Bunny will come wandering home, tired of her game. Unable to engage Walter, who continues to discuss his oppo-sition to bowling on Saturday with Donny, The Dude beats an exasper-ated retreat. Walter and Donny follow him out.

Walter tells The Dude to tell Lebowski that they made the drop. Donny remembers the venture and asks how it went. "Went all right. Dude's car got a little dinged up," Walter replies mildly. The Dude explodes, Wal-ter mocks his concern that the kidnappers will "kill that poor woman," and Donny directs random questions of religious practice toward Walter. Walter gloats over the million dollars in the trunk of "our car."

The three men leave the alley for the parking lot, where Walter and The Dude are stopped cold by what they do not see. The Dude's car is gone. The mobile phone rings again, loud in the silence of their shocked disbelief. The Dude begins his walk home, carrying the chiming telephone.

The ringing phone is a sound bridge to the next scene. Two police-men sit side by side, staring at The Dude and his pealing telephone. The younger of the two policemen is wide-eyed and earnest; the older is quiet and overtly intrigued by The Dude's home environs. The officers seem to wonder why Dude is pointedly ignoring the telephone but are too polite to ask. The Dude describes his car. One of the policemen asks about valuables that may have been stolen along with the vehicle. The Dude tells the man that the car contained a tape deck and "a couple of Creedence tapes." And, he adds, there was a briefcase filled with business papers. Also, The Dude says, his rug was stolen. There is some confusion as to whether or not the rug was in the purloined car until it is established that the thefts constitute "separate incidents."

An incoming telephone message for The Dude eliminates the mystery of the rug's disappearance. A female voice identifies itself as Maude Lebowski and, after informing The Dude that she took his rug, requests that he see her. She will send a car. Maude's voice is aggressively patrician, recalling Jennifer Jason Leigh's vocal stylings in *The Hudsucker Proxy*.

We cut to a puddle on an industrial-looking dark floor. A man-shaped shadow falls across the spilled liquid. The stylized contrast between the patterns of light and dark creates a noiresque image reminiscent of those in *Blood Simple*. The camera pans up as The Dude enters; he is wary as he moves toward what looks like an open area of a downtown loft. His ingress is accompanied by a panting, breathless, tuneless female voice on the soundtrack, the musical equivalent of the art we are about to encounter. The Dude pauses to gaze at a paint-spattered canvas that lies on the floor.

A sound not unlike the effects the Coens have used throughout the film for those of accelerating bowling balls begins to build. The Dude looks behind him and up, then ducks to avoid an overhead oncoming object. It is a naked woman suspended from a leather sling that has been propelled the long length of the building along a ceiling track. As the woman traverses the area above the canvas, she flings paint down upon it: the Coens' version of a 1960s-style Fluxus-inspired art happening. Two assistants then help the woman down and out of her gear. They cloak her in a heavy robe, then stand at attention.

Once clothed, the woman approaches The Dude. We recognize the voice from his message tape: it is Maude Lebowski (Julianne Moore). She embarks upon a discussion of her work, which has, she says, been "commended as strongly vaginal." She wonders why men in general are, and if The Dude in particular is, upset or offended by reference to female genitalia.

Maude, speaking with the clipped precision of a thirties screen debutante, delivers a wide range of information to our hero, who takes everything in stride while he secures the necessary ingredients for a White Russian. From Maude he learns that the rug was a gift from her to her

deceased mother and therefore had to be recovered; that she is aware of
the kidnapping and of his role in it and believes that "the whole thing
stinks to high heaven"; that feminists such as herself enjoy sex, believing
it can be a "natural, zesty enterprise"; that her stepmother, Bunny, is a
nymphomaniac and former porn actress, having appeared with the floater
in Lebowski's pool, aka Karl Hungus aka Dieter (Peter Stormare), in a
Jackie Treehorn production of *Logjammin'*; that Bunny is involved with
said porn producer; and that Maude believes the kidnapping to be a fake,
and her father's subsequent embezzlement of the million dollars ransom
from the Little Lebowski Urban Achievers Foundation to be the consequence of Bunny's scam. Rather than make her father's indiscretion a police
matter, she proposes to give The Dude ten percent of the ransom if he
will recover the sum for her. She also apologizes for the crack on the jaw
The Dude suffered during her reclamation of the much-coveted rug and
urges him strenuously to visit her doctor, free of charge.

Maude's loft is one of the film's most entertainingly imagined envi-
ronments. Much about Maude is strongly suggestive of the dominatrix,
and her cavernous, hard-edged lair is reflective of activities Maude might
find "zesty." The artwork that ornaments the place deserves special attention; a huge painting of a pair of scissors, which looms against one wall,
is a funny visual gag.

The Dude and Maude's driver get chummy during The Dude's ride
home; he is comically pleased with the latest turn of events and happy to
be curled up with a White Russian in the corner of Maude's limousine.
The driver tells The Dude that they've been followed and points out the
blue Volkswagen now parked half a block behind the stopped limo. Coen
fans will no doubt remember a similarly stalking Volkswagen in *Blood
Simple*.

Before The Dude can process this information, he and his White
Russian are strong-armed from behind by a large uniformed chauffeur.
The Dude is muscled into yet another limo within which The Big Lebow-
ski and his assistant Brandt lurk. They are perturbed.

"Her life was in your hands," shrieks Lebowski, concerned because
it has come to his attention that the ransom remains undelivered. The
Dude says that the money was, indeed, handed over. He waxes incoherent for several seconds, babbling about the complexity of the situation.
"New shit," he says, "has come to light." He tells Brandt and Lebowski
that Bunny kidnapped herself. Lebowski stares at The Dude, dumbstruck.
Encouraged, The Dude continues to map out his theory: young trophy
wife owes money all over town, including to known pornographers, angles
to get more than the agreed-upon million, etc.

Lebowski and Brandt look unconvinced. When The Dude requests his pay in cash (he fears, he says, that the money will bump him into a higher tax bracket, though he must check with his accountant), Lebowski orders Brandt to "give him the envelope."

While The Dude involves himself in the process of unwrapping the contents of said envelope, The Big Lebowski expresses his wrath. The Dude, he says, has stolen his money and unrepentantly betrayed his trust. He plans, he growls, to tell the kidnappers that they must recover the money from The Dude. And, he adds, as The Dude discovers that the envelope contains a little toe with emerald green nail polish cocooned in cotton, "any further harm visited upon Bunny shall be visited tenfold upon your head."

A cut to a brightly lit coffee shop finds Walter and The Dude discussing the severed toe. Walter maintains that there is no reason to assume that it is Bunny's; he can, he says, get The Dude a toe by 3 P.M. that afternoon—with nail polish. He reiterates his basic themes—the people they are dealing with are amateurs, things are not as they appear. The Dude voices his fear that the kidnappers will kill Bunny, then come after him. "That's the stress talking," Walter tells him. Their argument escalates. A waitress comes over and asks them to keep their voices down—they are in a family restaurant. This remark sends Walter into a Vietnam War–inflected tirade regarding his First Amendment rights. The Dude takes this as his cue to leave, which he does, after apologizing to the waitress. Walter makes a loud point of staying to finish his coffee.

An arresting shot of The Dude's soapy toes pressed against the side of a bathtub opens the following sequence. Our hero is taking a bath and smoking a joint, surrounded by small lit candles and the soothing murmur which emanates from the "Song of the Whale" tape in his deck.

The phone rings. It is the police with the news that they have located his stolen car. Just as The Dude begins to drowsily exclaim over his good fortune, the sound of wood splintering is heard. He looks up to see that two men have entered his apartment and are busy smashing up electronics in his living room. "Hey, this is a private residence, man," The Dude yells dreamily. A third man now enters. He has a small scurrying creature on a leash. All three men are dressed in black and wear black leather boots. Men and beast enter the bathroom. "Nice marmot," says The Dude. One of the men picks up the marmot, and we recognize the nihilist/porn actor. He throws the marmot into the tub with The Dude, where it goes crazy, screeching, splashing, and biting in a frenzied panic. "Ve vant ze money, Lebowski," one of the men says, holding The Dude down as he attempts to escape the tub.

The marmot is removed. The men make German-accented nihilistic threats to The Dude. They believe in "nossink," they tell him, and are therefore capable of anything. Including cutting off his "chonson," which they promise to accomplish on the morrow if The Dude fails to get them their money. The men leave, one pausing to smash a final offscreen object on his way out.

A crane shot swoops slowly toward The Dude's battered car. Not only is the briefcase missing, but the barely viable automobile reeks. A vagrant may have used the vehicle as a toilet, the policeman in charge surmises. "You're lucky they left the tape deck though, and the Creedence," the cop says consolingly. A funny exchange follows when The Dude inquires as to whether the police are working on any leads. "Leads, yeah," the cop laughs. "I'll just check with the boys down at the crime lab. They've assigned four more detectives to the case, got us working in shifts!" By the time the cop finishes, he is laughing uproariously, rocking back on his heels as The Dude sadly watches.

"My only hope is that The Big Lebowski kills me before the Germans can cut my dick off," The Dude intones. The line is a sound bridge connecting the scene at the auto yard to the next, which features The Dude, Walter, and Donny sitting at the bowling alley bar. Though Walter seems to consider such mutilation a remote possibility, The Dude remains disturbed. He laments the fact that had he not pursued the matter, a pee-stained rug would be his biggest problem. A discussion ensues as to whether the Germans in question are Nazis; Walter is uncharacteristically subdued by The Dude's allegation that the men are nihilists. Walter recovers enough to note the illegality of the Germans' pet marmot. The Dude is not interested in talking about the marmot's unlawful captivity, consumed as he is by what he determines are far more pressing concerns. When The Dude, in his extremism, minimizes the importance of the impending bowling tournament, Walter and Donny leave him to go find a lane.

The Dude orders another drink, and the camera pulls in close. "Tumbling Tumbleweeds" begins. When the camera pulls back, Sam Elliott is sitting on the stool that Donny has vacated. The Stranger wears a cowboy hat, denim shirt, and leather vest; his thick drawl matches the outfit. He orders a sarsaparilla.

The Stranger offers a sympathetic Western homily to The Dude, and mutual appreciation is expressed regarding each man's personal style. The cowboy has one criticism. He wonders why The Dude must "use s'many cuss words." At The Dude's "What the fuck are you talking about?" the cowboy smiles indulgently, bids The Dude "take 'er easy," and exits.

A phone call comes into the bar for The Dude; when he reaches for the phone "Tumbling Tumbleweeds" ends. Maude Lebowski is on the line. After noting that The Dude has not seen her doctor, she tells him that she would like to see him.

At Maude's warehouse space, The Dude meets a British friend of hers, a thin man with an extremely high-pitched giggle. This sound intermittently punctuates The Dude's subsequent conversation with Maude, who arrives home with what looks like found material for her art. The Dude says that it seems her mother really was kidnapped after all. Maude objects to both the theory and his use of the term "mother." She believes Bunny to be the perpetrator rather than the victim. The Dude tells her that he has evidence. She correctly identifies the source of his information—the head nihilist, Bunny's co-star in *Logjammin'*. She directs him to an album the man made with a group called Autobahn in the mid-seventies, a techno-pop recording called *Nagelbett*. Maude surmises that this man is pretending to be the kidnapper; she considers it unlikely that Bunny would be abducted by an acquaintance. When she asks if this man has the ransom, The Dude equivocates.

Maude changes the subject, suddenly urging The Dude to see her doctor lest he eventually suffer from "aftereffects." The scene closes as Maude and her friend take a phone call and commence to cackle together.

A short scene follows. The Dude visits Maude's doctor, where he is asked to slide down his shorts despite the fact that his is a jaw injury.

A little later, The Dude is seen driving, happily bobbing his head to a Creedence tape while simultaneously drinking and smoking. He checks his rearview mirror and discovers that the blue Volkswagen is once again behind him. He flicks the butt of his joint toward the window, which is closed. The butt bounces off the glass and lands on The Dude's lap. The Dude slaps at it and screams. The butt rolls between his legs, and The Dude, failing to fish it out, dumps his remaining beer on the afflicted area to douse the ember. An exterior shot observes The Dude's car as it runs a truck off the road, straddles the curb, and then plows into a garbage can before coming to a halt. The sequence is an amusing lampoon of the slick vehicular accomplishments of The Dude's counterparts in more classically formulated detective yarns.

The Dude collects himself behind the wheel before attempting to exit. He discovers that his passenger door will no longer open. He also discovers a piece of paper tucked between the front and back cushions of the driver's seat. The blue Volkswagen is gone. The Dude smoothes the paper and blinks several times at it. It is a piece of lined spiral notebook paper upon which is inscribed Larry Sellers' fifth-period History essay on "The Louisiana Purchase," an effort that has earned its author a D.

The screen whites out to be followed by the image of a white screen, behind which is performed a modern dance. The Dude's landlord emerges from behind the backlit screen, rotund and pale in a white bodystocking adorned with strategically placed foliage. A reverse angle shot captures Donny's open-mouthed attention to the man's awkward prancing; behind him The Dude gives the stage his serious attention. Walter, dressed in a brown suit and tie, enters the sparsely populated auditorium and sits down next to The Dude. He gives our hero an address. He has located the youthful car thief who, it seems, is the offspring of a television series writer known primarily for his work on "Branded." Walter's proposition, delivered along with his customary brutal and profane admonitions to the hapless Donny, is that they go to the ninth-grader's home (fortuitously near an In and Out Burger restaurant), recover what is left of the million dollars ransom, and cap the evening off with "some burgers, some beers, a few laughs." He tells The Dude that their troubles are over.

We are on a tree-lined neighborhood street. The Dude, Walter, and Donny park loudly at the curb, and we get a good look at the front of The Dude's car—it appears to be a bungee cord short of complete disintegration. Across the street a Corvette sits in front of a modest house. The Dude is quite unhappy about this fact, but Walter assures him that plenty of money may still be recovered.

At young Larry's house, Walter introduces himself and his associate, Jeffrey Lebowski, to the trusting woman who greets them. They've come to discuss little Larry, Walter tells her, and she cheerfully allows them in.

Walter is at once focused upon the man in the iron lung at the far end of the living room. The sounds of a rhythmic compressor fill the small space. Walter reverently identifies the writer to The Dude before loudly greeting the invalid. He asks the woman if the man still writes. She says no—he has health problems. Walter attempts a speech meant to laud the great impact "Branded" had on their lives; it is interrupted by the entrance of Larry, an implacable, rather large fifteen-year-old.

The woman tells Larry to sit down, these men are the police. Walter breaks in and says that he didn't mean to give her the impression that they were the police, exactly. They are, he says, hoping to avoid any police involvement.

An interrogation of sorts begins. Walter is point man. He dangles Larry's homework, now pressed in a ziploc bag, in front of the boy and asks him repeatedly to identify the page. The Dude gets fed up and opts for a more direct, typically profane approach. Their efforts elicit absolutely no response from the boy, who stares at them without expression.

Walter asks the boy if he has ever heard of Vietnam. He is, Walter tells him, about to enter a world of pain. The Dude threatens to castrate the young man, while Walter warns him that he is killing his father.

Walter replaces the homework in his attaché case and says that it is time for plan B. The Dude looks up uncomprehendingly. He follows Walter outside and stands on the front lawn. Walter screams continuously during the following sequence; he repeats an especially offensive, unprintably obscene phrase over and over again while attacking the red Corvette with a crowbar he has removed from the trunk of The Dude's car. The shadow of young Larry is discernible through the window of his house as he observes from his living room.

Lights go on in houses up and down the street as Walter escalates his ferocious assault on the car. A man in a tee shirt and shorts races over to Walter from the house next door and grabs the crowbar. He, too, is screaming. It seems the car is his—new the previous week. Walter is disconcerted. The man is enraged. He will, he shrieks, kill Walter's "fuckeen car." He takes the crowbar to The Dude's luckless vehicle; Donny leaps out, terrified. The scene, a nightmare version of *Raising Arizona*'s early precedent, ends on the sound of an especially violent crash.

After a fleeting blackscreen, we are peering into The Dude's car through its missing windshield. Donny and Walter are serenely munching In and Out burgers. The Dude drives with stoic resignation, staring straight ahead at the road, his shoulder-length hair blowing in the breeze created by the absent portion of his vehicle. A Santana pop song provides a jaunty musical counterpoint to the scene.

We cut to The Dude in his apartment. He talks on the phone while he pounds nails into a board. The Dude, we learn from his conversation with Walter, plans on handling the situation by himself from now on. We see that The Dude has nailed the board into his floor a few feet from and parallel to his front door. He braces a straightback chair underneath the knob of the door and against the board. Immediately the door swings open. It opens outward, away from the chair, which falls to the floor.

Two large men enter. They are The Dude's original intruders, the rug pee-ers. They issue a rather rude summons from Jackie Treehorn. The screen goes dark.

Against a black background, the night sky as it turns out, a young topless woman is blanket-tossed by a circle of men. After several angles of this activity, a long shot reveals a sixties-style bacchanal in progress on the beach. The revelry unfolds in slow motion; the effect is more grotesque than enticing. As the high and wide camera pans down, a man walks toward us. Tanned and well-dressed, he greets The Dude and introduces himself as Jackie Treehorn (Ben Gazzara).

Treehorn's home is admired by The Dude, for whom the 1960s minimalist modern decor holds great appeal. After a short conversation regarding the current state of the pornographic arts, Treehorn gets down to business. He wants to know where Bunny is. He doesn't believe the kidnapping story. He contends that Bunny's absence is related to the money she owes him. He believes that The Dude is involved in a plot to somehow extract funds from The Big Lebowski, and, he growls, he wants a share of it. In response, The Dude rambles in a noncommittal fashion.

A phone call comes in for Treehorn, who excuses himself and sits with his back to The Dude at a counter. While he talks in hushed tones he writes something on a pad of paper; that The Dude's eye is drawn to this pad is conveyed with an old-fashioned eye-line match to close-up sequence. Treehorn leaves the room. The Dude dances with exaggerated stealth to the counter and, in best spy tradition, traces over the top page of the pad with a pencil. Revealed is an obscene anatomical sketch. The Dude emits a small sound of surprise before a noise from the adjacent room sends him scurrying back to his place on the sofa, where he assumes a self-consciously nonchalant pose. He has stuffed the picture in his pocket.

Treehorn returns and fixes The Dude a White Russian. The Dude negotiates a ten percent finder's fee for locating the ransom money. He then tells Treehorn that the money is being held by a fifteen-year-old named Larry Sellers and describes where he can be found. He requests his fifty grand. When he tries to get up, he stumbles backward, prompting him to compliment Treehorn on the quality of his drinks. Treehorn expresses his dissatisfaction with The Dude's information. Meanwhile, The Dude is increasingly woozy. Treehorn has been joined by his two henchmen, who listen impassively to The Dude voice his regret over the loss of his rug, which, he reiterates, really tied the room together. He pitches forward and falls onto a glass coffee table. A shot from underneath the table affords us a view of The Dude's insensate, squished face. The image wavers and darkens toward blackout; Sam Elliott's cowboy drawl colorfully describes The Dude's loss of consciousness: "darker 'n a black steer's tuchus on a moonless prairie night. There was no bottom."

The Big Lebowski's second dream sequence begins with a black screen. What looks something like a lunar eclipse evolves into a bowling pin traveling past a gleaming bowling ball. A title appears: "Jackie Treehorn Presents." It is followed by three more titles that announce The Dude and Maude Lebowski's appearance in *Gutterballs*. The title logo is now a suggestively erect bowling pin flanked by a pair of bowling balls. Kenny Rogers and the First Edition perform "Just Dropped In" in the background.

The Dude enters a gargantuan stone alley; his dancing form throws a surreal shadow against the floor and wall. He is dressed as a cable repairman à la the protagonist in *Logjammin'*. The Dude is made ecstatic by a tower of rental bowling shoes that extends for miles upward toward the moon. He accepts a pair of shoes from Saddam Hussein, who wears a bowling shirt with his first name embroidered across the front pocket.

The Dude is performing a psuedoerotic dance down a black-and-white harlequin-checked staircase suspended against a starry night sky. Opposite him a troupe of Busby Berkeley–style, elaborately costumed female dancers are arranged around Maude Lebowski, who is dressed in an armored breastplate, Norse headgear, and pigtails. A trident is wielded with authority. The dancers perform an intricate routine around Maude; an overhead shot captures its circle-within-a circle design.

The Dude is now in the dancers' midst. He presses himself behind Maude and guides her as she releases a bowling ball. The dancers make their way onto a burnished bowling alley, where they straddle the lane, their legs becoming a tunnel leading to the bowling pins at the end. The camera begins to glide between the dancers' legs. Then, The Dude replaces the camera. Levitating inches off the lane, arms at his sides, The Dude sails between the dancers' legs, face down. He rotates in space, so that he faces upward, looking up the dresses of the chorines. An overhead shot records The Dude as he happily floats slowly down the lane. He spins again, heading toward the pins, which scatter as he hits them. The screen goes black. A topless woman falls into the frame, followed by the three German nihilists, dressed in red spandex. They run toward The Dude, brandishing hugely oversized scissors. He runs in slow motion toward the camera, the three nihilists behind him, the four figures stark against a black background. Headlights emerge from the dark. The Dude is running headlong down a freeway at night. A police car pulls up behind him. Then The Dude is in the squad car's back seat. His head lolls on his shoulders with the motion of the car, and he sings the theme to "Branded."

We cut to the interior of a police station. The Dude is thrown onto the police chief's desk; he banks off this object to land awkwardly in a chair. The Dude's wallet is thrown to the chief, who inspects its contents. He asks if The Dude's Ralph's Shopper's Club card is his only I.D. and unfolds the obscene drawing on Treehorn's personalized notepaper. The Dude requests the services of a lawyer, preferably Bill Kunstler. The chief attempts to impress upon The Dude the extent to which Treehorn is an esteemed resident of the beach community The Dude has defiled by his presence. Because The Dude fails to respond with the proper degree of deference, the chief bonks his coffee cup off The Dude's forehead, upends his chair, and kicks at him. He reiterates his request that The Dude stay out of Malibu. To add insult to injury, The Dude must endure the Eagles in the cab on his way home. He expresses his extreme dislike of this music to the cabbie, who then ejects him from the vehicle.

As The Dude stands stranded beside the freeway, a red convertible zooms past him. The driver is Bunny Lebowski, dancing and singing as she drives to "Viva Las Vegas." A shot of the car's footwell highlights Bunny's well-groomed toes, all ten of them.

Finally home, The Dude approaches his door warily, for it is ajar. The Dude pauses in his doorway and groans; his place has been searched and trashed. On his way in, he falls flat on his face. He has tripped over his useless floor brace. Bare feet below a bathrobe hem walk into the frame behind The Dude's prone form. It is Maude Lebowski, who drops the robe and voices a simple command: "Love me." The screen goes dark.

"Tell me about yourself, Jeffrey," Maude says. "Not much to tell," drawls The Dude. The sound of a match being struck coincides with the return of image to the screen. The Dude uses the match to light a joint, which he then smokes in bed, his arm around Maude. He tells her that he authored "the original Port Huron Statement," not "the compromised second draft." He was one of the Seattle Seven, he tells her, then worked briefly in the music business before his career "slowed down." His recreation consists of "the usual. Bowl, drive around, the occasional acid flashback."

The Dude gets out of bed and Maude rearranges herself, wedging a pillow behind her and reclining with her knees drawn up to her chin. Meanwhile The Dude apprises her of the latest turns of events—Treehorn, he believes, searched his apartment after getting him out of the way, Larry Sellers has the money, etc. He adds what he tells everybody he talks to. The case, he explains, is complicated. "Lotta ins, lotta outs." To cope he has, he says, "been adhering to a pretty strict, uh, drug regimen to keep my mind, you know, limber."

When he tells Maude that he is close to finding her father's money, she drops a bombshell. The Big Lebowski has no money. The wealth was Maude's deceased mother's. Maude explains that her father proved inept at running businesses and so is allowed to help administer the charities but nothing else. Maude has him on an allowance. The missing money belongs to the foundation, not to Lebowski.

The Dude notices Maude's contortions. He asks if it's yoga. When Maude explains that these positions increase the chances of conception, The Dude spits out White Russian onto the floor of his apartment. Maude explains her reasons for wanting The Dude to father her child. She does not want a partner, nor does she want to see the father socially, nor get involved with someone who will have an interest in raising the child. The Dude remembers his visit to Maude's doctor and his unlikely request, which now makes more sense.

The Dude has a revelation. He goes to the telephone in his destroyed living room and calls Walter. He wants Walter to pick him up. Walter protests. It is, he says, Shabbos eve, and he's not supposed to drive. He only picked up the phone because The Dude indicated on his message machine that it was an emergency. The Dude threatens to quit the bowling team unless Walter shows up. He slams the phone down and exits his place.

Once outside he notices the blue Volkswagen parked a half block away. He strides briskly toward the car. The driver attempts to quickly start the vehicle. When that fails, he pulls out a newspaper and hides behind it. The Dude yells for the man to get out of his car, and this the man does. He is a balding middle-aged man wearing a shiny dark suit. The two men face each other in the street, each assuming positions that vaguely suggest Eastern-style defense stances. The Dude keeps yelling at the man to identify himself.

The man tells The Dude to relax. He is, he says, a fellow shamus. The Dude is stymied. "Like an Irish monk?" he asks. The man is confused. He says his name is Da Fina (Jon Polito), and he is "a private snoop." Like The Dude, he says. The detective goes on to profess extreme admiration for what Da Fina describes as "playing one side against the other side—in bed with everybody—fabulous stuff, man."

In one of the film's most amusing exchanges, The Dude asks who Da Fina is working for—Lebowski? Treehorn? Da Fina looks mortified as he explains that he is working for the Knudesens—a wandering daughter job, he says. He shows The Dude a year-old picture of Bunny Lebowski, aka Fawn Knudesen, looking about sixteen years old and wearing a high school cheerleader's outfit. He also shows The Dude a snapshot of the most desolate farm imaginable, starkly filmed in black and white. Bunny's parents think the photo will make their daughter homesick. "How ya gonna keep 'em down on the farm when they've seen Karl Hungus," The Dude intones. He tells Da Fina that the girl is missing, possibly kidnapped. Da Fina wants to pool resources, a suggestion summarily dismissed by The Dude, who warns him away from Maude. Walter's van pulls up, and The Dude climbs in. The yappy sound of a small dog is heard; Walter has brought his ex-wife's Pomeranian.

We cut to a booth in a brightly lit pancake restaurant where the three Germans sit with a thin, blonde woman. Dieter, the head nihilist, speaks first, ordering pancakes from the waitress. Coen fans will recall that the actor playing Dieter, Peter Stormare, had quite a yen for this menu item in *Fargo*. The camera slowly travels to the woman's cowboy boot–encased foot. The top of the boot has been cut away to accommodate bare toes swaddled in a bandage, which is bloody at the site of her small toe.

Meanwhile, The Dude, Walter, and the Pomeranian speed along in Walter's van. The Dude lays out his current theory to Walter; dramatically composed hypothetical flashbacks punctuate his speech. He suggests that The Big Lebowski chose him to handle the kidnapping precisely because he judged him incompetent. Lebowski, he says, doesn't want his wife back. The Dude tells Walter that he thinks he may have substituted a ringer for a ringer; he thinks Lebowski never put the million in the briefcase. A quick flashback has Lebowski furtively stuffing the briefcase with phone books during a lightning storm that creates spectacularly sinister shadows around the man.

Walter finds The Dude's musings interesting but fails to see why they constitute an emergency of the sort that would allow him to "legally" break the Sabbath. There follows a spirited discussion of Walter's conversion to Judaism, which The Dude lumps together with Walter taking care of his ex-wife's dog as symptomatic of Walter's refusal to deal with the reality of his divorce. Their discussion comes to an abrupt halt when they reach the Lebowski mansion. A red convertible we recognize as Bunny's has plowed into the stone wall of a large fountain; "Viva Las Vegas" blares from the car stereo.

Inside the Lebowski manse they find Brandt picking up Bunny's clothing from the floor. Bunny herself can be glimpsed prancing naked in the garden. Brandt tells them that Bunny was visiting friends in Palm Springs and never bothered to tell anyone.

The Dude and Walter confront The Big Lebowski with their suspicion that he used the fake kidnapping mounted by the nihilists to cover his embezzlement of foundation funds. Lebowski snidely tells them that they have their story, and he has his. His is that The Dude stole the million dollars. The Dude accuses Lebowski of attempting to pin it on him because he judges him "a deadbeat, a loser, someone the square community won't give a shit about." "Well? Aren't you?" Lebowski sneers. "Well, yeah," The Dude says.

Lebowski yells at them to leave, which they do, but not before Walter, having bellowed that he knows spinal injuries and Lebowski is faking his, attempts to prove this theory by wrenching the man out of his wheelchair. Lebowski falls flat on his face; the Pomeranian cheerfully licks the groaning man's neck.

We dissolve to a slow-motion shot of Donny bowling. He looks stricken and confused when he bowls a spare rather than a strike, and he walks rather dejectedly back to the scoring table where Walter is regaling The Dude with the differences as he sees them between 'Nam and the Gulf War. The Dude barely bothers to respond. He is busy painting his fingernails.

Quintana and a buddy approach the trio. He begins yelling and gesticulating; every now and then he makes a threatening move forward and is restrained by his friend. His obscene diatribe is focused upon the idea that the tournament match date has been changed not to accommodate any religious principle but to accomplish "psych-out stuff."

The Dude, Walter, and Donny leave the bowling alley for the parking lot. There they find The Dude's car in flames. In front of the car are the three nihilists. One has a boombox under his arm; the rhythmic techno-pop it emits imbues the image of the torched car with a suggestion of performance art.

"Well they finally did it," groans The Dude. "They killed my fucking car." Dieter, the lead nihilist speaks. "Ve vant zat money, Lebowski," he says belligerently. He is in possession of a theatrical-looking curved sword. The Dude tells the man that they know the kidnapping is a sham. After conferring with his colleagues, Dieter informs them that they still want the money. Donny is scared. He is reassured, surprisingly gently, by Walter. Threatened with bodily harm, Walter explodes. No hostage, no money, those are the rules, he screams, peppering this communication with the usual obscenities. One of the nihilists whines loudly that Dieter's girlfriend gave up a toe in order to help them obtain the money. "Is not fair!" he croons. Walter responds with customary gusto.

Walter again reassures the terrified Donny. The nihilists decide to rob the three friends and "call it eefen." The Dude and Donny take out their wallets and count out what money they have. Walter repeats "what's mine is mine" a couple of times. He taunts the Germans, who, to Donny's horror and The Dude's extreme annoyance, charge the trio. A fight ensues. The nihilists are, despite their threatening look and demeanor, inexpert fighters.

The fight is grotesque and brief. Its macabre climax occurs when Walter bites off Dieter's ear and spits it high into the night sky. The bowlers prevail. As the nihilists lie bleeding, Walter shouts to The Dude that they have a man down. Donny lies on the pavement, gasping, his hand clutching his chest. The Dude initially thinks Donny has been shot; Walter says that Donny is having a heart attack and sends The Dude to call for help. The camera recedes upward and backward, away from Donny, who is gently cradled by Walter. The screen goes black save for the lit neon designs that adorn the side of the bowling alley. Then these bright lights go dark as well.

We cut to The Dude and Walter sitting side by side before a large desk, the former in bowling attire and the latter in his customary paramilitary garb. Footsteps echo behind them, the sound bouncing off the stone walls of a highly formal cavernous anteroom and office. A pale thin man in a dark suit introduces himself. The mortician hands Walter a tastefully elaborate bill. Walter becomes enraged at the suggestion that they pay $180 for an urn in which to transport Donny's ashes to the place where they will be scattered. He asks if there is a Ralph's nearby.

We transition to a windy bluff above the Pacific. The Dude and Walter pick their way down a narrow path to the bluff's edge. Walter carries a large coffee can with a plastic top under his arm.

Walter delivers Donny's eulogy, a tribute to Donny's love of surfing and bowling. He cannot restrain himself from referencing Vietnam as well. He releases the ashes, which blow not forward into what Walter has called "the bosom of the Pacific Ocean," but backward into The Dude, standing to the side of and behind Walter. The Dude stands motionless. Walter looks back and sees what has happened. He apologizes and attempts to brush the ashes off The Dude, who explodes, slapping Walter's hands away and yelling. He sounds near tears as he tells Walter that he has made a travesty of the ritual. He questions in most scathing terms the relevance of the Vietnam War to Donny's untimely death. Walter seems truly miserable and remorseful. The scene ends with an awkward hug between the two men and a suggestion that they go bowling.

The camera now glides along the gleaming wood of a well-polished lane. We watch a ball hit a strike and, in a visually arresting sequence, watch the behind-the-scene mechanics that govern the smooth flow of ball and pin return. A man painstakingly burnishes the surface of a lane.

We cut to a medium distance shot of a man with his back to us, bowling a strike. The Dude walks into the frame. He orders from the bartender, who offers condolences. The Dude responds with an aphorism we recognize from his earlier conversation with the laconic Stranger. Lo and behold, The Dude turns to find just this man at his elbow. They exchange pleasantries. The cowboy wishes The Dude well. "The Dude abides," drawls The Dude and leaves.

The Stranger closes the film with a monologue that drips with the same baroque Westernisms of his opening speech. Addressing the camera, he rejoices that The Dude is "out there … takin' her easy for all us sinners." He wishes Walter and The Dude success in the following day's tournament, laments Donny's death, relishes the story he has delivered, and wraps up a loose end—Maude will deliver "a little Lebowski." After a moment's reflection on "the way the whole durned human comedy keeps perpetuatin' itself," the cowboy catches himself and ends what he calls his "ramblin'." He hopes we have enjoyed ourselves. The camera moves over The Stranger's shoulder, and we hear him order a sarsaparilla; we watch the bowler from before bowl another strike. The ball finds its mark with an exaggerated crack of the pins, and the screen goes black.

"Raymond Chandler's stories are about a guy traipsing around L.A., but we changed the private eye into a pot-smoking loser," the Coens told a newspaper reporter in 1998.[3] This transformation, the exchange of a drug-addled sloth for the kind of elegantly haunted, obsessively driven sleuth played to perfection by actors such as Humphrey Bogart, represents the kind of idea that drives *The Big Lebowski*. In place of Chandler's characteristically crisp narration, we get The Stranger's bleary meanderings; in place of a Chandlerian femme fatale, we get a shrilly pontificating feminist who creates "vaginal art." And so on. Thrown in for good measure are various characters who fairly beg to be pegged "outrageous": toe-severing German nihilists, a Hispanic sex-offending champion bowler, a nymphomaniac trophy-wife cheerleader from the hinterland. The most grating of the bunch is Walter, embittered veteran extraordinaire. Goodman's religious, paranoid, obscenity-spouting provocateur is tiresome in the way that sophomoric jokes are: behind the Coens' wish to shock is a raw neediness that eclipses all.

In a way, that is the central problem with *Lebowski*. Never before have the Coens seemed so eager to please, so willing to cater to a lowest-common-denominator comic sensibility. The result is dummied-down Coen brothers. *Lebowski* is ultimately a caricature of their distinct style of filmmaking, a movie that showcases many of the Coens' motifs with little of the wit with which the filmmakers have typically deployed them.

The Coens' mix-and-match, slice-and-dice appropriation of generic tropes figures prominently in their seventh film. Western, screwball, noir, and buddy flick are but a few of the kinds of films that donate bits to *Lebowski*. Dream sequences have always been favored by the Coens, and the Busby Berkeley–inspired dance number (reportedly inspired by Berkeley's choreography for the 1930 film *Whoopee!*) is a high point in the film. But though this funhouse tribute to the genre is entertaining as a set-piece, like the other disparate generic components of *Lebowski*, it fails to contribute toward a whole that is greater than the sum of its diverse parts. There is a forced quality to this most familiar of Coen aesthetic strategies. As a result, *Lebowski* veers toward something that approaches formulaic self-parody.

Actually, the film contains so many references to the Coens' body of work that one might make the argument that self-parody was not unintended. Unfortunately, these references do nothing but significantly increase *Lebowski*'s unctuousness quotient, as do the broadly conveyed pop cultural references and the aggressively absurd plot twists, delivered with an unsavory amount of self-congratulation. The Coens' previous films conjure dreamworlds within which surreal events flow organically, one to the next, toward inevitabilities that exude their own pretzel logic. The bizarre story elements and characters of *Lebowski* are freighted with a calculation new to the Coens; the film is an exercise in overbranding.

As with their other films, *Lebowski* turns a great deal upon its language. In films such as *Blood Simple*, *Raising Arizona*, and *Fargo*, the Coens explore the intersections of regional and personal rhetoric. *Lebowski*'s L.A. milieu provides no overarching vernacular. It is rather a linguistic melting pot within which swim both those who have adopted a vocabulary during the process of reinventing themselves and those who have been adopted by a vocabulary that has come to define them. The two Lebowskis, for example, father and daughter, speak as they do in order to distinguish themselves from those with whom they reject affiliation, "bums" and those uncouth enough to employ "the parlance of our times." Walter, on the other hand, is shaped by both a political vocabulary evolved decades before and the lexicon of the therapy we can presume he has had for his lively case of post–traumatic stress disorder.

The Dude has an interesting way with language also. Though his communication consists primarily of Vietnam-era, hippie pot-head unfinished sentences, throughout the film he regurgitates the phrases of others. Like the acid flashbacks he includes in his list of recreational diversions, the words of others are apt to spring from his lips as though his brain synapses occasionally fire messages on tape delay.

Marring *Lebowski*'s particular discourse on the Coens' ever-present fascination with the geometries of language and self-construction is an abundance of gratuitous obscenities. The constant barrage of foul verbiage is at best annoying and boring. At its worst, as in the scene where Walter bludgeons a Corvette to death with a crowbar, it is repellent.

Lebowski is not without attractions. Its music, courtesy of Carter Burwell and T-Bone Burnett, often works wonderfully well within each context. And, like the Coens' other films, *Lebowski* unfolds with a good deal of visual aplomb. The slow reverence with which cinematographer Roger Deakins films the polished surfaces of the bowling alley which, in the parlance of The Dude, ties the film together, is one of the best reasons to watch *Lebowski*. Unlike their previous movies, each of which is marked by a distinctive and consistent visual aesthetic, *Lebowski*'s visual style varies greatly from one part of the film to the next. Deakins and production designer Rick Heinrichs have worked to skillfully blend various disparate visual tones together, from gritty realism to ultra-stylization, and much in between.

Perhaps the most interesting thing about *The Big Lebowski* is the fact that it boasts more truth than *Fargo*. "*Fargo*," clarifies Ethan Coen, "which was allegedly based on real events ... in truth contains mostly made-up stuff. Whereas *The Big Lebowski*, which purports to be fiction, actually is based on real people and events."[4] The Dude and Walter are loose composites of three of the Coens' friends, while a fourth real live person, a friend of a friend, was actually able to trace his stolen car to the joyriding teenage perpetrator through the youth's graded homework left behind in the vehicle. The homework was, as in the Coens' film, archived in a baggie. This story, says the Coens, was the seminal event that inspired the *Lebowski* project.[5]

Reviews of the film were mixed. Paul Tatara, reviewing the film for CNN, speaks for many when he notes *Lebowski*'s failure to reach a standard set high by the Coens themselves. The brothers, he says, usually deliver films that are "visually and verbally inventive. ... for some reason rampant, unamusing profanities have taken precedence over their usual warped wordplay." He goes on to accuse the Coens of "simply throwing 'weirdness' at the screen ... one of the oldest and least difficult tricks in the book."[6]

Jack Kroll, writing for *Newsweek*, calls the film a catastrophe, an "overboiled cinematic stew" which suffers from "Multiple Parodosis."[7] Roger Ebert liked *Lebowski*. Writing for the *Chicago Sun-Times*, Ebert enthuses over the film's "large cast of peculiar characters and its strangely wonderful dialogue." The film is, he says, "weirdly engaging."[8] Janet Maslin of the *New York Times* had mostly good things to say about the film, as did Carrie Rickey of the *Philadelphia Inquirer*. And many critics expressed in one fashion or another the opinion that a second-rate Coen brothers film is still better than most.

Audiences more or less agreed. *The Big Lebowski* was a profitable film, despite the fact that it harks back to the Coens' pre–*Fargo* mode of orchestrated estrangement. Apparently, the Coens' unique take on "the whole durned human comedy" bowled over more viewers than might be expected given its unusual status—not in the same league as vintage Coen nor as accessible as *Fargo*.

Filmography

Blood Simple (River Road Productions, 1984, USA)

DIRECTED BY: Joel Coen; PRODUCED BY: Ethan Coen; WRITTEN BY: Joel Coen and Ethan Coen; EXECUTIVE PRODUCER: Daniel F. Bacaner; ASSOCIATE PRODUCER: Mark Silverman; DIRECTOR OF PHOTOGRAPHY: Barry Sonnenfeld; PRODUCTION DESIGNER: Jane Musky; MUSIC BY: Carter Burwell; EDITED BY: Roderick Jaynes (Joel Coen, Ethan Coen) and Don Wiegmann; FIRST ASSISTANT DIRECTOR: Deborah Reinisch; CASTING: Julie Hughes and Barry Moss; COSTUME DESIGNER: Richard Hornung; SUPERVISING SOUND EDITOR: Skip Lievsay; ASSOCIATE EDITOR: Arnold Glassman

THE PLAYERS: Ray (John Getz), Abby (Frances McDormand), Julian Marty (Dan Hedaya), Private Detective (M. Emmet Walsh), Meurice (Samm-Art Williams), Debra (Deborah Neumann), Landlady (Raquel Gavia), Man from Lubbock (Van Brooks), Mr. Garcia (Señor Marco), Old Cracker (William Creamer), Strip Bar Exhorter (Loren Bivens), Strip Bar Senator (Bob McAdams), Stripper (Shannon Sedwick), Girl on Overlook (Nancy Finger), Radio Evangelist (William Preston Robertson), Voice on Answering Machine (Holly Hunter)

SPECIAL EFFECTS COORDINATOR: Loren Bivens; SOUND MIXER: Lee Orloff; BOOM: Peter F. Kurland; GAFFER: Joey Forsyte; KEY GRIP: Tom Prophet, Jr.; BEST BOY: Richard Creasy; MAKE-UP: Jean Ann Black; WARDROBE DESIGNER: Sara Medina-Pape; SPECIAL EFFECTS MAKE-UP AND PROSTHETICS: Paul R. Smith; SPECIAL EFFECTS MECHANICAL: Michael K. Sullivan; SET DRESSER: Nancy Griffiths; SPECIAL GRAPHICS: Beth Perry; SOUND EDITORS: Skip Lievsay, Michael R. Miller; SPECIAL SOUND EFFECTS: Fred Szymanski, Jun Mizumachi; MUSIC COORDINATOR AND PRODUCTION: Murri Barber; RE-RECORDING MIXER: Mel Zelniker; DIALOGUE COACH: Lizanne Brazell; NEGATIVE CUTTER: Victor Concepcion; TITLE DESIGN: Dan Perri

Raising Arizona (Twentieth Century–Fox, 1987, USA)

DIRECTED BY: Joel Coen; PRODUCED BY: Ethan Coen; WRITTEN BY: Ethan Coen and Joel Coen; CO-PRODUCED BY: Mark Silverman; EXECUTIVE PRODUCER: James Jacks; ASSOCIATE PRODUCER: Deborah Reinisch; DIRECTOR OF PHOTOGRAPHY: Barry Sonnenfeld; PRODUCTION DESIGNER: Jane Musky; EDITED BY: Michael R. Miller; MUSIC BY: Carter Burwell; COSTUME DESIGNER: Richard Hornung; SUPERVISING SOUND EDITOR: Skip Lievsay; ASSOCIATE EDITOR: Arnold Glassman; CASTING BY: Donna Isaacson C.S.A. and John Lyons C.S.A.

THE PLAYERS: H.I. (Nicolas Cage), Ed (Holly Hunter), Nathan Arizona, Sr. (Trey Wilson), Gale (John Goodman), Evelle (William Forsythe), Glen (Sam McMurray), Dot (Frances McDormand), Leonard Smalls (Randall "Tex" Cob), Nathan Junior (T.J. Kuhn, Jr.), Florence Arizona (Lynne Dumin Kitei), Prison Counselor (Peter Benedek), Nice Old Grocery Man (Charles "Lew" Smith), Younger FBI Agent (Warren Keith), Older FBI Agent (Henry Kendrick), Ear-Bending Cellmate (Sidney Dawson), Parole Board Chairman (Richard Blake), Parole Board Members (Troy Nabors, Mary Seibel), Hayseed in the Pickup (John O'Donnal), Whitey (Keith Jandacek), Minister (Warren Forsythe), "Trapped" Convict (Ruben Young), Policemen in Arizona House (Dennis Sullivan, Dick Alexander) Feisty Hayseed (Rusty Lee), Fingerprint Technician (James Yeater), Reporters (Bill Andres, Carver Barnes), Unpainted Secretary (Margaret H. McCormack), Newscaster (Bill Rocz), Payroll Cashier (Mary F. Glenn), Scamp with Squirt Gun (Jeremy Babendure), Adoption Agent (Bill Dobbins), Gynecologist (Ralph Norton), Mopping Convict (Henry Tank), Supermarket Manager (Frank Outlaw), Varsity Nathan Jr. (Todd Michael Rodgers), Machine Shop Ear Bender (M. Emmet Walsh), Glen and Dot's Kids (Robert Gray, Katie Thrasher, Derek Russell, Nicole Russell, Zachary Sanders, Noell Sanders), Arizona Quints (Cody Ranger, Jeremy Arendt, Ashley Hammon, Crystal Hiller, Olivia Hughes, Emily Malin, Melanie Malin, Craig McLaughlin, Adam Savageau, Benjamin Savageau, David Schneider, Michael Stewart), And Featuring the Amazing Voice of (William Preston Robertson)

STUNT COORDINATOR: Jery Hewitt; STUNT PLAYERS: Jery Hewitt, Bill Anagnos, Curt Bortel, Shane Dixon, Allan Graf, Cindy Wills Hartline, Gene Hartline, Jeff Jensen, Edgard Mourino, Ron Nix, Spanky Spangler; PRODUCTION MANAGER: Kevin Dowd; PRODUCTION SUPERVISOR: Alma Kuttruff; PRODUCTION AUDITOR: Barbara-Ann Stein; FIRST ASST. DIRECTORS: Deborah Reinisch, Kelly Van Horn; CAMERA OPERATOR: David M. Dunlap; PRODUCTION SOUND MIXER: Allan Byer; BOOM OPERATOR: Peter F. Kurland; RECORDIST: Greg Horn; RE-RECORDING MIXER: Mel Zelniker; GAFFER: Russell Engels; BEST BOY: Kenneth R. Conners; ART DIRECTOR: Harold Thrasher; SET DECORATOR/DRAFTPERSON: Robert Kracik; STORYBOARD ARTIST: J. Todd Anderson; MAKE-UP: Katherine James-Cosburn; HAIR: Dan Frey; COSTUME CONSTRUCTION: Mary Ann Ahern; SPECIAL EFFECTS: Image Engineering Inc.; SPECIAL EFFECTS COORDINATOR: Peter Chesney; ANIMAL ACTION BY: Karl Lewis Miller; ARIZONA CASTING: Sunny Seibel; EXTRAS CASTING: Becca Korby-Sullivan; DIALECT COACH: Julie Adams; SOUND EDITORS: Philip Stockton, Magdaline Volaitis, Ron Bochar; FIRST ASST. EDITOR: Michael Berenbaum; ASST. EDITOR: Kathie Weaver; ASST. SOUND EDITORS: Bruce Pross, Marissa Littlefield, Steven Visscher, Christopher Weir; SPECIAL ELECTRONIC SOUND EFFECTS: Frederick Szymanski, Jun Mizumachi, Carl Mandelbaum; FOLEY ARTIST: Marko A. Costanzo; NEGATIVE CUTTING: J. G. Films, Inc.; TITLE DESIGN BY: Dan Perri; MUSIC ENGINEERING: Sebastian Niessen; BANJO: Ben Freed; JEWS HARP, GUITAR: Mieczyslaw Litwinski; YODELING: John R. Crowder

Miller's Crossing (Twentieth Century–Fox, 1990, USA)

DIRECTED BY: Joel Coen; PRODUCED BY: Ethan Coen; WRITTEN BY: Joel Coen and Ethan Coen; CO-PRODUCED BY: Mark Silverman; LINE PRODUCER: Graham Place; EXECUTIVE PRODUCER: Ben Barenholtz; DIRECTOR OF PHOTOGRAPHY: Barry Sonnenfeld; PRODUCTION DESIGNER: Dennis Gassner; COSTUME DESIGNER: Richard Hornung; EDITED BY: Michael R. Miller; MUSIC BY: Carter Burwell; "DANNY BOY" SUNG BY: Frank Patterson; SUPERVISING SOUND EDITOR: Skip Lievsay; CASTING BY: Donna Isaacson, C.S.A. and John Lyons, C.S.A.

THE PLAYERS: Tom Reagan (Gabriel Byrne), Verna (Marcia Gay Harden), Bernie Bernbaum (John Turturro), Johnny Caspar (Jon Polito), Eddie Dane (J.E. Freeman), Leo (Albert Finney), Frankie (Mike Starr), Tie-Tac (Al Mancini), Mink (Steve Buscemi), Clarence "Drop" Johnson (Mario Todisco), Tad (Olek Krupa), Adolph (Michael Jeter), Terry (Lanny Flaherty), Mrs. Caspar (Jeanette Kontomitras), Johnny Caspar, Jr. (Louis Charles Mounicou), Cop—Brian (John McConnell), Cop—Delahanty (Danny Aiello III), Screaming Woman (Helen Jolly), Landlady (Hilda McLean), Gunmen in Leo's House (Monte Starr, Don Picard), Rug Daniels (Salvatore H. Tornabene), Street Urchin (Kevin Dearie), Caspar's Driver (Michael Badalucco), Caspar's Butler (Charles Ferrara), Caspar's Cousins (Esteban Fernandez, George Fernandez), Hitman at Verna's (Charles Gunning), Hitman #2 (Dave Drinkx), Lazarre's Messenger (David Darlow), Lazzare's Toughs (Robert LaBrosse, Carl Rooney), Man with Pipe Bomb (Jack David Harris), Son of Erin (Jery Hewitt), Snickering Gunman (Sam Raimi), Cop with Bullhorn (John Schnauder, Jr.), Rabbi (Zolly Levin), Boxers (Joey Ancona, Bill Raye), Voice (William Preston Robertson), Secretary (uncredited) (Frances McDormand)

STUNT COORDINATOR: Jery Hewitt; STUNT PLAYERS: Gary Tacon, Norman Douglass, Nick Giangiulio, Kurt Bryant, Bill Anagnos, Roy Farfel; PRODUCTION MANAGER: Alma Kuttruff; FIRST ASST. DIRECTORS: Gary Marcus; CAMERA OPERATOR: Barry Sonnenfeld; PRODUCTION SOUND MIXER: Allan Byer; BOOM OPERATOR: Peter F. Kurland; RECORDIST: Jean Marie Carroll; RE-RECORDING MIXER: Lee Dichter; ART DIRECTOR: Leslie McDonald; SET DECORATOR: Nancy Haigh; STORYBOARD ARTIST: J. Todd Anderson; MAKE-UP: Kathrine James; HAIR: Cydney Cornell; SPECIAL EFFECTS: Image Engineering Inc.; SPECIAL EFFECTS COORD.: Peter Chesney; FIRST ASST. EDITOR: Michael Berenbaum

Barton Fink (Twentieth Century–Fox, 1991, USA)

DIRECTED BY: Joel Coen; PRODUCED BY: Ethan Coen; WRITTEN BY: Ethan Coen and Joel Coen; CO-PRODUCER: Graham Place; EXECUTIVE PRODUCERS: Ben Barenholtz, Ted Pedas, Jim Pedas, , Bill Durkin; DIRECTOR OF PHOTOGRAPHY: Roger Deakins; PRODUCTION DESIGNER: Dennis Gassner; COSTUME DESIGNER: Richard Hornung; EDITED BY: Roderick Jaynes (Joel Coen, Ethan Coen); ASSOCIATE EDITOR: Michael Berenbaum; MUSIC BY: Carter Burwell; SUPERVISING SOUND EDITOR: Skip Lievsay; DIALOGUE SUPERVISOR: Philip Stockton; CASTING BY: Donna Isaacson, C.S.A. and John Lyons, C.S.A.

THE PLAYERS: Barton Fink (John Turturro), Charlie Meadows (John Goodman), Audrey Taylor (Judy Davis), Jack Lipnick (Michael Lerner), W.P. Mayhew (John Mahoney), Ben Grisler (Tony Shalhoub), Chet (Steve Buscemi), Garland Stanford (David Warrilow), Detective Mastrionotti (Richard Portnow), Detective Deutsch

(Christopher Murney), Derek (I.M. Hobson), Poppy Carnaham (Meagan Fay), Richard St. Claire (Lance Davis), Pete (Harry Bugin), Maitre D' (Anthony Gordon), Stage Hand (Jack Denbo), Clapper Boy (Max Grodenchik), Referee (Robert Beecher), Rustler (Darwyn Swalve), Geisler's Secretary (Gayle Vance), Sailor (Johnny Judkins), USO Girl (Jana Marie Hupp), Beauty (Isabelle Townsend), Voice (William Preston Robertson)

STUNTS: Ben Jensen; PRODUCTION MANAGER: Alma Kuttruff; FIRST ASST. DIRECTORS: Joe Camp III; CAMERA OPERATOR: Barry Sonnenfeld; PRODUCTION SOUND MIXER: Allan Byer; BOOM OPERATOR: Peter F. Kurland; RECORDIST: Jean Marie Carroll; RE-RECORDING MIXER: Lee Dichter; ART DIRECTOR: Leslie McDonald, Bob Goldstein; SET DECORATOR: Nancy Haigh; STORYBOARD ARTIST: J. Todd Anderson; MAKE-UP: Jean Black; HAIR: Frida Aradotter; SPECIAL EFFECTS: Stetson Visual Services, Inc.; SPECIAL EFFECTS SUPERVISOR: Robert Spurlock; FIRST ASST. EDITOR: Tricia Cooke; FOLEY ARTIST: Marko A. Costanzo; TITLE DESIGN: Balsmeyer & Everett, Inc.

The Hudsucker Proxy (Warner Brothers, 1994, USA)

DIRECTED BY: Joel Coen; PRODUCED BY: Ethan Coen; WRITTEN BY: Ethan Coen, Joel Coen & Sam Raimi; CO-PRODUCER: Graham Place; EXECUTIVE PRODUCERS: Eric Fellner and Tim Bevan; DIRECTOR OF PHOTOGRAPHY: Roger Deakins, B.S.C.; PRODUCTION DESIGNER: Dennis Gassner; COSTUME DESIGNER: Richard Hornung; EDITED BY: Thom Noble; MUSIC BY: Carter Burwell; VISUAL EFFECTS PRODUCED AND SUPERVISED BY: Michael J. McAllister; MECHANICAL EFFECTS BY: Peter M. Chesney; SUPERVISING SOUND EDITOR: Skip Lievsay; CASTING BY: Donna Isaacson, C.S.A. and John Lyons, C.S.A.

THE PLAYERS: Norville Barnes (Tim Robbins), Amy Archer (Jennifer Jason Leigh), Sidney J. Mussburger (Paul Newman), Waring Hudsucker (Charles Durning), Chief (John Mahoney), Buzz (Jim True), Moses (Bill Cobbs), Smitty (Bruce Campbell), Aloysius (Harry Bugin), Benny (John Seitz), Lou (Joe Grifasi), Board Members (Roy Brocksmith, I.M. Hobson, John Scanlon, Jerome Dempsy, John Wylie, Gary Allen, Richard Woods, Peter McPherson), Dr. Hugo Bronfenbrenner (David Byrd), Mail Room Orienter (Christopher Darga), The Ancient Sorter (Patrick Cranshaw), Mailroom Boss (Robert Weil), Mussburger's Secretary (Mary Lou Rosato), Luigi the Taylor (Ernie Sarracino), Mrs. Mussburger (Eleanor Glockner), Mrs. Braithwaite (Kathleen Perkins), Sears Braithwaite of Bullard (Joseph Marcus), Vic Tenetta (Peter Gallagher), Zebulon Cardoza (Noble Willingham), Mrs. Cardoza (Barbara Ann Grimes), Thorstenson Finlandson (Thom Noble), Beatnik Barman (Steve Buscemi), Newsreel Scientist (William Duff-Griffin), Za-Za (Anna Nicole Smith), Dream Dancer (Pamela Everett), The Hula-Hoop Kid (Arthur Bridges), Hudsucker Brainstormers (Sam Raimi, John Cameron), Mr. Grier (Skipper Duke), Mr. Levin (Jake Kapner), Mr. Bumstead (Jon Polito), Ancient Puzzler (Richard Whiting), Coffee Shop Waitress (Linda McCoy), Emcee (Stan Adams), Newsreel Announcer (Karl Mundt (John Goodman), Newsreel Secretary (Joanne Pankow), Norville's Goon (Mario Todisco), Newsboy (Colin Fickes), Drunk in Alley (Dick Sasso), Mailroom Screamers (Jesse Brewer, Sean Eichtenstein, Ace O'Connel, Frank Jeffries, Phil Lock, Todd Alcott, Richard Schiff, Lour Criscudio, Michael Earl Reid), Newsroom Reporters (Mike Starr, Willie Reale, Tom Toner, Dave Hagar, Harvey Meyer, David Fawcett), Newsreel Reporters (Jeff Still, Gil Pearson, David Massie, Peter Siracusa, Michael Houlihan, David Gould, Marc Garber, Mark Miller, Nelson George, Ed Lillard), New Year's Mob (Wantland Sandel, James Duter, Rick Peeples, Cynthia Baker), Stunts (Jery Hewitt, Don Hewitt, John Copeman, Dean Mumford)

PRODUCTION MANAGER: Alma Kuttruff; ART DIRECTOR: Leslie McDonald; SET DECORATOR: Nancy Haigh; FIRST ASST. DIRECTOR: Victor Malone; STORYBOARD ARTIST: J. Todd Anderson; PRODUCTION SOUND MIXER: Allan Byer; BOOM OPERATOR: Peter F. Kurland; RECORDIST: Jean Marie Carroll; RE-RECORDING ENGINEERS: Michael Barry, Lee Dichter; MAKE-UP: Jean A. Black; HAIR: Cydney Cornell; CHOREOGRAPHER: Wesley Fata; 2ND UNIT DIRECTOR: Sam Raimi; GRAPHICS DESIGNER: Eric Rosenberg; DIALOG EDITOR: Fred Rosenberg; ASSISTANT COSTUME DESIGNER: Mary Zophres; SPECIAL MECHANICAL EFFECTS: Design FX Company, Emmet Kane; VISUAL EFFECTS CO-PRODUCER: Kat Dillon; MINIATURE EFFECTS: Stetson Visual Services, Inc., Mark Stetson, Robert Spurlock; BLUE SCREEN UNIT MANAGER: Edward T. Hirsch; CHICAGO UNIT MANAGER: Terri Clemens; DIGITAL COMPOSITING: The Computer Film Company; MATTE PAINTINGS: Mark Sullivan, Rich Cohen; DIGITAL MATTE IMAGES: Industrial Light & Magic; FIRST ASST. EDITOR: Tricia Cooke; FOLEY ARTIST: Marko Costanzo; MAIN TITLE SEQUENCE AND OTHER COOL STUFF: Balsmeyer & Everett, Inc.; MUSICAL THEMES BY: Aram Khachaturian

Fargo (Gramercy Pictures, 1996, USA)

DIRECTED BY: Joel Coen; PRODUCED BY: Ethan Coen; WRITTEN BY: Ethan Coen and Joel Coen; EXECUTIVE PRODUCERS: Tim Bevan and Eric Fellner; LINE PRODUCER: John Cameron; DIRECTOR OF PHOTOGRAPHY: Roger Deakins, A.S.C.; PRODUCTION DESIGNER: Rick Heinrichs; COSTUME DESIGNER: Mary Zophres; MUSIC BY: Carter Burwell; EDITED BY: Roderick Jaynes (Ethan Coen, Joel Coen); ASSOCIATE EDITOR: Tricia Cooke; SUPERVISING SOUND EDITOR: Skip Lievsay; CASTING: John Lyons, C.S.A.

THE PLAYERS: Jerry Lundegaard (William H. Macy), Carl Showalter (Steve Buscemi), Grear Grimsrud (Peter Stormare), Jean Lundegaard (Kristin Rudrud), Wade Gustafson (Harve Presnell), Scotty Lundegaard (Tony Denman), Irate Customer (Gary Houston), Irate Customer's Wife (Sally Wingert), Car Salesman (Kurt Schweiskhardt), Hooker #1 (Larissa Kokernot), Hooker #2 (Melissa Peterman), Shep Proudfoot (Steve Reevis), Reilly Diefenbach (Warren Keith), Morning Show Host (Steve Edelman), Morning Show Hostess (Sharon Anderson), Stan Grossman (Larry Grandenburg), State Trooper (James Gaulke), Victim in Field (J. Todd Anderson), Victim in Car (Michelle Suzanne LeDoux), Marge Gunderson (Frances McDormand), Norm Gunderson (John Carroll Lynch), Lou (Bruce Bohne), Cashier (Petra Boden), Mike Yanagita (Steve Park), Customer (Wayne Evenson), Officer Olson (Cliff Rakerd), Hotel Clerk (Jessica Shephard), Airport Lot Attendant (Peter Schmitz), Mechanic (Steve Schaefer), Escort (Michelle Hutchinson), Man in Hallway (David Lomax), Jose Feliciano (Himself), Night Parking Attendant (Don William Skahill), Mr. Mohra (Bain Boehlke), Valerie (Rose Stockton), Bismarck Cop #1 (Robert Ozaskyu), Bismarck Cop #2 (John Bandemer), Bark Beetle Narrator (Don Wescott), Soap Opera Actor (Bruce Campbell)

STUNT COORDINATOR: Jery Hewitt, Jennifer Lamb, Danny Downey; PRODUCTION MANAGER: Gilly Ruben; ART DIRECTOR: Thomas P. Wylkins; SET DECORATOR: Lauri Gaffin; FIRST ASST. DIRECTOR: Michelangelo Csaba Bolla; STORYBOARD ARTIST: J. Todd Anderson; CAMERA OPERATOR: Robin Brown; SOUND MIXER: Allan

Byer; BOOM OPERATOR: Peter F. Kurland, Keenan Wyatt; UTILITY SOUND TECH-
NICIAN: Knox Grantham White; RE-RECORDING MIXERS: Michael Barry, Skip
Lievsay:; MAKE-UP: John Blake; HAIR: Daniel Curet; COSTUME SUPERVISOR: Sister
Daniels; SPECIAL EFFECTS COORDINATOR: Paul Murphy; DIALECT COACH: Eliza-
beth Himmelstein; FIRST ASST. EDITOR: Big Dave Diliberto; FOLEY ARTIST: Marko
Costanzo; TITLES: Balsmeyer & Everett, Inc.

The Big Lebowski (Gramercy Pictures, 1998, USA)

DIRECTED BY: Joel Coen; PRODUCED BY: Ethan Coen; WRITTEN BY: Ethan
Coen and Joel Coen; EXECUTIVE PRODUCERS: Tim Bevan and Eric Fellner; CO-
PRODUCER: John Cameron; DIRECTOR OF PHOTOGRAPHY: Roger Deakins, A.S.C.,
B.S.C.; PRODUCTION DESIGNER: Rick Heinrichs; COSTUME DESIGNER: Mary
Zophres; ORIGINAL MUSIC BY: Carter Burwell; MUSICAL ARCHIVIST: T-Bone Bur-
nett; EDITED BY: Roderick Jaynes (Ethan Coen, Joel Coen), Tricia Cooke; SUPER-
VISING SOUND EDITOR: Skip Lievsay; CASTING: John Lyons, C.S.A.
THE PLAYERS: The Dude (Jeff Bridges), Walter Sobchak (John Goodman),
Maude Lebowski (Julianne Moore), Donny (Steve Buscemi), The Big Lebowski
(David Huddleston), Brandt (Philip Seymour Hoffman), Bunny Lebowski (Tara
Reid), Treehorn Thugs (Philip Moon, Mark Pellegrino), Nihilists (Peter Stormare,
Flea, Torsten Voges), Smokey (Jimmy Dale Gilmore), Dude's Landlord (Jack Kehler),
Jesus Quintana (John Turturro), Quintana's Partner (James G. Hoosier), Maude's
Thugs (Carlos Leon, Terence Burton), Older Cop (Richard Gant), Younger Cop
(Christian Clemenson), Tony the Chauffeur (Dom Irrera), Lebowski's Chauffeur (Ger-
ard L'Heureux), Knox Harrington (David Thewlis), Coffee Shop Waitress (Lu Elrod),
Auto Circus Cop (Mike Gomez), Gary the Bartender (Peter Siragusa), The Stranger
(Sam Elliott), Doctor (Marshall Manesh), Arthur Digby Sellers (Harry Bugin), Lit-
tle Larry Sellers (Jesse Flanagan), Pilar (Irene Olga Lopez), Corvette Owner (Luis
Colina), Jackie Treehorn (Ben Gazzara), Malibu Police Chief (Leon Russom), Cab
Driver (Ajgie Kirkland), Private Snoop (Jon Polito), Nihilist Woman (Aimee Mann),
Saddam (Jerry Haleva), Pancake Waitress (Jennifer Lamb), Funeral Director (War-
ren Keith), Girl in "Logjammin'" (Asia Carrera [uncredited])
STUNT COORDINATOR: Jery Hewitt; STUNT PLAYERS: Lloyd Catlett, Vince
Deadrick, Jr., Jennifer Lamb; UNIT PRODUCTION MANAGER: John Cameron; ART
DIRECTOR: John Dexter; SET DECORATOR: Chris L. Spellman; FIRST ASST. DIREC-
TOR: Jeff Rafner; KEY SECOND ASST. DIRECTOR: Conte Mark Matal; STORYBOARD
ARTIST: J. Todd Anderson; CAMERA OPERATOR: Ted Norris; SOUND MIXER: Allan
Byer; BOOM OPERATOR: Peter F. Kurland; FOLEY ARTIST: Marko Costanzo; SOUND
EFFECTS EDITOR: Lewis Goldstein; RE-RECORDING MIXER: Michael Barry; MAKE-
UP: Jean Black; HAIR: Daniel Curet; CHOREOGRAPHERS: Bill and Jacqui Landrum;
COSTUME SUPERVISOR: Pamela Withers; VISUAL EFFECTS COORDINATOR: Janek
Sirrs; VISUAL EFFECTS: The Computer Film Company, Inc.; MECHANICAL EFFECTS
DESIGNER: Peter Chesney; FOLEY ARTIST: Marko Costanzo; TITLES: Balsmeyer &
Everett, Inc.

Chapter Notes

Introduction

1. Arthur Lubow, "Wowing Warren," *Inc.* (Mar. 2000) 76.
2. David Edelstein, "Invasion of the Baby Snatchers," *American Film* (Apr. 1987) 29.
3. William Preston Robertson, *The Big Lebowski* (New York/London: Norton, 1998) 69.
4. Robertson 55.
5. Robertson 55.
6. Robertson 55–56.
7. Judy Klemesrud, "The Brothers Coen Bow in with *Blood Simple*," p. 17, section 2, *New York Times* (Jan. 20, 1985).
8. Paul Zimmerman interview with the Coens for *Filmzone*.
9. John Hartl, "Big Winks in *Big Lebowski*," *Seattle Times* (Mar. 5, 1998).
10. Robertson 48.
11. David Handelman, "The Brothers from Another Planet," *Rolling Stone* (May 21, 1987) 61.
12. Handelman 61.
13. Klemesrud.
14. David Gritten, "Calendar," *Los Angeles Times* (Mar. 5, 1998) 8.
15. Robertson 26.
16. *Current Biography Yearbook*, ed. Judith Graham (New York: Wilson, 1994) 117.
17. Handelman 61.
18. Handelman 61.
19. Edelstein 56.

1. *Blood Simple*

1. Hal Hinson, "Bloodlines," *Film Comment* 21.2 (1985) 17.

2. David Handelman, "The Brothers from Another Planet," *Rolling Stone* (May 21, 1987) 59.

3. Hinson 18.

4. Peter Biskind, "Interview with the Coen Brothers," *Premiere* (Mar. 1996) 76–80.

5. William Van Wert, *The Film Career of Alain Robbe-Grillet* (Boston: Hall, 1977) 12.

6. John Harkness, "The Sphinx Without a Riddle," *Sight and Sound* 4.7 (1994) 8.

7. Hinson 17.

8. Hinson 17.

9. Hinson 14.

2. *Raising Arizona*

1. Eric Pooley, "Warped in America: The Dark Vision of Moviemakers Joel and Ethan Coen," *New York* Mar. 23, 1987) 45.

2. *Current Biography Yearbook*, ed. Judith Graham (New York: 1994) 118.

3. David Edelstein, "Invasion of the Baby Snatchers," *American Film* (Apr. 1987) 28.

4. Sarah Kozloff, *Invisible Storytellers* (Berkeley: Voice of California Press, 1998) 47.

5. Valerie Walkerdine, "Subject to Change without Notice: Psychology, Postmodernity and the Popular," *Cultural Studies and Communications,* edited by James Curran, David Morley and Valerie Walkerdine (London, New York: Arnold, 1996) 99.

6. Guiliana Bruno quotes Robert Venturi in her article "Ramble City: Postmodernism and *Blade Runner,*" in *Crisis Cinema,* ed. Christopher Sharrett (Washington, DC: Maisonneuve, 1993) 241.

7. Bruno 238.

8. David Denby, "Bringing Up Baby," *New York* (Mar. 16, 1987) 60.

9. Richard Corliss, "Rootless People," *Time* (Mar. 23, 1987) 86.

10. David Ansen, "Review of *Raising Arizona,*" *Newsweek* (Mar. 16, 1987) 73.

11. Sheila Benson, "Calendar," *Los Angeles Times* (Mar. 20, 1987) 1.

12. Edelstein 28.

13. *Current Biography Yearbook* 118.

14. Edelstein 28.

3. *Miller's Crossing*

1. John McCarty, *Hollywood Gangland* (New York: St. Martin's, 1993) 45.

2. Mark Horowitz, "The A–Z of the Coen Brothers," *Film Comment* (Sept.–Oct.1991) 26.

3. Richard McKim, "*Miller's Crossing,*" *Cineaste* (Spring 1991) 45.

4. Horowitz 27.

5. John G. Cawelti, "Chinatown and Generic Transformation in Recent American Films," in *Film Genre Reader II*, ed. Barry Keith Grant (Austin: University of Texas Press, 1995) 234.

6. Cawelti 237.

7. Robert Warshow, "The Gangster as Tragic Hero," in *The Popular Arts in America*, ed. William Hammel (New York: Harcourt, 1977) 129.

8. Louis Menand, "Get Unreal," *New Yorker* (March 17, 1997) 11.

9. Terrence Rafferty, "In Brief," *New Yorker* (Oct. 15, 1990) 32.

10. Sheila Benson, "Calendar," *Los Angeles Times* (Oct. 5, 1990) 10.

11. Peter Travers, "Miller's Crossing," *Rolling Stone* (Oct. 4, 1990) 50.

12. David Denby, "Hat's Off," *New York* (Oct. 8, 1990) 59.

13. Tim Pulleine, *Sight and Sound* (Winter 1990–1991) 64.

4. *Barton Fink*

1. William Preston Robertson, "What's the Goopus," *American Film* (Aug. 1991) 32.

2. Mark Horowitz, "The A–Z of the Coen Brothers," *Film Comment* (Sept.–Oct. 1991) 30.

3. Brian McHale, *Postmodernist Fiction* (London/New York: Methuen, 1987) 134.

4. J. Hoberman, "Hellywood," *Village Voice* (Aug. 27, 1991) 70.

5. John Harkness, "The Sphinx Without a Riddle," *Sight and Sound* 4.7 (1994) 7.

6. Stanley Kauffmann, "The Smothers Brothers," *New Republic* (Sept. 30, 1991) 26–27.

7. Nisid Hajari, "Beavis and Egghead," *Entertainment Weekly* (Apr. 1, 1994) 30.

5. *The Hudsucker Proxy*

1. Tad Friend, "Inside the Coen Heads," *Vogue* (Apr. 1994) 407–409.

2. Nisid Hajari, "Beavis and Egghead," *Entertainment Weekly* (Apr. 1, 1994) 31.

3. Peter Biskind, "Interview with the Coen Brothers," *Premiere* (Mar. 1996) 76–80.

4. Hajari 30.

5. Hajari 30.

6. Hajari 30.

7. Guiliana Bruno quotes Robert Venturi in her article "Ramble City: Postmodernism and *Blade Runner*," in *Crisis Cinema*, ed. Christopher Sharrett (Washington, DC: Maisonneuve, 1993) 241.

8. Fredric Jameson, *Postmodernism; or, The Cultural Logic of Late Capitalism* (Durham, NC: Duke University Press, 1991) 17–18.

9. Jameson 20.

10. Todd McCarthy, "Review of the Hudsucker Proxy," *Variety* (Jan. 31, 1994) 4.

11. David Ansen, "A Blast of Hollywood Bile," *Newsweek* (Mar. 14, 1994).

12. John Harkness, "The Sphinx without a Riddle," *Sight and Sound* (1994) 8.

13. John Powers, "Coen South," *New York* (Mar. 14, 1994) 74.

14. Peter Travers, "The Hudsucker Proxy," *Rolling Stone* (Mar. 24, 1994) 105.

15. Jack Matthews, "Another Send-up by Coen Brothers," *Newsday* (Mar. 11, 1994) 72.

16. Kim Newman, *Sight and Sound* (Sept. 1994) 39.

17. Tom Green, "Coens Return to Quirky Country," *USA Today* (Mar. 7, 1996) 10.

18. Biskind.

6. *Fargo*

1. Ethan Coen and Joel Coen, *Fargo* (London/Boston: Faber and Faber, 1996) x.

2. Peter Biskind, "Interview with the Coen Brothers," *Premiere* (Mar. 1996) 76–80.

3. Biskind 76–80.

4. William Preston Robertson, *The Big Lebowski* (New York/London: Norton, 1998) 17.

7. *The Big Lebowski*

1. William Preston Robertson, *The Big Lebowski* (New York/London: Norton, 1998) 19.

2. Robertson 44.

3. John Hartl, "Big Winks in Big Lebowski," *Seattle Times* (Mar. 1998).

4. Robertson 38.

5. Robertson 39.

6. Paul Tatara, CNN.

7. Jack Kroll, "All Purpose Parody," *Newsweek* (Mar. 16, 1998) 7.

8. Roger Ebert, "Review of *The Big Lebowski*," "Zone N.C." sec., *Chicago Sun-Times* (Mar. 6, 1998) 37.

Index

179